Fayez Sayegh
The Party Years 1938-1947

Adel Beshara

Fayez Sayegh
The Party Years 1938-1947

Adel Beshara

Copyright © 2019 Black House Publishing Ltd

All rights reserved. No part of this book may be reproduced in any form by any electronic or mechanical means including photocopying, recording, or information storage and retrieval without permission in writing from the publisher.

ISBN-13: 978-1-912759-22-4

Black House Publishing Ltd
Kemp House
152 City Road
London
United Kingdom
EC1V 2NX

www.blackhousepublishing.com
Email: info@blackhousepublishing.com

Fayez Sayegh 1922-1980

Contents

Preface	1
Introduction	5
1 - An Intellectual Portrait	11
2 - The Rise of Fayez Sayegh in the SSNP	39
3 - The Fall of Fayez Sayegh from the SSNP	67
4 - Disagreement with Sa'adeh	93
5 - The Question of Existentialism	137
Conclusion	173
Appendix	193
Bibliography	251
Index	257

Preface

This book provides an interdisciplinary introduction to the early writings and activism of Fayez Sayegh, whose passionate and prolific intellectual career was well known within academia (and probably also within the ranks of intelligence agencies anxious to keep outspoken and courageous critics of Zionism under surveillance). It is aimed at readers with diverse interests including nationalism, colonialism, Zionism, philosophy, ideology, humanism, and party activism.

Very little is known about Sayegh's early life. We remember him mainly as an articulate defender of the Palestinian cause: a subject that his work internationalized in words and deeds. However, we have only a faint idea of how and why he chose this life-long trajectory. The answer to the "how and why" lies in the roots that sustained his passion and got him there in the first place: the period between 1938 and 1947 when he was a political activist with the Syrian Social Nationalist Party (SSNP). This is the period of Sayegh's first intense intellectual development under two distinct and irreconcilable currents: (1) Antun Sa'adeh's nationalism and (2) Kierkegaard-Berdyaev's existentialism.

The tragedy that befell Sayegh when his soul became a battlefield for these two currents is an intrinsic part of this book. Its purpose is to unravel how Sayegh was woven into this intricate web and reveal how he managed or failed to disentangle himself from it. In the process, much light will be shed on his fallout with Sa'adeh in 1947, which led to his expulsion from the SSNP and the beginning of a new chapter in his life.

Fayez Sayegh - The Party Years 1938-1947

Those who knew Sayegh personally have confirmed that he consistently refrained from speaking about his dispute with Sa'adeh. They never understood why, and Sayegh never told them. He was so tight-lipped about the affair that he never referred to it in his writings or publicly spoke about it after 1948. Even more baffling is the absence of any reference to Sa'adeh in the entire mass of Sayegh's voluminous writings from 1950 to 1980. Even when the topic of discussion shared much ground with Sa'adeh (nationalism, Zionism, Communism) and the analysis bore his stamp, Sayegh did not mention him anywhere. Yet his publications show that, despite his evasive tactics and self-imposed ban on Sa'adeh, Sayegh never succeeded in completely disconnecting from his old leader.

In fairness to both of these men, this book recapitulates the dispute from the perspective of both parties. Independence and objectivity is maintained throughout the narrative by drawing on what both men said and wrote and what others close to them thought of the dispute. Naturally, in personal ideological disputes, the level of confusion and conflicting opinions is high. We attempt to cut through the maze of this confusion by deconstructing the dispute point-by-point rather than addressing it holistically. Analytically, because the book is largely about Sayegh, the focus is on his interpretation and explanations. Sa'adeh's response serves as a complimentary backdrop. The aim is neither to condemn nor to vindicate Sayegh, but to provide a novel entrance point into an obscure and forgotten phase of his life.

After Sayegh's death in 1980, his widow donated a large collection of his papers on Arab affairs and the Arab-Israeli conflict to the Middle East Library Division of the Marriott Library in the University of Utah, USA. In this collection there is a substantial amount of material on Sayegh's involvement with the SSNP. Some of this material, which has not been published, has enabled us to obtain invaluable insight into Sayegh's frame of mind, and to some extent, into his dispute with Sa'adeh.

Preface

We were also able to rebuild a coherent picture of Sayegh's years in the SSNP by drawing on his published writings between 1944 and 1947, especially in *Sada an-Nahda*, the Beirut-based newspaper he edited in 1946-1947. We are deeply grateful to the Jafet Library at the American University of Beirut for furnishing us with an electronic copy of *Sada an-Nahda*.

In the second half of the book, the reader is presented with translations of some of Sayegh's party writings from that period. The selected material in this section serves as an indicator of his sense of loyalty and deep commitment to the SSNP until his sudden downfall in December 1947.

As with the preparation of any book, several individuals deserve our thanks and praise: Dennis Walker, John Dayeh, Badr el-Hage, Michel Abs, and Ihsan al-Jamal.

Adel Beshara

Melbourne, March 25, 2019

Introduction

In 1963, the would-be ambassador of the United States to Qatar, Andrew Killgore, gave a speech on the Arab-Israeli conflict. He delivered the speech against a backdrop of mounting criticism in the American press of Gamal Abdel Nasser's program to build rockets to fire at Israel (ostensibly with the help of German scientists). During the speech, a young man in the audience interrupted Killgore furiously: "Mr. Killgore, when will the United States make Nasser get rid of his Nazi scientists?" Immediately, another man at the back of the room was on his feet saying, "Mr. Killgore, let me answer that question. Nasser will get rid of his Nazi scientists when the U.S. gets rid of its Nazi scientists".

The man behind that response was the distinguished professor Fayez Sayegh, who was teaching that year at Macalester College in St. Paul, Minnesota, US. The reference to Nazi scientists was to Werner von Braun and other German rocket scientists whom Washington had brought to the U.S. from Germany at the end of World War II to help with its military weapons program.

Despite his many well-known qualities, Fayez Sayegh remains a shadowy figure. No biography of him appeared either during his lifetime or after his death in 1980. Biographical snippets are readily available, but they are mostly of an inferior quality. Moreover, reference to the first major phase in his intellectual political career (1938 to 1947) is extremely rare. This is most unfortunate and highly negligent, because the foundations of Sayegh's acclaimed activism and intellectualism extended deeply and firmly into that period. He was a remarkable orator before he became known in the West. In addition, he was also:

- an outspoken political figure before he started lecturing abroad;
- an efficient analyst and researcher before he landed in the United States;
- a political activist before he joined the Arab bandwagon and the Palestine Liberation;
- a capable administrator before he worked at the United Nations and the Arab League; and
- a published writer long before his books started to appear around the world.

Intellectually, many of the views and opinions Sayegh developed after 1950 were an extension of his prior views and opinions. Even when he strayed from them, he retained some of the earlier qualities and values. For example, after 1950, Sayegh gradually drifted away from Syrian nationalism and joined the high tide of Arab nationalism. However, on closer scrutiny, we find that it was a partial rather than a full paradigm shift, as Sayegh continued to adhere to his pre-1950 notion of nationalism and to voice the same skepticism with which he characterized Arab nationalism. Similarly, his attitude towards Communism and Zionism after 1950 shows very strong continuity with his attitude and position before 1950.

We cannot understand the real Sayegh and his inner character and sense of reality by ignoring a sizable period in his life. The interval of 1938-1947 is crucial. During this time, Sayegh came of age as a political activist and a gifted orator with a thoughtful, reasoned mind. During those years, many young men and women expanded their intellectual and political horizons under the tutelage of Antun Sa'adeh (1904-1949), the founder of the Syrian Social Nationalist Party (SSNP), but none more than Fayez Sayegh. For almost a decade, he served the Syrian Social National Party with the utmost devotion. He rose from a junior role in the Party as a local branch executive to become the

INTRODUCTION

Party's leading spokesperson on cultural and political affairs, a public orator, and the chief editor of the Party's newspaper and internal publications. His published material on the Party prompted certain circles to regard him as the heir apparent to Sa'adeh.

At personal level, the period of 1938-1947 is Sayegh's first scholarly encounter with philosophical thinkers and themes. His academic record shows him studying and writing on various philosophical systems and ideas including Islamic and ancient Syrian philosophers such as Lucian of Samosata. Ultimately, Sayegh found his philosophical calling in existentialism. Existentialism is a philosophical theory or approach that emphasizes the existence of the individual person as a free and responsible agent determining his or her own development through acts of the will. It appealed to Sayegh's gentle nature and strong nostalgia for moral and spiritual betterment. He found in existentialism's philosophical and theoretical foundations an outlet from the evil problems that seem to drive the world from one adversity to another. Undoubtedly, the miseries and horrors of World War II (which sparked a renewed interest in existentialism and other moralist philosophies) influenced Sayegh, as did his coaching at the hands of the Christian existentialist, Charles Malik.

However, little did Sayegh realize that he was moving along two conflicting axes: (1) a nationalism soliciting his loyalty to the nation as the supreme value in life, and (2) an existentialism beseeching him to step back from collective ideologies that had brought nothing but suffering and disaster on humanity. Sayegh straddled these two currents blissfully unaware or perhaps in denial of what could happen if they collided. For almost three years (1944–1947), he was able to maintain a delicate balance between them by insulating himself from external interference. At one point, he attempted to reconcile the two and had mixed success. But the contradictions were too great to conceal, and they ultimately caught up with him.

The rupture occurred when Sa'adeh returned from exile in 1947 and admonished Sayegh to refrain from infusing the Party's national doctrine with existentialist themes. However, because Sayegh had developed an irreversible fondness for existential philosophy, he stood up to his leader. In the course of the polemical dialogue that followed between Sayegh and Sa'adeh, a wide range of issues beside existentialism was discussed concerning Sa'adeh's leadership, authority, prerogatives, and the Party's program. Fundamental intellectual and theoretical themes (e.g. freedom of thought, totalitarianism, and the relationship between ideology and philosophy) also came to the fore. The result was a complete break-up between Sayegh and Sa'adeh, but not before an intense debate that presented a multitude of questions few had seen coming.

Although Sa'adeh emerged as the clear winner of the dispute, it produced three primary results:

1. Sayegh was expelled from the Party.
2. Sa'adeh consolidated his position as the undisputed leader of the SSNP.
3. New insights into the ideology and worldview of the SSNP surfaced.

After this, Fayez Sayegh went on to become a renowned academic, writer, and political statesman. Although he moved well away from the SSNP, he continued to write and advocate for or against many of the same issues he had engaged in during his Party years: Zionism, Communism, nationalism, reformism, and the Palestine question. Syrian nationalism was perhaps the only topic he avoided. This omission and the fact that Sayegh never liked to talk about his interim Party years is probably why any reference to that period is sparse.

This book is a detailed reconstruction of that phase. It retraces Sayegh's meteoric rise in the SSNP, during which he was entrusted with two executive departments, oversaw the Party's newspaper, joined its Supreme Council, and became its leading spokesperson on national and international affairs. It also outlines the factors and circumstances that led to his spectacular fall from the Party. Until now, what little has been written about this obscure phase has followed two distinct trajectories. Some pieces are mindless pieces of rabid anti-Sa'adeh tripe that portray Sayegh as only a victim of intellectual suppression; while others blow him up into an ever-present figure and a hero of our times. We aim to present a more balanced assessment grounded in an intellectual and historical perspective rather than in sympathetic eulogies.

All the available facts will be considered carefully and both sides of the story will be presented. The point of the exercise is not to cast aspersions on Sayegh or Sa'adeh or to champion one over the other, but to provide a more accurate and detailed description of their disagreement, which will contribute to our understanding of other related issues.

By no means is this a definitive biography of Sayegh's early life. However, it does fill a gap in the existing literature. Although further detailed research is needed, the book should serve as a useful foundation for the writing of a full and comprehensive biography of Sayegh in the future.

1

An Intellectual Portrait

Born in 1922 in Kharaba, Syria, where his father was a Presbyterian minister, Sayegh was reared in Tiberias on the Sea of Galilee in what was then Palestine. Back then, people moved freely between modern-day Lebanon, Syria, and occupied Palestine either to search for jobs and opportunities or to visit relatives. Despite the division of the region between the French and British mandates, as pre-decided in the secret Sykes-Picot Agreement, there were no formal political barriers, no frontier checkpoints, and no visa requirements. A keen sense of territorial community made social mobility possible for most people.

Since the middle of the nineteenth century, Tiberias had been a popular destination for Western Christian missions. Its association with biblical narratives made it particularly appealing to the Church of Scotland mission to the Near East,[1] which shifted its Presbyterian project to the town around the 1880s after its failure and withdrawal from Aleppo and Damascus. Arguably, this background played a part in the decision of the Sayegh family to relocate to Tiberias.

From an early age, Sayegh leaned toward education. He attended the local school for his primary education and then went to Scots College: a secondary school in Safad, Palestine. He received a B.A. degree in 1941 and an M.A. degree in 1945 from the American University of Beirut (AUB) in Lebanon. His education was made possible with the help of scholarships from the Department of Education, the Government of Palestine, and

---

1 Michael Marten, *Attempting to Bring the Gospel Home: Scottish Missions to Palestine, 1839-1917.* (London: I. B. Tauris, 2005).

the Faculty of Arts and Science of the AUB. Fayez excelled in every field, especially in philosophy under the close supervision of Charles Malik.[2] In an anecdote often repeated it is said that Charles Malik once was talking to students about the impact of environment on the formation of individual personality and made a striking comparison between the Lebanese and the Hauranis (a reference to inhabitants of Hauran, a region in southwestern present-day Syria) as evidence of the superiority of the Lebanese over the Hauranis. Malik then turned around and ask sarcastically: "Can a clever young man like Fayez Sayegh come out of a backward country such as Hauran?". Fayez immediately rose to his feet and replied, "Yes. My father is Haurani and I am proud of my Haurani origin". The class burst into laughter leaving Charles Malik red-faced and gasping.[3]

In 1949, Sayegh earned a doctorate in philosophy at Georgetown University, Washington, DC, with a minor in political science. After receiving his degree, Sayegh spent most of his life alternating between public responsibilities and teaching. He worked for the Lebanese Embassy in Washington, DC, and as a research officer and adviser to the Lebanese delegation to the United Nations. He subsequently served as counselor to the Kuwaiti and Yemeni delegation to the U.N. and chief of the Arab States delegation to the U.N. His impressive résumé also included positions as program officer (Middle East) to the U.N. Radio Division and social affairs officer at the United Nations Division of Human Rights.

As a teacher and educator, Sayegh taught at Yale, Stanford, the AUB, University of Oxford, and Macalester College. He was an extraordinarily gifted teacher and lecturer. His teacher at the AUB and Acting Head of the Department of Philosophy, A. Kenneth Cragg, noted in a letter of recommendation:

---

[2] On Charles Malik see: Glenn Mitoma, "Charles H. Malik And Human Rights: Notes On A Biography." (*Biography*, Vol. 33, No. 1, winter 2010): 222-41.

[3] Sakr Abu Fakhr, "The triumph of Freedom over Ideology (Arabic). *Al-Safir* 'Palestine', 2012.

I formed the highest opinion of his academic ability and his capacity as a teacher. He showed great application and very considerable powers of exposition and had that ability to make a subject live and to enthuse students in its pursuit which is so important a part of classroom work.[4]

Sayegh enjoyed exchanges with students that faculty half his age could not match. He never forgot what it was like to be young. The exuberance of undergraduates charmed him and he, in turn, charmed them. His in-depth and extensive knowledge in philosophy and political science, of which he made effective use, gave him an edge over his colleagues and competitors. He could teach in both fields with considerable ease and fluency. His main courses centered on Arabic philosophy and current Middle Eastern affairs, especially during periods of political instability in the Middle East.

The number of books and articles that Sayegh wrote while teaching, as well as the wide variety of their subjects, is staggering. While he continued to produce material in stirring defense of the Palestinian question, he also began to write about the dominant themes and issues of the time: Neutrality, Arab unity, Arab socialism, propaganda, etc. Aroused primarily by Nasser's pan-Arabism and spectacular rise in world politics after the Suez crisis, these themes and issues became the research subject for many scholars around the world, and chief among them was Sayegh. His treatise "Arab unity: hope and fulfilment", which represents his first book-length work in English, was probably the highlight of this period. It stood out both for its thoroughness and insightful analysis:

In sum, *Arab Unity* is the only major treatment to date of the subject in English and is a serviceable and welcome contribution to western understanding of the modern Arab World.[5]

---

[4] Fayez Sayegh, 1922-1980 - Correspondence. (University of Utah - Fayez A. Sayegh Collection).

[5] Richard H. Nolte's review of *Arab Unity: Hope and Fulfillment* by Fayez A.

Sayegh participated in a symposium on Arab neutrality, from which another book surfaced: *The Dynamics of Neutralism in the Arab World*. He also co-authored a book entitled *Arab Socialism: A Documentary Survey*, which, in its time and place, reflected a universal push to provide a theoretical structure to "Arab Socialism". Together with an earlier essay on the "Arab mind" (published by the Organization of Arab Students in the United States in June 1953) and the various works on Zionist ideology, these books aimed to promote mutual understanding between the Americans and the Arab peoples. However, the message failed to get through. The gap of misunderstanding and mistrust continued to widen, especially in the United States where the Cold War had paralysed the ability to think and act outside the official line.

Attributing this anomaly to the effectiveness of Zionist propaganda, Fayez responded with a monograph on the rhetorical tools used by Zionist propagandists to shape political attitudes of Americans.[6] Drawing on his experience looking at American political habits and speech, Sayegh identified that certain patterns had appeared in Americans' acceptance or rejection of ideas. From this eight 'keys to the American mind' were recognized and discussed:

1. *The Underdog*: American instinctive sympathy towards and compassion for "the underdog" – the person who is exposed to superior power in such a way that he cannot be expected to resist, much less to survive, that power.

2. *Respect for Guts*: The admiration for the guts of the underdog in standing up to challenges which lesser people would avoid.

3. *"What about now?"*: The recognition that most Americans, like majorities everywhere, do not live in the world of abstractions and do not as a matter of habit think historically but are interested in the "now".

Sayegh. In *Middle East Journal*, Vol. 14, No. 1 (Winter, 1960), pp. 100-101.

6 Fayez Sayegh, Zionist Propaganda in the United States. (Pleasantville, NY: The Fayez A. Sayegh Foundation, 1983).

4. *Cause and Effect*: That is the effect of the causal sequence of events. They condemn the Palestinians for their hostility today without going back into its causes and linking effect with cause.

5. *Social Engineering*: Every social problem, the moment it comes to the consciousness of Americans, becomes a challenge for a solution. Americans want to know "Now what can we do about it or what must we do about it?" [. . .] As a result, he who can present an acceptable and plausible solution to the problem is more likely to find his version of the problem accepted by Americans than he who describes the problem and puts a full-stop and turns his back and goes.

6. *Simplification*: Reducing a message to very simple and compelling terms as "All we want is negotiations" or "it's about loving your own kind". Such terms are likely to strike a stronger note than going through the more sophisticated and more complex description of the solution.

7. *Belief in Compromise*: That every problem has two sides is an axiom of the American mind, and if every problem has two sides then every solution must be somewhere in between the two sides. Israelis stand before American audiences and declare that the Palestine problem is a conflict of two rights, not a conflict of right vs. wrong. Says the Israeli, "Don't the Arabs have other countries? We don't have another country and therefore we are entitled to Palestine". That almost ends his presentation.

8. *Realism*: This key to the American mind has been exploited assiduously and manipulated by Zionist spokesmen for years. The "realistic" often-repeated slogan, "Israel is there to stay", has far more effectiveness on the American mind than Arabs can even imagine.

Apparently, it was a wake-up call that Sayegh had received shortly after his arrival in the United States and which he never forgot that brought Zionist propaganda techniques to his attention: "I was called to make a speech on the Palestine problem. I started the speech with an historical review dating from World War I, and by the time the hour was up, I had not yet gotten as far as 1948. At the end of the speech my host came to me and said, [. . .] You loused it all up. Do you think any one of the people who came to listen to you came in order to listen to a history of Palestine? These people are too busy; they don't have time; they are reading that there is trouble in Palestine; they came to learn what it's all about. They did not come to get a course in history." I thanked him for his advice, and I never forgot it. [. . .] what they want to know is what the problem is all about now. . . It is much easier for them to begin with the present."[7]

By the late 1950s, Sayegh had carved for himself a reputation as 'the most articulate' exponent of the Arab point of view in the United States". This description comes from a flyer found among his personal papers. Ostensibly used to introduce him at public speaking events, it goes on to describe as "perhaps the best known Arab spokesman in America — having appeared on dozens of coast-to-coast television and radio programs and hundreds of local interviews, participated in over fifty conferences on the Middle East, and lectured widely on the campuses of all the major American universities and before diverse audiences in all parts of the country".

In 1965, Sayegh founded the Palestine Research Center in Beirut and became the Director General. Early that year, the Palestine Liberation Organization (PLO) had asked Sayegh to establish a research center on Palestine in Beirut. It took him less than three months, from February 1, 1965 to April 30, 1965, to complete the establishment of the Center. Upon completion of the task, Sayegh reported to the Organization and suggested the appointment of a permanent full-time director. Although it did appoint a full-time managing director, the Organization asked Sayegh to continue to "supervise" the work of the Center during the formative period of its infancy and be available to the

---
7   Ibid, 5.

Organization as a "technical consultant" on matters of research. Sayegh acceded to the request, but not before running into trouble with the AUB, which judged his "outside activity" as an intrusion on its academic independence. Fortunately, Sayegh was a first-rate persuader. He convinced the AUB Board that his extra-curriculum duties with the Palestine Research Center, limited to few hours a week with little to nothing in remuneration, would not conflict with his teaching responsibilities and research at the university. In his letter of appeal to the Board, Sayegh poignantly observed:

> Inasmuch as the Palestine Problem is an important international problem in its own right, inasmuch as it is also an important national problem for the people of this region, and inasmuch as very little has been done by way of scholarly research to illuminate and analyze the various aspects of the problem, the initiation of a program of responsible, scholarly research is both a contribution to the national cause that is of extreme importance to Arab youth (including many AUB students) as well as to the academic purposes of a university (particularly a university located in the Arab World). As a teacher of international relations, I feel that my participation (in a supervisory and consultative capacity, as well as a contributing author) in this program is an edifying asset . . . [Furthermore] my acceptance to continue with this activity will not interfere this year (as it did not interfere last year) with my full discharge of all my responsibilities as a member of the faculty.[8]

As a cultural and educational institution, the Palestine Research Center helped to document various aspects of the Palestine problem. It conducted academic research on all aspects of Palestinian and Zionist politics, and it acquired large numbers of books, documents, and publications relevant to the Palestinian question. Subsequently, the Center became the largest research

---
8   Sayegh at the American University of Beirut 1954-1966: Letter to Adnan Iskandar, October 29, 1965. (University of Utah - Fayez A. Sayegh Collection).

institution specializing in the Palestinian problem. Its library included over 25,000 volumes. The Center published a monthly journal entitled *Shu'un Filastiniyyah* (*Palestine Affairs*) and over 400 books and other publications. As a frequent contributor, Sayegh published at least two of his well-known titles through the Center: *Zionist Colonialism in Palestine* and *Discrimination in Education Against Arabs in Israel*.[9]

Sayegh devoted much of his life to building a better understanding of fundamental human problems. His gentle personality, simple style of speaking and strength of character won him many friends and admirers:

> Fayez Sayegh was different. I enjoyed his intellectual coolness, which was not without passionate conviction and commitment to the cause of justice and political rights for the Palestinians. Fayez was then simply a junior associate of Charles Malik of Lebanon, who, at the time, was "the White Arab" for Americans. But diplomatic rank was not important to me - nor, I think, was power-brokerage Fayez's first concern. We each had some things to learn from the other. And without ever saying so, we explored each other's thinking.[10]

Sayegh pushed himself hard for meanings and explanations. He allowed nothing to affect his resolve or deflect him from his course. Even on the bleakest of days, he never gave up trying to make sense of the world and his place in it. In the pursuit of

---

9   On September 15, 1982, as Israeli troops invaded West Beirut, they ransacked the offices of the Palestine Research Center confiscating all its possessions and transporting them to Israel. Despite its official diplomatic status granted by the Lebanese government, the Center was subjected to a series of attacks by Israeli troops and their Lebanese allies aimed at closing the Center and ending its activities. During these attacks, several members of the staff were killed, including Hanneh Shahin, the wife of Sabri Jiryis, who was the Director of the Center.

10 Elmer Berger, "Memoirs of an Anti-Zionist Jew." (*Journal of Palestine Studies*, Vol. 5, No. ½, Autumn, 1975 - Winter, 1976): 3-55.

this objective, he built a stellar reputation for which he is still remembered. First, both his admirers and detractors grant that he was a prolific writer. A cursory review of his works presented to the University of Utah is enough: four to five hundred written works, several hundred tape recordings and films of his speeches and interviews, and a personal library of four to five thousand volumes, including collections on theology (Islam, Christianity and Judaism), international law, U.S. foreign policy, world history, and philosophy. The quality of his output was of such high standard that some of his works were translated into 16 languages including English, Arabic, French, Spanish, German, and Russian. No doubt, his prodigious knowledge, memory, and vast archive gave him a crucial edge: "Fayez was famous for citing, by heart, paragraphs of given UN resolutions, dates of issuance, and books with page numbers. He kept excellent archives of his own cross references long before the computers became popular."[11]

Second, Sayegh established an international reputation as a masterful speaker and debater. His thoroughness, incisiveness, brilliant analysis, and ability to present logical and coordinated arguments in a pleasing manner were phenomenal. He spoke with vigor and adroitness and seemed to have a politician's sense of the right phrase at the propitious moment. One could describe him as a "natural born speaker" whose eloquence and simplicity embodied the power of the spoken word and who exemplified that rhetoric can be used to both reflect and shape reality.

Sayegh developed and perfected his oratory skills during his involvement with the SSNP. He was fond of choosing simple, direct words to convey his meaning and he usually spoke with the objective of persuading his audience. Indeed, his power of persuasion was often decisive in steering the views of the majority in his direction. He even swayed the hard-hitting

---

[11] Anis F. Kassim, (Ed.), *The Palestine Yearbook of International Law, 1998-1999*. (Brill: Martinus Nijhoff 1984-): 245.

"Jewish" television presenter, Mike Wallace,[12] to a Palestinian perspective at the height of Zionist influence in the U.S. During an appearance on "Larry King Live", Wallace made a startling confession when King asked him whether it was tough for a Jewish reporter to be objective about Israel:

> Wallace: It shouldn't be if you're a professional reporter... I was fortunate enough as a young, much younger reporter back in the 50s, I met a man by the name of Fayez Sayegh who was a Palestinian, and he was really a Palestinian to his roots, and he helped to let the scales fall from my eyes about the relationship between Palestinians and Israelis, between Arabs and Jews. And you take on quite a chore when you go against your own religion, go against what you learn, what I learned from my folks growing up, but if you are a professional reporter, you do it.[13]

Wallace provided a little more detail about this "Palestinian" who "helped to let the scales from my eyes" in his 1984 memoir *Close Encounters*. Co-written with Gary Paul Gates, the book alternated between Wallace's first-person reminiscences and Gates's third-person narrative. Gates wrote about the evolution of Wallace's thinking and Sayegh's lasting influence on it:

> As a Jew growing up in America, [Wallace] had been taught to believe that the gospel according to Israel was almost as sacred as the Torah itself. Yet the more deeply he delved into the savage desert politics of the Middle East, the more he came to recognize that the Israeli view of the region's past, present and future was not the only defensible position.

This shift to a more balanced perception of Israel's historic dispute with its Arab neighbors was gradual and evolved over

---

12 *LIFE*, Jan 28, 1957, p. 57.

13 http://www.jewishpress.com/indepth/media-monitor/media-monitor-51/2002/08/07/0/?print

many years. During that time, Wallace made a dozen or so trips to the Middle East, where he interviewed almost every major leader... But no interview on the subject was more important, in terms of its effect on Wallace's own thinking, than one he conducted in New York back in 1957. For that was his first serious encounter with a spokesman for the Palestinian cause, and it left an enduring impression on him.

The individual who impressed him so greatly was an Arab scholar named Fayez Sayegh whom Wallace had first met when he was a guest on [Wallace's program] "Night Beat" ... Wallace was so impressed and stimulated by Sayegh that he invited him home to dinner the following week: a social courtesy he seldom extended to guests on the program. The two men talked for several hours that night, first over dinner and then over coffee. To be more accurate, Wallace listened as Sayegh elaborated on the tragic dilemma of the Middle East from a Palestinian point of view.[14]

In 1967, an exchange on television with the sharp Zionist TV host David Susskind established Sayegh as a masterful debater. His "encyclopedic knowledge of the Middle East, his marvelous facility in English and his passionate honesty left the cocksure Susskind at a loss for words."[15] Susskind found it impossible to provoke Sayegh and was surprised by Sayegh's calm and logical presentation. As As'ad Abu Khalil pithily put it, "He presented his case with the precision of a jeweler".[16] The following excerpts from that interview will suffice:

David Suskind: What effective role can the U.N. play, finally, in the Arab-Israeli issue?

---

14   Mike Wallace and Gary Paul Gates, *Close Encounters: Mike Wallace's Own Story.* (William Morrow & Co, 1987).

15   Andrew Killgore, "25 Years After His Death, Dr. Fayez Sayegh's Towering Legacy Lives On." (*Washington Report on Middle East Affairs*, Dec 2005, Vol. 24, Issue 9): 22.

16   As'ad AbuKhalil, "Before Edward Said: a Tribute to Fayez Sayegh." (*Al-Akhbar*, Tue, December 9, 2014).

Fayez Sayegh: Well, let's not forget that it was the role of the United Nations, to begin with, that created the present troubles in the Middle East, by recommending the establishment of a Jewish state on what was Arab Palestine—or, on a portion of what was Arab Palestine. So we feel that if the United Nations can be effective for ill, it certainly should be able to be effective for good....

DS: How do you think you've fared so far, compared to the Israeli presentation at the U.N. [regarding the Six-Day War]?

FS: The United Nations system represents a progressive concept of world order which, until 22 years ago, was still a dream in the minds of many people. Under this system, no state can take arms against another state, invade its territory, occupy its land, and retain that land. Therefore, under this system, which is the only hope of mankind today, what the Arabs are demanding, that Israel withdraw unconditionally from Arab territory occupied by force, is, far from being an irrational demand, the only rational demand, and the only demand consistent with a system of law and order, which can give this world any peace, and any hope of peace.

DS: Is it your contention that Israel commenced war against the Arab countries?

FS: It is not even the contention of Israel that it did not, sir. Israel certainly sent its Air Force across the demarcation lines and the borders, into Arab air bases, and at a time when Arabs were being told by the United States, by France, and by the Soviet Union, "As long as you do not invade Israel, don't worry about Israel invading you." And the Arabs were assuring these great powers that we shall not invade first...

DS: Dr. Sayegh, why will the Arab countries refuse to sit down, at this point, with Israel to negotiate peace?...

FS: For the simple reason that, when Israel asks for negotiation, it says it wants to negotiate with the Arab states. It so happens that the party primarily responsible for discussing the fate of that area is the people of Palestine. We, in Kuwait, Syria, the UAR, Iraq, all the Arab states, have no right to dispose of a portion of Palestinian territory. It is up to the Palestinians to decide what they agree to and what they do not agree to, by way of ultimate disposition of their land. Israel wants to negotiate with non-parties, rather than with the party to the problem.

Secondly, by saying, "let us negotiate directly," Israel is saying—in a whisper—"keep the United Nations out of the picture". This is the virtual implication of the demand for direct negotiations: the ouster of the United Nations, the blockage of the way of the United Nations to intervene.

Now, let me remind you, the United Nations has been responsible for the creation of every stage in the evolution of the Palestine problem, from 1947 until today. Israel cannot, having benefited from a partial implementation of U.N. recommendations in the past, having benefited from U.N. actions, and from U.N. inaction, Israel cannot now say, "Let the U.N. stand out of the picture; I want to deal directly with the Arab states". It cannot at one time say, "The whole problem should be decided upon by the U.N.", and then, at another stage, say, "The U.N. has no say in the matter."...

Now, you say we refuse to recognize Israel. Yes, we refuse to recognize Israel because the Israel you are speaking about is an act of usurpation of an Arab territory, and Arab land; an act of ouster of an Arab population. Every Israeli who is in Israel today is living in the home of an Arab who has not been compensated for his property. Every Israeli who is in Israel today is there because an Arab has been ousted. Israel is, because Palestine has been made not to be. The being of Israel is the non-being of Palestine. We do not endorse the non-being of an Arab country called Palestine. We will not recognize Israel as long as that means non-recognition of Arab Palestine. ...

DS: If she's a usurper state, and inhabiting your land, the only successful conclusion, from your point of view, would be her final demise, or defeat?

FS: Not necessarily.

DS: What else would accommodate your ambition?

FS: I—what would accommodate my ambition will be—my hope—and I say this now in the utmost earnestness, whether you like to believe me or not—my hope [is] that the human conscience will still wake up among the Zionists living in Israel, and will make them realize that they have usurped someone else's land, and will make them accept to live as human beings in a democratic Palestine, where they and the rightful inhabitants have a place, rather than to live in an exclusively Zionist state, at the expense of the rightful inhabitants of Palestine.

DS: Give up statehood?

FS: Give up statehood, but not give up existence.

DS: Well, that's charming. Don't die, but go away.

FS: Well, sir, you have done that—Israel has done that to the Arabs of Palestine. And I believe that human beings are human beings everywhere. I believe that the human conscience of many people in Israel will still awaken to the tragedy that they have been instrumental in inflicting upon another people that was never guilty of their suffering, that was never guilty of their persecution in Christian Europe....

DS: Turn over the state to an Arab country, is that it? The state of Israel?

FS: While they're there, it will not be an exclusively Arab country. Any Jew who has no place else to go will be able to stay in Palestine; the rightful inhabitants of Palestine must be allowed to come back to their country; and you will have a bi-national state of Christians, Muslims, Jews, Druse, Baha'i, atheists; all in Palestine, as Palestinians, leading a Palestinian life.

For years after that interview, no Zionist or pro-Israel debater would appear with Sayegh publicly.[17]

Finally, Sayegh was a political social activist of a primary kind. His vast personal history in activism began during his days as a member of the Syrian National Party in the 1940s. Whether advocating for Syrian nationalism, pan-Arabism, or Palestine, he stood up for what he believed in with unbreakable confidence. Many people around the world admired his resilient spirit and unwavering commitment.

Sayegh carefully and consciously created for himself an image as a public speaker. He never missed an opportunity to speak out or state his case. He gave public lectures, participated in symposiums, appeared on television shows, spoke on radio programs, and partook in live debates. As a result, he became one of the most visible spokespersons of the Palestinian cause in the West.

The highlight of Sayegh's activism was the passing in 1975 of UN Resolution 3379, which determined that Zionism is a form of racism and racial discrimination. Sayegh was the chief architect of that resolution. Representing Kuwait, he made four oral statements to the Third Committee of the General Assembly of the UN (Social, Humanitarian, and Cultural) and to the General Assembly in support of that decision. Sayegh argued the case with objective, empirical sense. He asked the Committee and the Assembly to consider the matter not from an Arab or strictly Palestinian perspective, but from the standpoint of the UN's own definition and standards of "racial discrimination":

---

17   Killgore, op. cit. In 1974, Sayegh appeared on the television show *Firing Line* with William F. Buckley Jr. who was not a Zionist by any means.

We do not come before this Committee today with a new, arbitrary definition of our own invention and ask it to adopt our definition in order to determine that Zionism is a form of racial discrimination. On the contrary, we come to this Committee with its own long established and universally-accepted definition of "racial discrimination", and ask it to judge whether or not Zionism, as defined by the Zionist movement itself, constitutes a form of racism and racial discrimination, as defined by the Committee itself long ago.[18]

With precision and the power of repeated proof, Sayegh then tore into Zionism's inherent racism. He highlighted terms like "distinctions", "exclusions", "Jewishness", "restrictions" and "preferences" and exposed them as essential elements of the Zionist agenda and worldview. Almost instantly, this rendered Zionism racist because these elements were essential to the universal and scientific meaning of the term.[19] At the risk of being labeled anti-Semitic, Sayegh continued to repeat his lifelong opinion that Zionism, in both its fundamental ideas and tactics, bore all the marks of the Nazi system:

> The Zionist concept of the final solution to the Arab problem in Palestine, and the Nazi concept of the final solution to the Jewish problem in Germany, consisted essentially of the same basic ingredient: the elimination of the unwanted human element in question. The creation of a Jew-free Germany was indeed sought by Nazism through more ruthless and more inhuman methods than the creation of an Arab-free Palestine accomplished by the Zionists: but behind the difference in techniques lay an identity of goals.[20]

---

18 Fayez A. Sayegh, *Zionism: "A Form of Racism and Racial Discrimination" Four Statements Made at the U.N. General Assembly."* (Office of the Permanent Observer of the Palestine Liberation Organization to the United Nations, 1976).

19 See *The Link*, Published by Americans for Middle East Understanding, Inc. (Volume 36, Issue 2, April-May, 2003): 7.

20 *Ibid.*

Yet, as a testament to the power of his analysis and reasoning, Sayegh could not be tarnished with the anti-Semitic tag. He did, however, cope with a tirade of hysterical abuse and name-calling, especially from representatives of the United States. His response was vintage Sayegh: "I am not chagrined and I am not disconcerted. Long, long ago, in my first elementary course in philosophy, I was told by my professors: 'Only he who has no argument resorts to name-calling.' "[21]

In December 1991, the United States, using all the diplomatic power it could muster, pressured the UN to repeal Resolution 3379. Sayegh did not live long enough to fight this repeal. It was achieved not through an objective re-assessment of Zionism, but through sheer political pressure and expediency: "The vote reflected the shifting political currents of recent years, the Persian Gulf war in particular, which split the Arab and Islamic worlds, and the changes in the former Soviet bloc, fostered by the collapse of Communism."[22]

Politics can distort the truth, but can never take its place. The events since the repeal of Resolution 3379, especially the spread of Jewish settlements and calls for the recognition of Israel as a "Jewish state", indicate that Zionism has lost none of its racist underpinnings. It might be some consolation for Sayegh to know that an "Arab Committee Against Zionism and Racism" was established to defend UN Resolution 3379 and that the Committee was spearheaded by In'am Raad, a fellow student from AUB and also a three-time president of the Syrian Social Nationalist Party.

Because Sayegh crafted his ideas with uncommon care and diligence, Zionists scrambled for cover when he spoke. They feared the power of his spoken word, the historical and theological knowledge he commanded, and the confidence he possessed to

---

21 *Ibid*, 39.
22 Paul Lewis, "U.N. Repeals Its '75 Resolution Equating Zionism With Racism." (*The New York Times*, December 17, 1991)

develop fresh proposals and to bring them forward usefully. If not for Sayegh's resilience and strong academic credentials, they would have succeeded in their attempts to isolate him from the public limelight. But Sayegh always stood his ground. He knew that they were after him, but he refused to bow down or back away.

Sayegh passed away in 1980 at the tender age of 58. He left behind his wife, Ariene, and daughter, Rima. He could not have died at a more critical time. With Israel posing to invade Lebanon and expel the PLO to Tunisia and with secret negotiations for the Oslo Accords in 1993 approaching, the Palestine cause would have gained much insight and benefit from his wisdom and energy. But whether Sayegh would have relinquished the fight against Zionism in favor of a truncated Palestine is open to conjecture. Be that as it may, having denounced Zionism as a colonial project all his life, it does seem very unlikely Sayegh would have changed his views on Zionism and Palestine.

Intellectual Development

Sayegh's portrait as developed here underwent significant changes. Since he lived in continuous contact with the realities of a world experiencing rapid transformations, the changes in his thinking followed an inherent logic. At least four changes in Sayegh's thinking, which we shall refer to as phases of his intellectual development, are clearly evident.

The First Phase

From 1938–1947, Sayegh accepted nationalism as the basis of his thinking and his interpretation of sociocultural reality. He embraced the iron logic of Antun Sa'adeh's unifying national doctrine and immersed himself in its philosophical and cultural values. Appearing at the height of national and sectarian divisions in the mid-1930s in Lebanon, Sa'adeh became a magnet for a whole and confused generation of people. His integrative and highly secular doctrines reverberated with the burgeoning new intelligentsia and provided an alternative course of action to the suffocating politics of communal and sectarian formations. For an aspiring intellectual like Sayegh, Sa'adeh's totalizing philosophy provided a practical answer to the political and national confusion that wreaked havoc on his generation. Its systematic analysis, ambitious ideals, novel approach, and accent on change resonated well with Sayegh's nationalist ego, as it did with many of his contemporaries, and it opened a wide field to his inquisitive and ambitious young mind. He subsequently set out not only to fathom the key topics of this new philosophy, but also to infuse them with doses of his own thinking and sentiments. Eventually he became one of its most visible spokespersons and principal tactician; a position he would occupy until 1947.

THE SECOND PHASE

Around 1945, Sayegh developed a distinct fondness for existential philosophy. This fondness arose from his philosophical studies at the AUB and his affiliation with Charles Malik's philosophical circle. As a result, nationalism was married to a new interest in life. The spirit of collective existence popularized by Sa'adeh in a sociological endeavor that accords society a central place in human development suddenly appeared less attractive than it once had been. Sayegh began to lean toward the existentialist perspective that each individual—not society or religion—is solely responsible for giving meaning to life. While not completely discarding the societal perspective, he began to focus on human existence as the product of personal experiences and the theatre for the actions and feelings of the individual. By 1945, his conversion to existentialism was complete. It was capped off with a Master's thesis entitled "Personal Existence: Its Contents, Its Tragedy, Its Paradox" in which Sayegh gave "a powerful though not unflawed defense of radical individuality and personality under the rubric of what he terms 'personal existence.' "[23]

---
23 Habib C. Malik, "The Reception of Kierkegaard in the Arab World." In Jon

Existentialism embodies a perennially recurring philosophic theme: the significance of the individual person and the problems and peculiarities that face individual human beings. Accordingly, it tends to distrust abstractions and overgeneralized formulations of "human nature" because each of us, in some important sense, makes his or her own nature. The idea appealed to Sayegh so much that, without hesitation, he wrote a monograph about it: *nida' al-aamak: nadharat fi al-insan wa al-wujud* (*A Call from the Depth: Reflections on Man and Existence*). Published in 1946, the monograph can be described as an intimate call for re-self-discovery and personal rejuvenation in an age of great uncertainty and constant change: "The need is critical to discover the human in every person, after that human element has been dispersed and replaced by the citizen, the economic being, the social creature, or reduced to the abstract mind, the pure feelings, or the raw instincts."[24]

To discover the human in us in a seemingly inhumane world is not only noble but also essential. The process might be fraught with ambiguities and unavoidable landmines, but it is the only way to achieve a meaningful life in an absurd and unfair world. The key is not to be willed towards fruitless endeavors and therefore excluded from creating a better world for ourselves.

In his PhD dissertation "Existential Philosophy: A Formal Examination", Sayegh articulated a theory of existential philosophy without restricting himself to any particular existentialist or non-existentialist philosopher. Speaking "as an existentialist", he set out not to defend and justify a specific mode of existential philosophizing but to demonstrate that

---

Stewart (ed.), *Kierkegaard's International Reception: The Near East, Asia, Australia, and the Americas.* (London: Ashgate Publishing Limited, 1989): 39-96.

[24] Fayez Sayegh, *Nida' al-Aamak: Nadharat fi al-Insan wa al-Wujud*. (Beirut: Dar al-Fikr, 1947): 11. Though published in 1947, Sayegh prepared the ground for this monograph in 1946.

> ... the tendency [that existential philosophy] is born from, and the choice from which it gets rise, and therefore its own formal character, are in strict conformity to the requirements determined by the nature and situation and destiny of man, and the conditions of human knowledge.[25]

According to Habib Malik, "the exposure to [Existentialist] philosophy became a life-changing experience"[26] for Sayegh. But it was not as smooth a transition as Malik portrayed. Before his conversion to existentialism, Sayegh faced serious problems about his own insecurities regarding existentialism and endured occasional bouts of anxiety and self-doubt arising from the anti-rationalist bias of existentialist theorists like Kierkegaard and Berdyaev. He particularly found their assault on rationalism and religious truth too unbearable to sustain, and he persevered only by counterbalancing this assault with the realism and rationalism of Jacques Maritain and the Aristolean-Thomistic mode of philosophizing. By his own admission, his inner doubts and fears of existentialism were soothed by the additional information afforded by the post-war flow of European books and English translations of existentialist texts.[27]

Why Sayegh chose existentialism as his preferred choice of philosophy remains a matter of conjecture. Some claim that his professor, Charles Malik, a noted Christian existentialist, played a key role in luring him to the existential position: "During the early 1940s, Sayegh ... immersed in the Malik philosophical circles and had imbibed a sufficient dose of existential philosophy to enable him to write with passion his master's thesis on the topic of personal existence."[28] This explanation is not entirely implausible, but it does not explain how Sayegh could have

---

25 Fayez Sayegh, "Existential Philosophy: A Formal Examination." (Georgetown University, 1949): xvi.

26 Habib C. Malik, op. cit.

27 Fayez Sayegh, "Existential Philosophy: A Formal Examination." (Georgetown University, 1949): xvi.

28 Habib C. Malik, op. cit.

remained involved and strongly committed to the Party and to Sa'adeh in 1946 despite Malik's aversion to Sa'adeh's ideological orientation and political taste. Moreover, the evidence suggests that Sayegh did not always find Charles Malik agreeable and openly criticized him. Among his many essays from that period is one in which Sayegh stands up to his teacher after attending one of his public lectures on nationalism. Echoing Western critics of nationalism as regressive and hegemonic, Malik stated:

> Nationalism maintains that man in himself is a nationalist ... that his existence is not complete unless he belongs concretely to a specific nation. Moreover, man to the extent he wants to fulfill his being must direct all his duties and loyalties to his nation alone.[29]

In the essay, Sayegh took issue with Malik over this parsimony and narrow description. "As a 'nationalist', I do not see myself exclusively through the restricted prism implied by the lecturer."[30] The fact that a nationalist owes his primary duty to the nation does not necessarily preclude the nationalist of life's larger duties and loyalties to the groups and institutions that form the nation, the broader community of nations, universal literature and art, and the noble ideals of right and justice. Thus, according to Sayegh, man is not a "nationalist" but a social entity first. He becomes a "nationalist" or has become a "nationalist" because man has arrived at a stage in life where the "nation" has come to represent the perfect and most complete expression of his social existence. The logic he followed was intended to serve the cause of "positive nationalism"; a concept he would develop and remain committed to for most of his life. In fact, in his response, Sayegh invoked the concept of "positive nationalism" several times to distinguish his conception from Malik's distinctly negative tag that juxtaposes all that is nationalist with all that is supposedly obnoxious.

---

29 Quoted in Fayez Sayegh, *al-baath al-qawmi*. (Beirut: Dar Fikr, 2nd ed. n.d.): 76.
30 *Ibid.*

After obtaining his PhD, Sayegh produced several essays from an existentialist perspective, but they were trifling in comparison with his output in political writings. The scale and speed of political developments in the Middle East, especially in Palestine and Egypt with Nasser's rise to power, compelled him to return to politics.

THE THIRD PHASE

In this phase of Sayegh's intellectual development, which spanned much of the 1950s and 1960s, Sayegh developed a reserved admiration for pan-Arab nationalism. Stepping away from the Syrian nationalism of the 1940s, he embraced the cause of Arab unity and took up the mantle of the League of Arab States. In 1956, following the Suez fiasco and Nasser's emergence as an undisputed leader of Arab nationalism, Sayegh jumped on the Nasser pan-Arab bandwagon. Like many others, he believed that the moment of deliverance for Arabs had finally arrived:

> For the first time in centuries, Arab forces have now appeared on the stage of Arab life ready and able to remake Arab history. For the first time in many centuries, Arab leadership has asserted itself as the principal actor on the stage of Arab life, abandoning alike the observer's seat and the spectatorial role formerly assigned to it. No longer is Arab society content with reciting a script written by someone else, or with suffering meekly during a performance, supposedly its own but actually designed neither for its enjoyment nor for its edification. At long last, the Arabs have now emerged, in their own homeland, as the makers of their own history.[31]

The formation of the United Arab Republic (UAR) in 1957 added mightily to Sayegh's interest in the Arab idea. The pace of his writing and lecturing on Arab unity intensified and

---

31 Quoted in Betty S. Anderson, *The American University of Beirut*. (University of Texas Press, 2011): 16.

he contributed a comprehensive ideo-historical account and analysis of the Arab national movement: *Arab Unity: Hope and Fulfillment*. Hailed for its "grace and dignity of scholarship",[32] the book elevated Sayegh to new academic heights and enhanced his reputation as chief spokesman in America of Arab political aspirations. In his public talks and addresses, he began to promote the concept of "dynamic nationalism" as the "only real alternative, both to untenable reactionary system at home and to unwanted domination from the outside (whether direct or indirect)",[33] and to apply it to Nasser:

> It is beginning, nowadays, to dawn on those who had maligned him viciously in the past, that President Nasser symbolizes this type of nationalism, which moves forcefully to eliminate backwardness and corruption, through introducing reform and thus averting Communist-exploited eruptions of popular discontent; and which also moves effectively to eliminate vestiges of degrading domination by the Colonial Powers while averting — through its dynamic policy of non-alignment — Soviet domination.[34]

Nonetheless, it is necessary to point out two closely related issues concerning Sayegh's pan-Arab inclinations. First, despite the exhilaration evoked by Nasser and the surge of Arab nationalism under his leadership, Sayegh did not join any pan-Arab movement or political party: Nasserist or non-Nasserist. He remained politically independent and did not cross the moral threshold in his appraisal of Arabism. Second, Sayegh did not convert to Arab nationalism in the full ideological sense. He was more inclined to the concept of "Arabism" than to the doctrine of "Arab nationalism". His discourse was "political" rather than "national". It advocated for a "unified political system" for the "Arab lands" (anything from federal to

---

[32] Zafar Ishaq Ansari, "The Movement For Arab Unity: A Review Article." (*Pakistan Horizon*, Vol. 13, No. 3 (Third Quarter, 1960): 240-45.

[33] Fayez Sayegh, "For the Record." (*The Caravan*, Brooklyn, N. Y., Thursday, January 15, 1959): 7.

[34] *Ibid.*

confederal to commonwealth) rather than union in a national sense. Sayegh called it "Arab dynamic nationalism" (as opposed to Arab nationalism), and he defined its frame of reference primarily in terms of positive constructs such as independence, social progress, unity, neutralism, and socialist reforms.

THE FOURTH PHASE

This phase, which overlaps with the previous three phases, was Sayegh's most intense phase. It is the stage of the Palestine cause. Apart from Syrian nationalism in the early part of his life, no other issue captured Sayegh's attention like Palestine. Its cause became his life quest. He dedicated his time and work to almost entirely attempting to debunk Zionist myths. Hardly a claim passed without capturing his attention or investigation. As a proficient writer, Sayegh did not disappoint.

The amount of literature on Palestine that flowed from Sayegh's pen was vast and scrupulously impartial. He was very methodical and left no stone unturned in the pursuit of his objective. He managed his responses with great regularity. Still, it was not always pleasant for him, nor did he expect it to be. As a large organization with infinite resources, the Zionists were always there to block his efforts. The attacks came from all sides and in every conceivable form. However, Sayegh's ability to present his case with logical and commonsense knowledge and to convince his audience and readers that he was morally and intellectually qualified to address the topic at hand proved too problematic to be overcome by appeals to traditional tactics. Repeatedly, Zionists would attempt to paint him as an anti-Semite, but Sayegh was too clever for them. He would not be drawn into that kind of introspection. His incisiveness and total dedication thwarted every effort to deflect him from the central issues.

One does not have to read far through Sayegh's various works to appreciate his intense commitment to countering Zionism's misguided mythology. His central argument, which he continued to develop and streamline all his life, was very clear and precise: as an exclusivist political movement of the Jewish people, Zionism is a process of systematic colonization based on the combined form of forcible dispossession of the indigenous population, their expulsion from their own country, the implantation of an alien sovereignty on their soil, and the speedy importation of hordes of aliens to occupy the land thus emptied of its rightful inhabitants. For Sayegh, nothing could be more inhuman and racist. The physical and human losses of such an enterprise might be unimaginable, but they were dwarfed before the longer-term repercussions on the displaced Palestinians:

> The people of Palestine has lost not only political control over its country, but physical occupation of its country as well: it has been deprived not only of its inalienable right to self-determination, but also of its elemental right to exist on its own land.[35]

Depictions of Zionism as a colonial project may be as old as the Zionist movement itself. Sayegh was the one who established the right theoretical foundation for it. By making it a primary research interest, he delivered a critical assessment of Zionist ideology and built a comprehensive discourse that rationally-countered and brilliantly illuminated a host of problems and issues. Its wide acknowledgement by researchers and decision-makers reveals the power and credibility of his analysis, as does his success with United Nations General Assembly Resolution 3379. Sayegh's tireless personal quest to inform the misguided American public about Zionism also deserves attention. Drawing on his extensive experience looking at American political habits and speech, he could determine the patterns in Americans' acceptance or rejection of ideas and use them to great effect to

---

35 Fayez A. Sayegh Collection, University of Utah, Box 222, Folder 4. Sayegh analyzed the violent nature of Israel as a settler colonial state informed by a racist ideology in his 1965 book *Zionist Colonization of Palestine*. (Beirut: Research Center, Palestine Liberation Organization, 1965).

convey the facts. He did not achieve much success on this front, but neither did anyone else.

Conclusion

Fayez Sayegh developed a keen sense for the important constellations in sociopolitical reality early in his life. In its evolving forms and character, this sense exemplified a life spent in pursuit of justice and political awareness at various levels. In the process, Sayegh left a body of lasting literature that is probably greater than that of any other Near Eastern writer. What makes this literature so exciting is its thematic and aesthetic diversity. One cannot help but be struck by its peculiar intellectual consistency and painstakingly detailed and informative analysis.

The excellence of Sayegh's literary output was overshadowed only by his reputation as a skillful public speaker and debater. On this level, as well, he gave outstanding performances and displayed exceptional skills regarding the working and application of his ideas. He had the knack to dodge information rhetoric and he always strove to remain current and up-to-date. His ability to be the first to take charge and prevent his opponents from drawing him into futile polemics was another strong feature.

That much is pretty well known and established. Nonetheless, large gaps in Sayegh's biographical profile requires attention before a more complete picture of his life can be obtained. The largest gap in this profile appertains to Sayegh's eight-year spell as an active senior officer with the Syrian National Party between 1939 and 1947.

2

The Rise of Fayez Sayegh in the SSNP

Fayez Sayegh hailed from a family that understood the practical value of education. Despite the family's involvement in political struggles, it strove for the highest standard of education and the worldly enjoyment of its members. The family was also deeply steeped in the patriotic spirit and open to the values and perspectives of secular life despite its Presbyterian tradition. Therefore, it was only natural that, when the Sayegh brothers relocated to Beirut in the mid-1930s to pursue their education at the American University of Beirut, they would mingle with groups that embodied the values and ideals of their upbringing the most. Before long, they found their calling in a tightly organized and highly ideological group called the Syrian Social Nationalist Party (SSNP). Headed by the erudite and charismatic Antun Sa'adeh, the SSNP had several engaging features: a strong accent on social unity, a penchant for secular values, a hardnosed opposition to Zionism, an antipathy for religious sectarianism, an appetite for modern ideas, and a flair for discipline and ethics. The Party resonated strongly with young idealists discontented with the status quo and the existing divisions. It particularly attracted intellectuals and university students despite an official ban on political parties and the numerous risks to which it exposed members.

The Sayegh brothers joined the SSNP in quick succession: Yusif in 1936, Fuad in 1937, and Fayez in 1938. Of the three, Fayez was the brother who left a profound and lasting mark on the Party. For almost nine years (1938–1947), nothing occupied his mind and soul more compellingly and intensely than the SSNP. In conjunction with his academic studies, Fayez served its cause, promoted its principles, and garnered support for its vision with flawless dedication and loyalty.

As his first Party responsibility, Fayez served as head of the AUB student branch at the tender age of 20.[1] This was a dangerous position to hold with war raging and the ruling French cracking down on political activists. The war also brought the wrath of the Arab nationalists and other active groups on the campus with it.

Fayez's tireless efforts were noticed and certainly appreciated by the Party. In near record time, he was elevated to a senior rank and appointed as officer-in-charge of its cultural department.

Two factors facilitated Sayegh's rapid rise in the Party's hierarchy:

1. Antun Sa'adeh's departure in 1938 to South America on a diplomatic mission for the Party and the incarceration of the Party's senior cadres and functionaries soon after the outbreak of World War II. This rapid depletion of leadership opened the door wide for the induction of "new blood" into the Party's leadership, and Sayegh happened to be in the right place at the right time.

2. Sayegh's proficiency and engaging style were too good to pass up. His academic style and ability to articulate complex thoughts and convey them with interpersonal efficacy and confidence gave him a clear edge over others, including some of the more established members of the Party.

By all accounts, Fayez handled himself with the utmost competence and integrity. He did not waver from his convictions and maintained a high standard of conduct. He was always reliable and hardworking. Despite the unpleasant atmosphere of intimidation, fear, and persecution unleashed by the ruling French, Fayez did not deviate from his commitment to the Party. He continued to invest his time and energy in it, even

---

[1] Adib Qaddura, *Haqa'iq wa Mawaqif.* (Beirut: Dar Fikr, 1989): 99.

when the situation looked bleak and hopeless. According to his brother, Anis, Fayez's dedication exposed him to the wrath and indignation of the French authorities, but somehow he managed to escape from them. His other brother, Yusif, recalls: "During that period, Fayez was in hiding for almost a year; the French wanted him because of his fiery speeches. He grew a beard and put on a monk's habit. That is why his Master's took longer than it should. He lived in the mountains, in the houses of Party members."[2]

After Lebanon gained independence in 1943, Fayez's name and stature spread like wildfire. He developed a formidable reputation as a competent public speaker and an authority and writer both on Party and non-Party issues. Marveling at his amazing ability, the Party leadership reciprocated by furnishing him with a platform to exercise his skills and showcase his talent:

> From the age of 15 or 16, Fayez could write articles with an engaging content and a lively mind and a foresight that exceeded his age. He won the admiration of all of us, including Sa'adeh, and we came to anticipate his development and academic attainment eagerly so that we could utilize him for the Party on a full-time basis.[3]

Fayez did not disappoint. He proved his worth and rose to the challenge with grace and dignity. He was an extremely gifted and generous speaker and very capable in executing a range of different activities and tasks. He was so effective and invaluable that the SSNP's constitution was amended to promote him to the Party's Supreme Council before he had met all the required conditions for joining it.

After 1944, Fayez held several executive posts in the Party. He rose in 1946 to the dual positions of Dean of Culture and Dean

---

2 Rosemary Sayigh (ed.), *Yusif Sayigh: Arab Economist Palestinian Patriot, A Fractured Life Story.* (Cairo: The American University in Cairo Press, 2015): 132.

3 Abdullah Qubersi, *Memoirs*, Vol. 2. (Beirut: Dar Fikr, 1982): 192.

of Information. This catapulted him into the political limelight and made him one of the most visible faces in the Party's top hierarchy. A four-part breakdown and review of his duties and responsibilities in 1946 will demonstrate his performance and stamina in the SSNP.

1. NEWSPAPER SUPERVISOR / EDITOR

As chief of the SSNP Information Department, Fayez was responsible for the Party's publications. This included the regular bulletins and internal missives issued directly by the department as well as the Party's official newspaper *Sada an-Nahda*. Between 1946 and 1947, assisted by a team of capable writers and columnists and with the full backing of his peers, he oversaw the publication of *Sada an-Nahda*. He attended to this duty with the same care and attention that he had given to previous collaborations. Fayez's name did not appear on the paper's editorial board, but he was effectively the person in charge because the Party's internal by-laws placed all publications under the jurisdiction of the Information department.

As overseer, Fayez's role was to ensure the strict adherence of the paper to the Party line. He could not have had much trouble with this because the editors and contributors were almost all Party members with varying degrees of journalistic and ideological experience. Some of them, like paper's first editor, Farid Mubarak, had worked on previous Party publications. Adherence to the Party line meant, in the first place, observance of the Party's policies in both internal and external matters - from the Party's policy of "openness" on the Lebanese regime, to its opposition to Zionism and Communism, and to its aversion to sectarian politics. In the handling of this responsibility, Sayegh showed both leadership and maturity. He delegated issues of a strictly Lebanese nature largely to the Party's "Lebanon" experts, like Asad al-Ashqar, Abdullah Qubersi, and Mustapha Abdul Satir, while he then concentrated on issues which he could accomplish more since they were germane to his interests.

As for his own contribution to the paper, it was as generous as that of anyone else. First, the paper's regular second-page editorial column, published under the pseudonym "an-Nahda", came entirely from Sayegh's pen. In 1946, he contributed two editorial series. The first consisted of 44 commentaries from February 9 to April 30, and the second consisted of 26 short reviews from July 11 to August 10. In both cases, he introduced and discussed elemental issues of society (national struggle, reform, political parties, role of culture, freedom of thought, independence, etc.) from the national perspective of the Party. Occasionally, Fayez would insert his own personal opinions and views, but not forcefully enough to take him beyond the Party's ideology.

Second, Fayez contributed regular reviews and features either in anticipation of certain events or in response to sensitive situations. He was extremely efficient at composing fast responses under pressure. For example, in 1946 he managed to produce a detailed response within a few days from the release of the report by the Anglo-American Committee of Inquiry into conditions in Mandatory Palestine. In his response, he mercilessly berated the report's recommendations with factual refutations. Furthermore, Fayez's feature articles covered a wide range of issues including labor rights, independence, political freedom, concepts of reform, Communism, Zionism, and of course, nationalism. The frequency and intensity of the articles reflected the measure of his commitment to the Party.

Third, Fayez carefully avoided radical excesses and usually preferred to write in a composed and moderate tone. When a situation arose, however, he could write forcefully, which he did on several occasions. His assertiveness struck primarily and most directly in his routine "responses" to press rumors and political gossip about the Party and in his commentaries on Communism and Zionism. A case in point is the hard-hitting response Fayez wrote to a government suspension order against *Sada an-Nahda* on June 5, 1946, in which he berated the authorities for banning newspapers that dared to broach the issue of corruption in an attempt to deflect public attention from the corruption devouring the state.[4]

Fayez omitted no opportunity to strike back at the Party's critics, even when others were present to answer back. He was always there and ready to provide vigorous refutations. His duty was to monitor the press and to correct misconceptions and falsehoods, and he certainly fulfilled this role. He spared no one. Even the "Syrian" and "Egyptian" press came under his microscopic scrutiny.

Fayez Sayegh's supervisory management of *Sada an-Nahda* enabled him to maintain the public presence he had accomplished through other mediums of the Party. It gave him exposure and the perfect opportunity to parade his pen and react quickly to political events. It also afforded him a forum in which to communicate the viewpoints and beliefs of the Party without impinging on his private life. Through the paper, he could stay in touch with political realities and prove his worth to the Party. The result was a positive outcome for both himself and the Party.

2. Public Speaking

In addition to serving as newspaper administrator, in 1946, Fayez Sayegh served as the Party's front man in public and ideological matters. He dominated the rostrum for the entire year with one incredible performance after another. The power of his commanding oratory came to the fore, and he tantalized audiences with his range and improvisational skills. According to those who knew him, Fayez was overly confident in his own intellectual abilities and obtained a strong sense of pleasure and satisfaction from using them. He was unquestionably aware of his oratory gift, and his unparalleled ability to connect with people was widely acknowledged.

---

[4] *Sada an-Nahda.* (Beirut: 5 June 1946).

The Rise of Fayez Sayegh in the SSNP

A cursory look at Fayez's public engagements for 1946 is enough to form an approximate picture of his dynamic personality and achievements:

DATE	PLACE	SUBJECT
26 March	Damascus	Our Primary Enemy
11 April	Beirut	Communism
16 April	Beit Meri	Religious Sectarianism
20 April	Damascus	Independence Day
1 May	AUB	Thought and Society
22 May	Beirut	SSNP and Arab Cause
22 July	Mt. Lebanon	Meaning of Nation
25 July	South Lebanon	SSNP Program
22 August	Haifa	The Path
28 August	South Lebanon	Political Parties
2 September	Dhur Shweir	Reform in National Life
10 Sept.	Hakour	Farmers' Rights
17 Sept.	Dhur Shweir	SSNP Mission
17 Sept.	Munsif	Ethical Reforms
29 Sept.	Baalbek	SSNP Principles

This schedule lists only the lectures and addresses reported in *Sada an-Nahda* in 1946. It is incomplete since Fayez's speaking roster for that year included, in addition to the above engagements, a series of talks to the Party's student branches in Beirut and Damascus. *Sada an-Nahda* did not report those talks fully but made passing references to them. Collectively, the speeches reveal several striking features about Fayez: (1) he enjoyed the challenge of public speaking and gave it all the skills and oratory abilities he commanded; (2) although he spoke on a wide variety of subjects, he almost always reverted back to the National Party and spoke in the light of its ideology; (3) his speeches tended to draw large crowds and admiration to the point that political and intellectual groups beyond the Party sometimes invited him to address them on certain topics; (4) he did not mind travelling back and forth between Lebanon, Palestine, and al-Sham (Syrian Republic) to speak; and (5) he was, *par excellence*, the SSNP's most eminent public speaker.

As popular as he was with the audience, Fayez often invited wrath from political adversaries. The Communists were particularly menacing. They pursued him with vengeance and great eagerness in their attempts to prevent or obstruct him from talking. This speaks volumes about Fayez's rhetorical skills and the power of his spoken word. The Communists confronted Fayez because his knowledge and insights into the Marxist/ Communist system and his ability to present effective and coordinated arguments against Communist beliefs hurt them far more than the demagoguery and xenophobia of other groups. At least three times (twice in Lebanon and once in Palestine), the Communists tried to cut him off either by trying to shout him down or by engaging in scaremongering tactics. Yet Fayez remained firm and true to his cause. Despite the risk to his life, he continued to speak out against Communism and to critique its errors and adherents.

Fayez's speaking engagements constituted yet another benchmark in his Party career. The intensity and frequency of his oratory is a testament to the steadfast zeal with which he held and defended the SSNP, and it is a reflection of his deep conviction in the aim and principles of its program. Fayez did not mince words or veil his feelings. Nor did he disguise his disdain for the Party's political opponents. He deftly tackled controversial issues and spoke candidly and directly, aided by the sound logic and critical, realistic analysis that would become the hallmark of his entire oeuvre. Nonetheless, the SSNP is entitled to much credit for placing its entire Information apparatus at his disposal and for giving him all the support it could muster to help him develop and perfect his skills.

3. Information and Cultural Responsibilities

In addition to serving as newspaper administrator and public speaker, Fayez's appointment as Dean of the SSNP's Cultural and Information Departments could not have come at a more challenging time. 1946 was the year of the French evacuating from Lebanon-Syria and the beginning of political independence in both states. It was also the year of planning and preparation for parliamentary and presidential elections. Those developments, coming so close to the end of World War II, coincided with a period of great political turbulence in the region marked by the rise of Communism as a powerful and frightening ideology and by the advance of Zionism as a real force of Jewish colonialism in Palestine.

As a national movement, the SSNP had a direct stake in local and regional developments. It could not afford to look on passively while the destiny of the nation it purported to represent was being determined and shaped by forces beyond its control. Traditionally, the task of responding to fateful moments and dramatic changes was left entirely to Sa'adeh, but as he was barred from re-entering the country, it became a shared responsibility between the Party's legislative body (the Supreme Council) and its executive body (the Deans' Council). After the war, the greater part of that responsibility was delegated to Fayez Sayegh due to his information skills, wide knowledge and accurate, clear way of thinking. Furthermore, his proven proficiency in writing also confirmed his eligibility for the task.

Though he was only 25 years old, Fayez proved a capable and effective choice. He showed a profound awareness of ideological complexities and handled political challenges with great dexterity and nimbleness. As head of the named departments, he performed many functions and fulfilled a variety of roles both behind the scenes and publicly. In addition to his obligation as editor of *Sada an-Nahda*, Fayez was tasked with:

1. Publishing and contributing to the Party's internal bulletin "*Nashrat Imdat al-Iza'ah*".

2. Issuing regular guidelines to the Party branches on the conduct of indoctrination and initiation sessions.

3. Answering and clarifying queries received from members on ideological issues.

4. Organizing and speaking at Party conventions and public rallies and celebrations.

5. Giving press conferences, interviews, and replying to press reports about the Party when needed.

6. Representing the Party at general political meetings and official engagements.

Moreover, in 1946, Fayez produced two significant memorandums on behalf of the Party. The first, "Note on the Palestine Problem", was written in English to convey the Party's message quickly and accurately. It was submitted to the Anglo-American Committee of Inquiry on March 19, 1946. The following day, *Sada an-Nahda* published an Arabic version of the memorandum. Upon the release of the Committee's report at the end of April 1946, Fayez was asked to respond to its findings and recommendations. He did so with an extensive analysis. He tore into the report for its simplistic logic and blanket judgments and criticized the Committee for backing away from the hard facts to appease influential Zionists. Fayez used the occasion to call for the formation of a "United Front" and for an urgent meeting of the recently founded League of Arab States to save Palestine.

The second memorandum, addressed to the Arab League, took aim at King Abdullah's Greater Syria Scheme. Fayez argued, somewhat carelessly, that the scheme was a British ruse to consolidate and further Britain's imperial domination of the Near East through the agency of Emir Abdullah. He affirmed:

The Greater Syria scheme is a threat to the independence of the two states in the region it seeks to unite [namely Syria and Lebanon]. It relinquishes the territories of Cilicia and Alexandretta, consecrates sectarianism in Lebanon, and seeks to turn the country into a religious safe haven for a particular group. Conversely, it endeavors to establish a Jewish home in the heart of a dear sector, which has struggled hard to defend itself from the alien Jews. In addition to all of this, the scheme calls for a system of government that it is inimical with the foundations of modern civilization and its concepts as well as with all the values that every open-minded person cherishes.[5]

The Jordanian government took offense to this memorandum and issued a public statement reprimanding Fayez for attempting to vilify the scheme. Fayez countered that he could provide the documentary evidence to confirm both the memorandum and his subsequent statement to United Press. The matter ended there. In fairness, it should be said that the memorandum was written at the behest of the Party's Supreme Council, which, having veered the Party in a Lebanonist direction in 1945, was determined to stay the course by doing whatever it took to appease the Lebanese State, whose objection to the Greater Syria Scheme was paramount.

4. Monographs

Given the plethora of tasks he carried out simultaneously, as described above, it is quite incredible that Fayez's writing output was so enormous. Yet this output does not represent the full magnitude of his literary oeuvre. Between 1946 and 1947, Fayez also published three monographs from a distinctly Party perspective. The first, *al-Tariq* or *The Path*, grew out of a lecture organized by the Orthodox Club in Haifa on August 17, 1946. It is essentially an odyssey into the "Path" that passionate and

---

5   Fayez Sayegh, *The Greater Syria Scheme*, The Syrian National Party (Information Bureau), Beirut, 6 December, 1946: 26.

sincere reformers of society must conquer in their attempt to eliminate social maladies and achieve correct reforms. However, according to Fayez, not everyone qualifies for such an undertaking. The "path" is reserved for only the strongest and most determined individuals: those with the right vision and the highest standard of ethical conduct who can endure the challenge of reform and stay its full course. It is neither a utopian ideal nor an unreachable phantom, but it does pass through ranges of precipitous heights and deep gorges. There is also a logical sense of indispensability associated with the "path" arising from and justified by the need to move forward and to attain excellence. *The Path* captures the essence of this odyssey and reminds us how we are all connected in a common endeavor.

Fayez intended this monograph as a wake-up call for the people of Syria. It is essentially a civilized appeal to their good senses to take the "path" of genuine reform and progress without looking over their shoulders or waiting in vain. If others could do it, so could they, but they first had to master the inherent value of the "path" and learn to resist the temptations of compromise and mediocrity. The message is clear and straightforward, but its underlying theme is precisely the meaning that Sa'adeh had already imparted. On reading the monograph, Sa'adeh remarked:

> *The Path* is a product of the school of Syrian Social Nationalist thought. It is infused with the spirit of national revival and the ideals of the ethical philosophy of our movement. Indeed, I detected a keen response in it to my call for great heroism as described in my second missive from Argentina. *The Path* abounds with faith, heroism, and self-confidence. It is a book for the generation of the new life – the social nationalist life – that we aim to create.[6]

Fayez's second monograph, *al-taifiyah* or *Sectarianism*,[7] is

---

6   SSNP Information Bulletin, No. 4, 15 August, 1947.

7   Fayez A. Sayigh, *Al-ṭa'ifiyya: Bath fi asbabiha wa-akhṭariha wa-'ilajihaā* (*Sectarianism: A Study into its Causes, Dangers, and Treatment*) (Beirut:

considered one of the first conceptual and methodological approaches to examine, diagnose, and propose treatments for the problem of sectarianism. According to Max Weiss, in this monograph, Fayez succeeds in shifting the discourse on sectarianism from a legalistic analysis of its administration to a broader social perspective relating to Lebanese society and culture:

> Echoing the historical amnesia often observed in contemporary Lebanon, Fayez argued there was no need to recount historical events contributing to the present context of Lebanese sectarianism. In his words, 'The important thing is for us to attend the reality of [sectarianism], to be aware of its manifestations.' Recognizing that political and social reality might be separable from the essential qualities constituting sectarianism – what might be called sectarian effects – he was more concerned with the fact that sectarianism resides in "popular life" and in the "popular consciousness" (*al-nafsiyya al-sha'biyya*). The latter is both its "principal headquarters" and its "greatest danger". If not for such a popular dimension, moreover, "the institutions focused on [sectarianism] would not have developed in the first place". Nevertheless, according to Fayez, sectarianism resided in institutions, which "are a mirror of society, expressing the desires of its constituencies (*fi'at*) and embodying the different interests that play a role in its life".[8]

In *Sectarianism*, in keeping with the Party's secular outlook, Fayez proposed understanding the phenomenon of sectarianism as anathema to the ideal-type modern state. He argued that, through the interference of religious leaders in the affairs of state, "sectarianism strikes its final blow against the structure of the state: here sectarianism strikes with a harsh hammer the

---

Manshurat Maktabat al-Wajib, 1947).

8   Max Weiss "The Historiography of Sectarianism in Lebanon." (*History Compass* 7/1, 2009): 141–54.

skull of the civilized state (*al-dawla al-madaniyya*) without mercy, here the state is subjected to powers and interests, not aiming at the highest level towards the good of society". With the Party's national program in mind, Fayez concluded with the ominous warning that sectarianism stands as an "obstacle" to the "progress and advancement of the nation and as a shameful stain on the forehead of its history".[9]

The third monograph, *al-baath al-qawmi* or *National Resurrection*, is a collection of essays and speeches Fayez delivered between 1941 and 1946. These essays and speeches cover topics across the social, cultural, and national spectrums from the standpoint of the Party's nationalist conception. Some were original interpretations while others were mere restatements of Sa'adeh's already published ideas. The significance of *National Resurrection* derived from its ability to provide much needed explanations and helpful hints about the Party, although some members judged it as an exercise in self-promotion. Fayez's choice of topics (nationalism, reform, Zionism, national revival, Communism) reveals that (1) Fayez took the Party very seriously and was deeply committed to everything it stood for and (2) Antun Sa'adeh acted as the single and most dominant influence on his burgeoning intellect. Fayez's commitment to both Sa'adeh and the Party can be gauged from the positive and strong ideological orientation of this monograph and its clear advocacy for national reform.

THE CONTENT AND TRAJECTORY OF FAYEZ'S PARTY WRITINGS

Although he showed glimpses of independent thinking, Fayez stayed within the ideological perimeters established by Antun Sa'adeh. He did not attempt to question the validity and authenticity of Sa'adeh's ideas or tamper with the broad outlines of his ideological system. To the contrary, he looked to Sa'adeh

---

9   (http://www.al-akhbar.com/node/7770). 20 July, 2017.

as his mentor and role model, often speaking reverently of him and tapping into his expertise and guidance. Above all, Fayez openly admired the courage and resilience of Sa'adeh and highly appreciated his insight. In November 1946, for example, he held a large banquet at his residence to mark the tenth anniversary of Sa'adeh's first arrest and imprisonment. The banquet, attended by the *crème de la crème* of Lebanon's political and intellectual establishment, served as a sobering reminder of Sa'adeh's bravery in the face of danger and adversity.[10]

The trajectory of Fayez's writings also speaks volumes about his commitment to the Party. Beginning in 1941, he set out to develop a theoretical framework for the concept of reform stipulated in the Party's national program. The endeavor was initiated with a lecture to the Reform Club in Beit Shabab at the end of 1941 in which Fayez identified the constituents and stages of reform as:

1. Awareness of the extant corruption

2. Defining the target

3. Drawing up practical plans

4. Implementation

For six years, Fayez wrote and spoke on the subject of reform with passion, honesty and perseverance. Under the patronage of the "national institution" (*al-mu'assassa al-qawmiyah*) of the SSNP, he travelled around Palestine, Lebanon, and the Syrian Republic to speak on the nature and fundamentals of reform and the Party's program of national revival. Following his lecture at Beit Shabab, he set out to describe and analyze each constituent element individually.

Fayez addressed the first constituent in a lecture delivered at the Catholic Club in Haifa under the rubric "A Nation Crying for

---

10   Full coverage of the banquet can be found in Sada an-Nahda, 19 November, 1946.

Help". He addressed the second constituent in a lecture at the Nahda Club in Nazareth.[11] Next, Fayez published 44 consecutive articles in the Party's newspaper, *Sada an-Nahda*, in which he explored and analyzed the practical plans needed to accommodate the regulatory requirements of reform. Almost simultaneously, he published a five-part series on the implementation aspect of reform in the Party's internal cultural bulletin.

A fair share of Fayez's public engagements on behalf of the Party was also taken up by the reform issue. In 1945, he delivered two major speeches on reform: one in the Lebanese town of al-Mtayn and the other in Baaklin. He gave at least three equally reform emphasizing speeches in 1946. The pace and tone of his writings on reform increased towards the end of 1946 in anticipation of parliamentary elections in Lebanon. No less than thirty-three short articles on the role of "political parties in national reform" flowed from his pen during this period. In all cases, Fayez used his insights and analytical skills to improvise and develop the reform vision proposed by Sa'adeh. He did not attempt to introduce a different vision or develop a new conceptual framework for the analysis of reform. Like others in the Party, he considered Sa'adeh's perspective correct and beyond challenge. Thus, feeding directly from Sa'adeh, Fayez began by reaffirming the Party's view that reform was not only healthy but also necessary:

> Regardless how difficult it may be, reform is a human necessity. It is a requirement of refined human life in all its stages. It is the rescuer of human life from its natural disposition to lapse into decadence ... Reform is indispensable as long as man is incomplete, and since man will forever remain incomplete, there will always be a need for reform.[12]

No doubt, the improved understanding of reform was vital for

---

11 This lecture was subsequently revised, expanded and published in the Lebanese daily *Beirut* in 1941.

12 *Al-baath al-Qawmi*, 84.

its effective implementation and sustainability. Fayez focused his mind on the issue of reform not only to draw attention to some of its salient features, but also to suggest and facilitate further investigation into it. After a careful examination, he concluded (1) reform, like any other human manifestation, is governed by laws that cannot be wished away or abrogated at will; (2) the management of reform in a divided and crisis-ridden society like Syria's cannot be left to politicians who thrive on the decadence of the status quo or whose actions are dictated by expediency and self-interest; and (3) as a tapestry of profound responsibilities and duties, reform should be entrusted to visionary reformers acknowledged for their devotional integrity and high ethical and moral standards.

When read against the initial themes developed by Sa'adeh, it becomes evident that Fayez, in addition to willfully framing his analysis with Sa'adeh's vision in mind, was maneuvering to promote Sa'adeh as the ideal reformer for the nation. He could easily be mistaken for talking about himself, but the myriad of praises and admiration he heaped upon Sa'adeh in his speeches and writings indicates otherwise.

The second major theme in Fayez's political writings during that period was the threat of Communism. Nationalists and Communists were bitter rivals. Therefore, it was only natural for the "nationalist" Fayez to take a stand against Communism. He literally tore into local Communists, accusing them of incompetence and a lack of loyalty and slating their radical views as a pernicious creed that created more division than it pretended to solve. While recognizing the existence of class struggle, Fayez developed a very low opinion of Communism. He dismissed Marxist dialectical materialism as pseudo-science and accused local Communists of accentuating class division by attempting to superimpose the interests of the working class on the rest of society. He argued that this was both inimical to social unity and deceiving, because it merely reshuffled the hierarchy of class struggle instead of eliminating class struggle altogether.

Playing on popular sentiments, Fayez went on to describe Communism as a godless creed. He cast the theory and practice of Communism as not only opposed to all religions, but as expressing only hatred toward faith as taught by all religions. The question of the incompatibility of communism and religion is neither new nor uncommon. However, Fayez went beyond the sentimental approach of presenting the issue in purely rhetorical terms. He applied himself to the Marxist system and invoked vivid examples of religious persecution under Communism. He also drew on contemporary Communist literature to prove that Communism is antireligious and utilized direct quotes from Marx and Lenin.[13] At one point, he published a series of front-page captions on the difference between the Communist creed and the Nationalist creed on various issues. The Communists were far from impressed.

However, nothing appalled Fayez more than the spectacle of seeing Communists blindly and with a total disregard to the national interest following Moscow's instructions. The local Communists received a heavy dose of criticism over this. They were depicted as godless puppets under Moscow and traitors of the national cause in the name of class solidarity and higher interests of the Soviet Union. Fayez did not have much trouble articulating this depiction. Soviet tacit endorsement of the Zionist colonial project in Palestine and the local Communists' own sympathetic response to it, which saw them extend a fraternal hand to Jewish workers while Palestinian workers and peasants were being dispossessed of their rights and land, gave him enough ammunition to build a strong case and mount a tenacious campaign against local Communists.

Fayez attacked the Communists with every means at his disposal, but he was most scathing in his public speeches and

---

13 Marx dubbed religion the "opiate of the masses," and opined that "Communism begins where atheism begins." Speaking on behalf of the Bolsheviks in his famous October 2, 1920 speech, Lenin stated matter-of-factly: "We do not believe in God."

appearances. His ability to express his views with clarity and force and to present them in a scholarly fashion was so deeply disturbing that the Communists tried to kill him:

> While Fayez was studying for his master's and doing a lot of work for the PPS [the French acronym for Parti Populaire Syrien, or SSNP], there was an attack on him that could have been fatal. He criticized the Arab Communists a great deal because of their position on Palestine. He was riding on a motorbike behind a friend of his who also had some high responsibility in the PPS. They were going to this person's home. On the road to Jal al-Deeb and Antalias, they were ambushed by three or four men with sticks. The men hit the rider on the motorcycle, the motorcycle spun around, and Fayez fell off. They concentrated on beating Fayez until he was unconscious. The young man who was with Fayez was wounded too, but the blows that Fayez got were mostly to his head. In fact, they thought that he was dead, and that is why they left him. We found out about this later because there was some jubilation in their circle over his death. But the other young man, the owner of the motorcycle, managed to get a lift, reach Jal-al-Deeb, and get the word out so that people could go and help Fayez. A couple who were very loyal PPS members – I think his name was Khalil Abu Jawdeh and his wife Linda – rushed in a car to pick Fayez up. When he woke up, he was in their home and he did not know what had happened to him, because he was still concussed. He refused to go to hospital because he was hiding from the authorities. He stayed there for two or three weeks until he recovered.[14]

The near fatal beating did not dissuade Fayez from attacking the local Communists and developing and defending the national idea of the SSNP. In April 1946, he gave a critical lecture on Communism at the American University of Beirut. The lecture

---

14 Rosemary Sayigh (ed.), *Yusif Sayigh: Arab Economist Palestinian Patriot, A Fractured Life Story*: 133.

precipitated a call for a live debate between Fayez and a Communist ideologue. A week later (on April 18, 1946), Fayez responded affirmatively to the call in writing in *Sada an-Nahda* on the condition that a transcript of the debate would be made public. The Communists did not respond, but a rumor spread that they accepted the challenge and offered to meet Fayez halfway. Fayez dismissed the rumor as baseless and the matter petered off after the Communists were unable to produce a copy of the letter of response.

The third and perhaps most important theme for Fayez was the question of Palestine. No other issue dominated his life and writings as much as this issue both during and after his involvement with the SSNP. One thing is certain, though. The seeds of his voluminous writings on the Palestine question, which contained some of the most profound reflections of our time on the nature of Zionism, were planted largely while he was active in the SSNP between 1938 and 1947. Moreover, they were planted by and cared for by the perception established by Antun Sa'adeh. This does not take away from the importance of Fayez's contribution and intellectual legacy: it merely puts them in the right perspective.

Sa'adeh developed an undisguised contempt and loathing for Zionism at an early age. In 1924, he wrote: "Despite that the Zionist movement is not rotating around a natural axis, yet, this movement has been able to make significant progress. If no other systematic movement is organized to counter it, it will eventually succeed".[15] By the early 1930s, Sa'adeh's attitude toward Zionism had changed from opposition to outright rejection. The entire Jewish and Judaist legacy came under scrutiny and was juxtaposed with Zionism as a common enemy. Sa'adeh was totally convinced that Zionism was a colonial settler ideology representing a danger of epic proportions not only for Palestine but for geographic Syria as well. He thought that this perception should be enshrined in the aim and program of his political party:

---
15   Antun Sa'adeh, *Complete Works*, vol.1: 8-25.

The principle [of Syrian nationhood] cannot be said to imply that Jews are a part of the Syrian nation and equal in rights and duties to the Syrians. Such an interpretation is incompatible with this principle that excludes the integration of elements with alien and exclusive racial loyalties in the Syrian nation. Such elements cannot fit into any homogeneous nation. For large settlements of immigrants in Syria, such as the Armenians, Kurds, and Circassians, assimilation is possible given sufficient time. These elements may dissolve in the nation and lose their special loyalties. Nevertheless, one large settlement cannot be reconciled, in any respect, to the principle of Syrian nationalism: the Jewish settlement. It is a dangerous settlement that can never be assimilated because it consists of a people that has remained a heterogeneous mixture, although it has mixed with many other peoples, instead of a nation with strange stagnant beliefs and aims of its own, which are essentially incompatible with Syrian rights and sovereignty ideals. It is the duty of the Syrian Social Nationalists to repulse the immigration of this people with all their might.[16]

Fayez was indoctrinated into this belief system at a very young age. He accepted its assessment and conclusions without question and went on to dissect and analyze the Zionist movement according to its reference system. His conclusions, which he never ceased to develop and revise, were repeatedly published in the Party's newspaper and used by critics of Zionism everywhere. A sense of his mindset can be obtained from the memorandum he wrote and presented to the Anglo-American Inquiry in 1946 on behalf of the SSNP:

> The traditional conception of the Palestine Problem as a dilemma with which the Promising Authorities are confronted, due to their simultaneous declaration of contradictory and irreconcilable promises, must be

---

16 Antun Sa'adeh, *The Ten Lectures*, p. 87.

exchanged for the alternative view of the Problem as an injustice which the Palestinians have been made to suffer through the introduction, into their country, of an alien people ambitious enough to look upon this country as their own and to seek to transform it into a national home wherein they will be not only the numerical majority, but the ruling power of the state as well! For, indeed, this is the problem, and it has to be viewed from this angle.[17]

Fayez utilized every opportunity to disparage Zionism. His blazing speech to the Christian-Islamic Conference in 1946 at Aley is a case in point. With sheer fury and force, he tore into Zionism and Judaism by describing them as a "danger to civilization and spirit". "Let it be understood", he told the participants, "Zionism is not a national movement in the contemporary sense but a pseudo-religious ideology that derives its principles fundamentally from 'Jewish mentality, Jewish history, and material culture'". He went on to characterize the Jewish worldview as a legacy of humiliation, retribution, and cultural fossilization of the most primitive kind. It is unclear why Fayez brought up this matter at the Conference. One can only assume that he did it to thwart any attempt to use the conference to build bridges with Judaism while Jewish immigration and land confiscation were expanding in Palestine.

Fayez's early writings on Zionism also included detailed analyses of the Balfour Declaration and he was ruthlessly uncompromising in his judgment. With analytical precision and attention to historical detail, he tore into the Declaration, labeling it as a blot on human history and a statement of injustice bordering on the denial of fundamental rights. He dismissed the Balfour Declaration as invalid, citing its contradiction with the very elemental rights of national existence and sovereignty: "Our rejection of the Balfour Declaration arises from this starting-point: the trespassing against the national rights of the Palestinian people. What we reject is precisely the arbitrary

---

17 See "Note on The Palestine Problem" in the appendix section of this book.

treatment of Palestine, and the determination of its destiny by powers not authorized to interfere in the fate of that country".[18] However, he did find one good thing about the Declaration: it inadvertently exposed the Zionists for what they really were – not the peace-loving and charitable group they had been made out to be, but a "gang of bloodthirsty, trigger-happy warmongers intent on a destructive course that may be irreversible". [19]

Philosophical Themes

Toward the end of 1945, a complex and contentious theme began to crop up in Sayegh's writings. Without declaring it to the Party, Sayegh began to promote a philosophical perspective centred on Berdyaev's existential concept of 'personalism'. In the process, nationalist values, such as power, loyalty, order, sovereignty, statehood, etc. were 'dressed-up' or 'toned-down' to accommodate this new concept. Without tampering with the Party's Aim and Program, Sayegh sought to inject a refreshing element into the Party's national political discourse consistent with the new moral order created by World War II.

This shift toward moral philosophy occurred soon after Sayegh completed his Master's thesis: "Personal Existence: Its Contents; Its Tragedy; Its Paradox". Drawing largely on Berdyaev's personalism, the thesis firmly stood for a conception of 'personal existence' as the highest perfection before which all social and political barriers must tumble and fall. The term 'personal existence' is used in a very strict sense to denote an inward self-realization of the individual personality as opposed to the general terms 'individual' and 'individuality':

> To exist as an individual is the minimum of human existence; it is the condition for attaining the maximum, for achieving the fullness of being which is personality...

---

18   *Sada an-Nahda*, 2 November, 1946.
19   *Ibid*.

Individuality is separateness, singularity. Personality is the fullness, the plenitude of achievement of the individual.[20]

According to Sayegh, true human existence is contingent on true personal existence, which in turn is contingent on the growth of the human personality. The latter is unconcerned with the "outward" or the "external" and resides in the inward recesses of the soul. It is the response of the self to, and its participation in, truth and beauty with a pure will and pure intentions. By locating the secret of true existence in personal existence, Sayegh basically elevated the 'person' to the highest order in life: "Man is truly only insofar as he is 'person'". [21]

The social and political implications of such a conception cannot be underestimated. On the one hand, it subordinates individual and social existence to personal existence and elevates the 'personality' to a supreme level. Accordingly, both the individual and the society must always be ready to serve the demands of the human personality, willingly or unwillingly. Conversely, the conception exalts the personality and renders it an end itself over and above the social personality. It is independent of the social personality and takes precedence over the needs and desires of society. Social personality, as much as it is a fundamental objective of national politics, is rendered in Sayegh's visualization as inconsequential and, in fact, as a potential impediment to the true nature of the individual personality.

Sayegh then lifted these theoretical themes from his thesis and superimposed them on the Party. The topics he took up after 1945 and the framework of his interpretations and emphases clearly attest to a dramatic turn in his writing style. The Party's precepts continued to attract his attention, but they were increasingly remoulded to assimilate existentialist notions. This is clearly reflected in the tone of his speeches and lectures, which

---

20 Fayez Sayegh, "Personal Existence: Its Contents; Its Tragedy; Its Paradox." (Unpublished Master Thesis, AUB, 1945): 12.

21 *Ibid*, 36.

intermittently included reference to the existentialist concepts used in his thesis:

> Accordingly, the Nationalist Party has deemed that individual personal reform, which lies in the depths of every citizen, is the one and only course to meaningful reform![22]

Two major studies from that period found among Sayegh's private papers are also indicative of this transformation. The first is an undated and untitled study on the conflicting tendencies that emerged after World War II and presently confronted the "national revival". An existentialist tone is interwoven throughout its complex and sometimes tediously extended philosophical discussions:

> The two tendencies are not mere philosophical notions or purely artistic or scientific outlooks. Rather, they are ontological attitudes that man holds up toward himself. Thus, he sees himself, appreciates his values and activity, and interprets society and civilization. Accordingly, he determines the type of society to live in, the form of its institutions, and its principle orientation. Hence, the two tendencies represent man's attitude towards his entity as a human being. In light of them, he decides all the efforts and deeds that emanate from his human entity. The soul of each person is, thus, the place where these two tendencies contend and compete, and the identity of man is their subject matter.[23]

The essay is permeated by references to the 'human being' and the 'human soul'. In contrast to the early SSNP writings, it contains little if any reference to nationalist symbols even though the

---

[22] His speech "Reform in National Life." In *Sada an-Nahda*, Beirut, September 2, 1946.

[23] "Man is a Social Being", an unpublished essay (n.d.). See Sayegh's Collection. J. Willard Marriott Digital Library, The University of Utah.

"national revival" was clearly on Sayegh's mind: "Our nation, standing as it is at a crossroad today, finds in our national revival a decisive decision that we will be a human society, that we will have human spiritual courage, and that from the heart of this nation, real humans will emerge instead of deformed creatures who have decided to eliminate their own humanity".[24] Sayegh can be clearly seen to be trying to free himself from the shackles of nationalist rhetoric by swinging the pendulum of commentary and critique in the direction of the 'human person'. The social or individual or national unit as nucleus of national politics gradually receded into the background.

The second study is a longer and more convoluted essay. Entitled "Man is a Social Being", it was intended for publication as part of a Party-related series, but for some inexplicable reason did not get published. In it, Sayegh moves from a largely "historical" demonstration to a mainly "philosophical" inquiry. The philosophical import of the material presented is developed and pursued in a way that is consistent with an existential perspective. At the same time, the essay adheres in its general argument to the Party's social theory developed by Sa'adeh in *The Rise of Nations*, that society alone is the physical realm for human life. Sayegh framed the argument as follows:

> Man is social from his existence ... He is social in his development... social in his endurance ... social in his thinking and production ... social in the fullness of his moral entity ... Outside social life, he is not a human being and cannot exist at all. Where there is no social life there is no human being![25]

Ultimately, Sayegh back-paddles to an Existential position: "The only acceptable theory of social life is that which regards sociality as embodied in the depths of the human soul and at

---

24 *Ibid.*

25 *Ibid.*

the root of its humanity." The emphasis in the essay on the "human" departs from Sa'adeh's perspective, which imparts a transcendental value to the "social" and subordinates all other forms of existence, including "personal existence", to its exigencies.

In many ways, the pervasiveness of philosophy in Sayegh's post-1945 writings was both inevitable and predictable. His penchant for philosophy and the years of studying the subject at the AUB, and his exposure to the post-War tide of moral philosophies could not possibly have passed without exercising some incidental influence on his writings. Were it not for the deteriorating situation in Palestine and the surging demand for independence elsewhere, his philosophical input would probably have been more omnipresent than he had hoped.

Perspective

Fayez's almost verbatim adherence to Sa'adeh is a telling reminder of just how much influence Sa'adeh had over him, and at the same time, an unstinting testimony to Fayez's loyalty and service to the SSNP. As a superb orator who spoke extemporaneously and with great elegance and ease, Fayez served the SSNP with utmost dedication and sincerity. He took its national message very seriously and invested a great deal of his time and effort promoting and demonstrating its potential usefulness. This earned him respect and admiration from both admirers and detractors, with the exception perhaps of the Communists. Even cynics inside the Party have acknowledged his drive and energy at least once in their lives.

Fayez did not live inside the Party: the Party lived inside him. For almost a decade, nothing else occupied as much of his mind and soul. The Party became the one great passion of his life. However, like all things in life, it had to end. With Fayez, the end came far sooner than he and many others had anticipated. It happened unexpectedly and quickly. By the end of 1947, his association with the SSNP had all but ended. The once respected and influential leader suddenly and meteorically became a Party outcast and a *persona non grata*. His downfall was swift and clinical. It was as if he had never been a member of the Party.

How someone as valuable and resourceful as Fayez could end up on the outside with remarkably little resistance or difficulty is still a matter of conjecture and debate. We will discuss the issue in the next chapter.

3

The Fall of Fayez Sayegh from the SSNP

In December 1947, the Syrian Social Nationalist Party (SSNP) woke up to the news that Fayez Sayegh had been expelled from its ranks. Apart from some senior Party officers, very few people inside or outside the SSNP were apprised of the dispute that had developed between Fayez and Sa'adeh, who had returned to Lebanon and was back in charge of the Party. The news surprised everyone, not the least the Party's political foes who had never thought that Fayez would face expulsion after years of dedicated service to the SSNP. Some, like the Communists, were extremely delighted by the news; others were more ambivalent, and in a sense, more deceptive about it. They were not unhappy to see him go, but they feared the worst from his departure.

The curious aspect of Fayez's expulsion merits further investigation. An outsider could easily dismiss it as the drama of a power struggle between two brilliant minds or as a pure exercise in dictatorial authority. In fact, most interpretations have fallen on one side or the other of this divide. Additionally, the focus has tended to center on the personality dimension rather than on the reasons and issues at the core of the dispute.

HISTORICAL BACKGROUND

From the outset of his political career in 1932, Sa'adeh consciously pursued a series of clearly discernible policy initiatives connected by one fundamental and common objective: to change the life of a nation whose development had long ceased and whose objective potential for movement in new directions had subsided to almost nothing. Accordingly, he conceived the SSNP as a creative transforming agent of this change rather than a party that seeks to attain political power within a government. Also, from the outset, he structured the aim of the SSNP around three supreme and exclusive goals:

1. The establishment of an independent state in "Greater" Syria.

2. The modernization of the nation according to a new outlook on life.

3. The formation of an Arab front.

For almost six years, from 1932 to 1938, Sa'adeh devoted his time and energy to sustain this perspective. He developed an entire ideology around it, mentored Party members, and set up a Cultural Forum (*al-nadwa al-thakafiyya*) and a newspaper (*an-Nahda*) to promote it. Persecution then struck, and in 1938, he ended up in forced exile in South America.

During Sa'adeh's absence, the SSNP's home-based leadership deviated from their ideological commitments and began to meddle with the Party's stated objectives. In the 1943 presidential campaign, the Party leadership broke away from its original policy of neutrality in Lebanese electoral politics and sided with Beshara Khoury. The other contender, Émile Eddé, was seen as a symbol of French influence.[1] In exchange for the Party's support, Khoury promised that, if elected, he would release its imprisoned members and allow the Party to resume political activity. He deferred the issue of Sa'adeh's return to Lebanon, however.

Khoury's goodwill freed the Lebanese government from an important responsibility, but it proved to be tactical and self-serving. The nascent Lebanese State lacked both the strength

---

[1] Gibran Jreige, *Haqa'iq Ain al-Istiqlal: Ayyam Rashayya*, 4th edition. (Beirut: Dar Amwaj, 2000): 22. It is claimed that the Party played a decisive role in getting Khoury elected to Parliament for the Maronite seat in Mount Lebanon.

and the adaptability of the French colonialists to grapple with the SSNP, and using repression after the Party had pledged to respect the new independent state would have been unwise. Pacifying the SSNP could benefit the government by (1) serving as an incentive for a softer attitude towards the status quo from the Party; (2) assisting in fostering factional fighting inside the Party over its new direction; and (3) enabling future governments to manipulate the Party.

With these objectives clearly in mind, the Lebanese leadership reached a formal compromise with the SSNP's local leadership in 1945. The government agreed to grant the Party an official permit. In return, the Party pledged:

1. To work within the political framework of the National Pact, the unwritten agreement between Khoury and Solh, to consolidate Lebanon as an independent state within a power-sharing arrangement between the various sectarian groups.[2]

2. To tone down its pan-Syrian rhetoric and turn the Party into a "Lebanese" organization.

By the end of 1946, the government's strategy bore fruit on two fronts. First, it succeeded in splitting the SSNP into two factions: (a) a pro-faction of "talented men"[3] agreeing to the new policy

---

2 The main principles of the Pact were: (1) Lebanon was to be a completely independent state; (2) the Christian communities were to cease identifying with the West, and in return, the Muslim communities were to protect the independence of Lebanon and prevent its merger with any Arab state; (3) Lebanon, though an Arab country, can still maintain its spiritual and intellectual ties with the West; (4) Lebanon, as a member of the family of Arab states, should cooperate with the other Arab states and remain neutral in conflicts among them; and (5) public offices should be distributed proportionally among the recognized religious groups. See Farid el-Khazen, *The Communal Pact of National Identities: The Making and Politics of the 1943 National Pact.* (Oxford: Centre for Lebanese Studies, 1991).

3 Nadim Makdisi, *The Syrian National Party: A Case Study of the First Inroads of National Socialism in the Arab World.* (PhD dissertation, American University of Beirut, 1960): 31.

direction and (b) an anti-faction (or "old guard") of men and women who remained committed to the ideological and administrative foundations of the Party.[4] The two factions did not contest their differences openly but "decided, grudgingly, to wait for the return of the Leader [Sa'adeh], which they hoped would restore them to their lost status".[5] In the meantime, the government's plan to turn the SSNP into a "Lebanese" organization advanced rapidly. By 1946, fundamental changes had rendered the SSNP almost indistinguishable from the other Lebanese parties and nothing like the SSNP of the previous decade. Outwardly,

1. The word "Syrian" was removed from the Party's name. It was now called "The National Party."

2. The flag of the Party was modified and its colors were changed.

3. The Party's head-office in Beirut began to exercise greater autonomy from the Party branches in Palestine and the Syrian Republic.

4. The Party's manner of salute was toned down.

5. Sa'adeh's title was expunged.

Inwardly, the Party was "directed more toward the domestic problems of independent Lebanon than to the national problem as defined by Sa'adeh".[6] Its leadership began to emphasize local Lebanese issues and accommodate the newly independent state. The Party's new trajectory peaked in November 1946 with the release of a public statement affirming its opposition to King Abdullah's Greater Syria Scheme:

1. The National Party condemns the "Greater Syria Scheme" and rejects it outright.

---

4   Ibrahim Yammut, *Ḥasad al-Murr: Qssat tafattut qiyadat ḥizb wa-tamasuk 'aqidah*. (Beirut: Dar al-Rukn, 1993): 121.

5   Makdis, op. cit., p. 31.

6   Labib Zuwiyya Yamak, *The Syrian Social Nationalist Party: An Ideological Analysis*. (Harvard University Press, 1966): 61.

2. The National Party calls on all good citizens in the states projected in the proposed union to resist and to fight the scheme.

For a political party that had struggled solely for Syrian unification, the Greater Syria Scheme declaration was a clear ideological reversal and a measure of how far the Party had gone down the road of Lebanonization. Sa'adeh's initial reaction to this development from his exile in Argentina was surprisingly mild and cautious (the proverbial calm before the storm). He affirmed that nothing should deflect the Party from its national objectives, but he did not discipline the deviationists because they might have conspired with the government to keep him out of Lebanon indefinitely. Moreover, a showdown with the deviationists from afar might have split the Party. Sa'adeh's strategy did not stop the perpetrators, but it did spare the Party the pain of an internal split.

In March 1947, Sa'adeh was finally re-admitted into Lebanon. It is claimed that, by giving assent to Sa'adeh's return, President Khoury expected to draw political capital from the SSNP in the general elections scheduled for May 1947.[7] However, on the day of his arrival, Sa'adeh restored the Party to its original principles and nullified the tacit agreement between the government and the "Lebanonist wing" in the Party. He then reconsolidated the Party around him and restored its original name, flag, salute, etc. He purged and expelled the deviationists from the administration; reinstated the Cultural Forum; issued a regular cultural bulletin; set up press organs strictly connected to the Party; and utilized dailies that closely (but not officially) identified with the Party's views and goals. In addition, the Party's "ideology" became again the organic sphere of its political struggle, and Sa'adeh re-emphasized the benefit of ideological consolidation in building a sustainable society to the Party members. The primary concern for Sa'adeh was to bring the varied Party ranks into a disciplined body that would march towards its goal with great certainty and decisiveness.

---

7   Walter L. Brown, (Ed.), *Lebanon's Struggle for Independence*, Part II, 1944-1947 (Documentary Publications, North Carolina, 1980): 142.

Fayez versus Sa'adeh

The confrontation between Fayez Sayegh and Antun Sa'adeh developed principally during this reconstruction phase. Previously, on March 2, the Party had commissioned Fayez to deliver the welcome address on Sa'adeh's long-awaited day of return. Fayez did not disappoint. Standing in front of Sa'adeh, he uttered loudly:

> Our honorable leader,
>
> If I am standing here on this very momentous and happy occasion, it is because every Party member is absolutely delighted to have you back and to see you once more, and I am no exception.
>
> If I stand right here to describe to you how much they have missed you, I am trying to do the impossible. The feeling that this massive crowd expressed is impossible to describe in words. I think that you understood that from the moment your plane touched the ground at the airport and we were looking at you wherever you went. At the midst of all this, there is one thing that expresses everybody's wish: We are ready. No vote of confidence is stronger than that given by the hearts and souls of this large crowd. Very near to where we stand rests a martyr in peace. He was our first martyr and he will vouch for what I say. It is in his deep silence that our martyr cries, "Sa'adeh! We are true to our oath. We are prepared to march behind you till death, so that the nation can walk on our bodies toward life".

At the end of the speech, Sa'adeh hugged Fayez warmly with an appreciative smile on his face. The crowd erupted in loud cheers in an expression of support for Fayez's speech.

At the time, Fayez was oblivious to the plans that Sa'adeh had in store for the Party. He was doubtlessly apprised of the brewing dispute between Sa'adeh and the Party's Lebanonist clique, but not of the measures that Sa'adeh intended to take against them. These only became clear to him in May when Sa'adeh began to purge the Party. As the deviationists were brought before Sa'adeh to account for their ideological transgressions and then expelled after refusing to repent, Fayez looked on with a strange emotion of hope mingled with foreboding and almost with affright. At first, he was edgy about the sudden turn of events, but after listening to Sa'adeh, he gradually came around to his side. He took note of Sa'adeh's logical explanations and he was touched by his flexibility and egalitarian approach. Still, the loss of close friends and comrades with whom he had worked for almost a decade was deeply agonizing. It pained him severely to lose his former president, Naimet Thabet, who was widely respected and loved in the Party. In the end, Fayez put the Party before friendship and persevered.

Apparently, Fayez had opposed the idea of "Lebanonizing" the Party in 1944, but he was coaxed into accepting it as a matter of necessity. In return for his silence, he was made Dean of Culture in the Party and given almost a free hand to run the Cultural Department. This was a kind of "gentleman's agreement". Fayez jumped at the opportunity and immediately turned the Department's bulletin into a portal for his own agenda. The bulletin was revised to conform to a new policy subject to his "own" direction and to the "High Ideals" as defined by Fayez rather than to the Party's aim and teachings. Fayez also designated himself as the "final" person-in-charge of the bulletin. The editorial for the first issue of the bulletin stated:

> It remains to be said that this bulletin – which is one of several projects undertaken by the Cultural Department – is subject to the basic policy of the Dean as stated in his basic declaration on the front page, especially in relation to the thinkers outside the Party ... The Cultural Department is pleased to welcome every sincere thinker seeking to convey his cultural message. It is prepared to set aside

an uncensored platform in its bulletin from which he can express his thought and art freely.[8]

Upon learning of the changes, Sa'adeh's blood pressure went up. From his Argentine exile, he sent a strongly worded letter to the Party's Supreme Council demanding it to put an immediate stop to Fayez's transgressions. The letter described the "basic policy of the Dean" as "tinted with a strong personal and individual bias that does not take into consideration the development of the Department and the centrality of the basic cultural idea in the social national doctrine and its explanation".[9] For Sa'adeh, the disquieting aspect of this bias was that it rendered the Cultural Department subject to Fayez's 'basic policy and declaration' rather than to the basic aim for which the Department was created – i.e. the Aim of the Party. The potential danger of such an act cannot be underestimated. Not only did it set a bad precedent for other departments to pursue a similar independent course but also seriously undermined the entire hierarchy of the Party.[10] Sa'adeh's demands were met tentatively. Fayez toned down his ego, but retained full control of the bulletin.

Internally, Sa'adeh remained woefully unhappy with Fayez, but he took no further action for the time being. He did not want to intimidate Fayez anymore than he had and he preferred to postpone the matter until he returned home. However, things did not transpire as Sa'adeh wished. The pressure of political circumstances, beginning with the issue of a warrant for his arrest upon his arrival in the country on March 2, 1947, and the building tension of an approaching election, forced Sa'adeh to shelve the matter. The Lebanonist affair, which flared up in May 1947, deferred the matter even further.

Towards the end of August, Sa'adeh swung the lever in Fayez's

---

8   A. Sa'adeh, *Collected Works*, vol. 13, (1946): 55.

9   *Ibid.*

10 Suheil Rustom, *al-Nidham al-Markazi wa Wihdat al-Amal* (The Central System and Work Uniformity). Beirut: Dar Fikr, 2014, pp. 34-40.

direction. Though still the Party's Dean of Information, Fayez's public appearances had become fewer and he wrote considerably less after Sa'adeh's return. During the Lebanonist affair, he observed the proceedings from the sidelines and went about his business quietly and without drawing attention to himself. Likewise, he watched the confrontation between Sa'adeh and the government from a safe distance. He was more an onlooker than a participant. The once outspoken and fiercely confident Fayez suddenly turned uncharacteristically quiet and pensive. His voice seemed to disappear in the cacophony of voices and emotions generated by Sa'adeh's presence.

Fayez's case came up after Sa'adeh carefully scrutinized his writings and found them dangerously awry from the Party's central ideology. Particularly, Fayez's brazen attempt to remold Sa'adeh's teachings into an existentialist context despite some serious and inherent contradictions between them and the Party's official ideology caught Sa'adeh's attention. At least three issues troubled Sa'adeh, and he quickly confronted Fayez about them:

1. Fayez's emphasis on the concept of human individualism despite earlier warnings to desist.
2. Fayez's prioritization of essentially existentialist ideas over his own doctrines in Party literature.
3. Fayez's application of existentialist ideas not only in the bulletin of the Cultural Department, but in almost all of his inter-party publications.

When confronted by Sa'adeh, Fayez conceded to the "charges" but argued, in self-defense, that since the Party did not advocate a philosophy of its own, then his conduct, correspondingly, could not be deemed to violate the sanctity of its national program. Sa'adeh retorted with great virulence that this was not necessarily the case. He told Fayez that a "philosophical outlook" was embedded in the Party's principles, and that, had he studied and pursued them with the same ardor as existentialism, it would have become apparent to him. Fayez remained stubbornly unconvinced. This triggered a series of long discussions and debates between the two men. One session took place under the pine trees of Sa'adeh's hometown of Dhur Shweir on a warm August night and lasted thirteen hours, but it failed to break the deadlock.[11]

With the conflict with the Lebanese government still unresolved, the exchange between the two men was kept under the strictest secrecy. Only a few Party officials were privy to it. However, the longer the exchange dragged on, the worse it became for everyone. It irked those who saw it as an inappropriate use of valuable resources and time. One such person was Fayez's secretary, Shawki Khairallah. He wrote Fayez an impassioned letter appealing to him to drop the issue out of consideration for the general national cause:

> For the sake of the idea (cause) which is more important than him, you, me, and any person...
>
> For the sake of the mission that is under threat of persecution in this serious stage...
>
> For the sake of the nation, for which alone we worked and will continue to work and for which we will die...
>
> For the sake of the values we believe must prevail in the land...
>
> In the name of every grain of sand in this inspiring land and every stubborn rock in its mountains...
>
> In the name of every mighty eagle in its skies and hurricanes, and every sullen tormented face...
>
> In the name of every sigh coming from the infinite depths in the chests of the oppressed...
>
> In the name of Palestine, the land of struggle, where injustice, hate, and struggle materialize, and where we must exert all our efforts for the sake of the truth...

---

11   Abdullah Qubersi, *Memoirs*, Vol. 2. (Beirut: Dar Fikr, 1982): 196.

In the name of every child born without a safe certain future…

In the name of every robust forearm in the mountains and valleys that builds and constructs, carrying on, for thousands of years, the most ancient mission known to civilization…

In the name of every homeless child, every orphan, every hungry belly, and every unlettered person…

In the name of the mighty ones who remain silent and steadfast throughout the days and the unknown soldiers in these broad profound social depths in every village, every cave, and every school and laboratory…

For their sake and in their name…

…I beg you to stop discussing the matter now and to agree with him (Sa'adeh) even if only in principle, until we see what transpires after this phase.

I beg you to do so and to at least believe in him. Try, no matter how much it costs, to keep the ranks unified and to silence the gloaters and to foil the plots of those who fish in murky waters.

Despite this powerful appeal, nothing changed. Fayez continued to pursue the issue with vigor at a heavy cost to his image and reputation. Party members and neutral officials, long captivated by his oratory skills, were deeply irritated by his obstinacy during a political confrontation that demanded every ounce of his strength and intelligence. They expected to see him on rostrums and in newspapers leading the charge against the government instead of behind the scenes fighting with their beleaguered leader over a philosophical principle. Later, Sa'adeh would bemoan, perhaps in an indirect reference to Fayez, that the confrontation with the government was left almost entirely to him, while those he expected to step up and speak out in his defense remained reticent.

To complicate matters, Fayez's attitude hardened further when Sa'adeh amended some sections of the Party's principles and general program. Three particular amendments were introduced:

1. Syria's national boundaries were redefined to include Iraq and Kuwait in the east and Cyprus in the West.
2. The aim and program of the Party were reworked slightly to accommodate a social philosophy.

Sa'adeh did not consult the Party's high councils before introducing these amendments: as undisputed leader of the Party, he was vested with the legislative and executive powers to act independently of them. For Fayez, though, the amendments amounted to a blatant misuse of personal powers. He quickly seized on the opportunity to extend the dispute beyond the bounds of existentialism. Sa'adeh's "leader principle" was called into question and the Party's constitution was invoked to undermine any thoughts of "absolute power". This sparked a long discourse during which Fayez touched on previously uncontested matters of authority, rights, and constitutional powers.

At the height of this discourse, Fayez left for the Gold Coast (today's Ghana) on a Party mission. Sa'adeh tried to send someone else, but the head of the Party's branch in the Gold Coast, unaware of the internal controversy, insisted on Fayez. Fayez's intellectual energy and speaking ability were deemed vital for the success of the mission in a social landscape dotted with divisions and political landmines. Apparently, Fayez's performance on the mission was exemplary, but on his way there, he engaged in bizarre behavior. He wrote two quixotic letters to an imaginary lover and carelessly had them published in the bulletin of the Information Department (of which he was in charge). The first letter, entitled "To the one silent soldier", sparked a wave of confusion in the Party as members debated among themselves whether the "soldier" in question was Sa'adeh. The second letter was less ambiguous and more direct. Its explicit poetic tone and expressions of unbridled passion quickly dispelled the fleeting thought that they might be about Sa'adeh. For example, Fayez wrote:

> Between you and me are miles, seas and clouds, and yet, despite all that, I am with you and you are with me in a union that distance cannot undo and in a condition that farness cannot dissipate ... I almost can hear two whispers, one that frightens me and the other alarms me. The first is the echo of a faint humming emanating from a natural weakness in you and me. It is the whisper of despair rising to challenge the faith in you and the confidence, bliss and hope, and to thwart as well the determination and perseverance you have shown...

The letters infuriated Sa'adeh. It was not so much the poetic nature of the letters that aggravated him, but Fayez's use of an internal Party bulletin to promulgate a very personal and intimate matter. For Sa'adeh, the letters served as a sober reminder of Fayez's earlier transgression when the Party's cultural bulletin was used as a platform for existentialist ideas. The present transgression was just as, if not more, serious. It flew in the face of political exigencies, made a mockery of the cultural standards on which the SSNP had prided itself, and most importantly, vindicated the muted suspicion in the Party that Fayez regarded the cultural bulletin as a private enterprise rather than a party publication with a broad readership.

What was Fayez thinking? What could possibly have prompted him to use a political party publication for intimate contemplations? Did Fayez intend to intimidate Sa'adeh, and if so, why? There are no clear-cut answers to these questions because Fayez remained tight-lipped about the whole affair. If intimidating Sa'adeh was the intended objective, then Fayez clearly succeeded, but to his own detriment. The letters proved to be the 'straw that broke the camel's back'. Sa'adeh's response was swift and decisive. He abolished the "Bulletin of the Cultural Department" and replaced it with the "Official Bulletin of the Social Nationalist

Movement". An internal Party missive committing the new publication "strictly to Party affairs" was circulated to members to contain any potential fallout. That missive indicates the aura of doubt and skepticism that had begun to form around Fayez:

> During the Leader's absence [in exile], the Party's reality, cause, and message, which the Leader had established and defined in his wide-ranging teachings, suffered from significant oversight. As a result, major deviations from this basic fact developed in the high echelons of the Party in politics and at various Information, cultural and purely administrative levels and the Social National Movement ... descended to the nadir of a perspective that considers the Movement a sheer number of individuals who randomly joined a regulated corps thought to be fit as a current for the various tendencies and goals no matter how conflicting they are with each other and with the national social doctrine.[12]

In another indirect swipe at Fayez, Sa'adeh infused the new bulletin with elaborate statements of his own philosophical vision. His opening article in this regard, "The Group and Society", can easily be construed as a sort of repudiation of Fayez's thesis of existential individualism:

> Our ideology believes in a basic and total human reality, which is the social reality par excellence: the group, society, and community. Social life is imperative for human existence and necessary for its survival and continuity. Society is perfect human existence and total human reality. Moreover, supreme human ideals cannot possibly exist and be effective except in society. Society is the sole direction of all values and it is their source and their aim.[13]

---

12 SSNP, *Al-Nashrah al-Rasmiyah lil Harakat al-Qawmiyyah al-Ijtimae'yah*. (Beirut: Vol. 1, No. 2, December 1947).

13 *Ibid.*

The Fall of Fayez Sayegh from the SSNP

The following passage is decidedly even more anti-existential:

> Social life cannot be determined electively by individuals living without or outside society. Social life is also not a social contract whereby individuals choose to live together and decide to form a society or agree to the terms of the social contract by choosing to stay within the society. Never. Social life is nothing of the sort. It is not a selective phenomenon.[14]

With energy and focus, Sa'adeh then turned to Fayez's writings and carefully highlighted where they violated the Party's constitution and teachings. The passages cited for this purpose came largely from Fayez's *National Resurrection* and more specifically from his essays "al-Hadaf" (The Objective) and "al-Qawmiyyah al-Ijabiyyah" (Positive Nationalism) in the monograph. Infused with a subtle existentialist spirit, both essays accentuated the "individual person" as the centre of all human actions and focused upon the subjective, personal lives of individual human beings rather than on society as an objective reality. Thus, they contradicted the most fundamental roots of the "society first" concept for which the SSNP was conceived and prepared.

The promulgation of such ideas jolted Sa'adeh into action. He drew up an elaborate statement outlining the facts and issues as he saw them and handed it to Fayez on his return from the Gold Coast. It was not so much a letter, as an ultimatum. In it, Sa'adeh bluntly asked Fayez to observe the following directives:

1. Put an immediate and full stop to any reference to teachings of Berdyaev and Kierkegaard, which until now have not been formally submitted to the Party's councils and the Leader for consideration and assessment.
2. Confine your duties strictly to the Social National movement and only to those dimensions that give concrete *expression to its reality or perspective.*

---

14 *Ibid.*

Fayez's reaction to the letter was somewhat muted. He conceded that a strong note of existentialist fervor had permeated his writings, but he argued in self-defense that it was harmless and legal. He reiterated his previous argument that, since the Party does not espouse a philosophical position, promoting an existentialist worldview does not contravene its objectives or the functionality and application of its program. Sa'adeh reacted with caution and modesty. He asked Fayez to brush up on the Party's ideology and to reconsider carefully the negative aspects of his "untamed ideas". Fayez was instructed to report back, but was granted an extended amount of time to do so.

On December 4, 1947, Sa'adeh gave the Party's high councils a lowdown of the situation. He assured them that the matter was being attended to with the utmost urgency and care, and he instructed them to give Fayez room to consider his options. The briefing was more about preparing them for the worse than about anything else. It indicated both how delicate the situation was and of how far Sa'adeh was prepared to go to retain Fayez. Losing Fayez immediately after the losses already incurred from the Lebanonist affair had the potential to split the Party wide open, and Sa'adeh had to consider this possibility very carefully in view of Fayez's popularity inside the Party and the philosophical complexity of his case. Intellectual differences are, largely, more convoluted than political differences, and thus more difficult to explain or predict. Also, the after-effects of an intellectual controversy can be wide ranging and progressively debilitating, especially when it comes to one's reputation.

Two days later, on December 6, 1947, Sa'adeh heard that Fayez was whipping up a frenzy against him. Surrounded by several important figures in the Party (Yusif al-Khal, Ghassan Tueini and Fuad Suleiman), all of whom were philosophically formed in the spirit of the Charles Malik School, Fayez had apparently spent the previous evening exhorting his supporters, who had come to bid him farewell, to stand up to Sa'adeh. Abdullah Qubersi, a senior Party official and a personal friend of Fayez, later recalled:

The Fall of Fayez Sayegh from the SSNP

Fayez turned up at my house near al-Kabushiyyah Church in Hamra Street accompanied by Yusif al-Khal and Fuad Suleiman. They were intent on convincing me that Fayez was right and Sa'adeh was wrong ... The trio tried to persuade me to stand by Fayez and to defend him ... on the grounds that Sa'adeh's attitude contravenes the principle of intellectual freedom in the Party.[15]

A lawyer by profession, Qubersi suddenly found himself between the hammer of his leader (Sa'adeh) and the anvil of his friend (Fayez). Not wanting to lose either of them, he proposed a compromise under which Fayez would suspend all intellectual discussions with Sa'adeh and use the extra time to ponder matters (Fayez was preparing to leave for the U.S. to study for his PhD). In return, Sa'adeh would refrain from taking any further action against Fayez.

Both Sa'adeh and Fayez pledged their support. The following day, December 6, Qubersi went to bid Fayez goodbye. To his astonishment, he found him in a grumpy mood angrily defending his views and urging others to rebel against Sa'adeh: "I stood up and told the comrades: those of you who believe in Syria and Sa'adeh follow me and those who believe in Fayez can stay. I remember only two remained and the others walked out with me ... Then, from the nearest phone, I called Sa'adeh and told him that Fayez had ditched his pledge".[16] On December 7, Fayez was expelled from the Party and a notice of his expulsion was quickly circulated to Party members to contain any potential fallout.

Fayez responded swiftly to the news of his expulsion. On December 10, the highly respected Beirut daily, *an-Nahar*, carried a hard-hitting front-page response from him declaring the "demise of the Syrian Social Nationalist Party".[17] The tone

---

15 Qubersi, *Memoirs*, Vol. 2: 199.

16 *Ibid.* 200.

17 *An-Nahar*, December 10, 1947.

of the response was biting. Fayez accused Sa'adeh of:

1. Deviating from the Party's aim and program.
2. Breaking his oath.
3. Abrogating the "Contract" on which the Syrian social Nationalist Party was founded.
4. Creating a new political party without swearing an oath of allegiance to its principles.
5. Introducing changes to the Party's program without consulting the members.

The response concluded with Fayez brazenly announcing his "withdrawal" from the Party (a subtle insinuation that he left of his own accord).

THE FALLOUT

If Fayez thought that his "expulsion" or "withdrawal" would cause a mass exodus from the Party, he grossly miscalculated, as the episode passed almost without a hitch. Only a handful of members left the Party, and the rest remained firmly united behind Sa'adeh. Fayez's assertiveness proved no match for Sa'adeh's decisiveness. He was more able to present strong and rational arguments than other Party members were, but Sa'adeh always had the right response to every argument. In retrospect, Fayez did not count on Sa'adeh working equally as hard to prevent him from flirting with extraneous ideas inside the Party.

Fayez made two cardinal mistakes. The first was to go public with the dispute. This opened the floodgates to a tidal wave of criticism and condemnation from elite intellectuals who had been quietly observing the proceedings from the sidelines. Dumbstruck by Fayez's sudden outburst, they quickly closed ranks and rushed to Sa'adeh's defense. The unity of the Party was deemed too important to be jeopardized by unnecessarily dragging disagreements. Among the respondents was his former "secretary" and "student", Labib Yamak Zuwiyya. He tore into Fayez with a most stinging reply:

> Fayez, I wish you had never published your statement because the words you said to me in Dhur al-Shweir last summer still echo in my ears. Have you forgotten that you said, "The Leader is the only person who must be a role model for the whole nation"? Unfortunately, the teacher deviated from the right path and claimed that he had been in the dark. I, your student and friend of yesterday, am sorry to be the first to confront you and say: "Everything you said and claimed is nonsense!" Pretense has blinded you, and pride has destroyed you. I, your student whom you cared for and whom you taught the principles of philosophy, am sorry to tell you that you have been deceitful, concerned with fame, and craving acclaim, and that as a philosopher, you have been an unctuous meddler.[18]

The long chain and weight of the responses quickly dispelled any pity for Fayez. It added credence to Sa'adeh's perspective and brought many borderline members back in line with the Party. It was one thing to disagree with Sa'adeh, but another to attack him publicly. The strong impression of treachery fostered by Fayez's public announcement obscured the real issue and strengthened the general perception of Sa'adeh as the real protector of the Party. Any sympathy or credibility that Fayez may have had dissipated quickly because of the public announcement.

The second mistake made by Fayez was his ill-fated decision to drop his bombshell on the very last day. Deserting a battlefield after declaring an intellectual war on an adversary is not exactly smart politics. It is self-defeating, especially when the enemy is an intellectual giant in his own right. By declaring war on Sa'adeh on the day he was due to leave the country, Fayez inadvertently undermined his own cause, as the announcement was seen as a measure of political insensitivity and a gratuitous breach of

---

18 Reproduced in the "Letters" section of this book.

Party trust unbefitting his record as a person, writer, and public speaker. It made him look weak and desperate. Conversely, it made Sa'adeh look grand and imposing, just the way he liked.

With Fayez not around to defend himself or to answer questions from the press and the public, a few dissidents were left to pick up the pieces. Genuinely loyal to Fayez, they saw the saga as an opportunity to strike a fatal blow to Sa'adeh. Calling themselves the "Free Nationalists", they issued a couple of press releases to the *an-Nahar* newspaper, whose owner-editor, Ghassan Tueini, was a sympathizer and an active member of their ring. The first statement, reiterating Fayez's announcement of the previous day almost verbatim, appeared on December 11. Another followed on December 18 with a slightly modified theme. This time, the dissenters, seeking new attention, claimed that their disagreement with Sa'adeh was not over existentialism but over Sa'adeh's "totalitarian" and autocratic style of leadership. The campaign petered out as quickly as it had begun. The dissenters could not rise to the challenge, and like Fayez before them, deserted the battlefield as the sound of their enemy's artillery approached.

In this regard, Sa'adeh's response deserves careful study. Instead of joining the battle himself, which would have given the dissenters more attention than they deserved, he sent in a couple of his 'intellectual generals': Abdullah Qubersi and Hilmi Maluf. These generals contributed two superb rejoinders which *an-Nahar* could not refuse to publish having proclaimed itself a champion of "intellectual freedom".[19] Maluf's rejoinder was particularly engaging because it posited the issue from a dispassionate perspective:

> In the past week, and specifically in the intellectual circles of the country, a clamor could be heard "fight Sa'adeh; fight him because he violated his own fundamental principles; fight him because he wants to superimpose his own philosophy on the country; fight him because he is an

---

19 Seen *An-Nahar*, December 13 and 19, 1947.

enemy of free thinking." For my part, I tell thee, "Yes, go ahead and fight him. It is your right to fight him with all the power you command, but fight him on anything but on these grounds".[20]

As the protagonists were fighting it out, Sa'adeh looked on with satisfaction and approval. He instructed one of his aides to "advise them [i.e. Free Nationalists] that, despite their resignation, expulsion, and disagreement with the Party's beliefs, he would award them a Party medal for instigating a splendid ideological intellectual battle in the press, but would never forgive them if they turn the debate into a platform for vituperation and hostile polemic".[21] Obviously, Sa'adeh was reaping good rewards. The campaign gave him plenty of publicity and projected him as a confident and uncompromising leader. Sometimes bad publicity is good publicity in disguise, depending on how it is handled. In this case, contrary to the intended purpose, Sa'adeh came across as highly convivial and open to intellectual discussion rather than as a maniacal dictator. Moreover, by putting others in charge of the exchange, Sa'adeh created the impression that the dissenters' discord was not with him but with the Party at large.

Another factor worth considering is the composure of Sa'adeh's response. Rather than going public about the dispute, as Fayez and his sympathizers did, he pitched his position directly to the Party members. He wrote two instructive articles in the Official Bulletin that quickly helped to dispel any apprehension or lingering doubts. The first article provided insight into the saga based almost entirely on Sa'adeh's version of events. It gave the Party members some crucial facts that, until then, had been carefully kept under wraps, and it also accentuated the firmness and equanimity shown by Sa'adeh. Fayez himself was not maligned or discredited in any significant way, but he was depicted as a Party renegade who had broken ranks.

---

20 *An-Nahar*, December 19, 1947.
21 Shawki Khairallah, *Memoirs*. (Beirut: Dar al-Jadid, 1990): 95.

The second article was in the form of an analytical essay on Berdyaev's doctrine of individual personalism. The Russian philosopher and author of *Slavery and Freedom* saw every dogma or orthodoxy, whether political, religious, or any other, as the authority of an organized society over a free individual and the free spirit of a person. This was something that he could never accept. To the collectivist Sa'adeh, such a view appeared as not only unreasonable, but as a concept that bordered on the danger of "selfish anarchism". In a key passage, he wrote:

> Personalism is a very subjective doctrine, a perpetual revolt that propels the individual to object and rebel in order to assert his personality, and for fear that their acceptance of any thought or judgment or convention may be understood as implying acquiescing in a decision stemming from society or the state or God. Disobey and gain! This is the trademark of individual personalism! Disobey and gain; disobey relentlessly to gain even more! It is the golden rule of this unusual creed.[22]

In addition to projecting Sa'adeh as a competent writer on philosophical issues, the second article provided the first "ideological" justification for Fayez's expulsion based on intellectual considerations rather than personal or internal Party ones. It fostered an aura of relief and satisfaction among the Party's rank-and-file and helped to consolidate the Party even more firmly behind Sa'adeh. Likewise, it reflected unfavorably on Fayez, who was not there to contest its claims.

Towards the end of December, Fayez released a detailed monograph on the dispute. Entitled *Whither To?,* the monograph was circulated to various Lebanese newspapers for maximum impact, but to no avail. By the time it reached the press, public interest in the dispute had more or less fizzled out. Fayez's absence from the scene and the timing of the monograph's release

---

[22] A. Sa'adeh, "The School of Selfishness." (*In al-Nashrah al-Rasmiyyah lil Harakah al-Qawmiyyah al-Ijtima'eyah,* vol. 1, No. 3, 1948).

on the eve of the Festive Season also contributed to its lukewarm reception. In the end, *Whither To?* received scant attention and recognition. Fayez's sympathizers found nothing new in it to be enthusiastic about, and the only newspaper that seemed to care, the dedicated anti-SSNP newspaper *Beirut Telegraph*, scarcely mattered.

About one month after the publication of the monograph, Sa'adeh launched a series of lectures on the Party that led to the almost sacred manual *The Ten Lectures*. Although we cannot ascertain if *Whither To?* was a factor in triggering the lecture series or if the series started independently, Fayez's case was referred to in the first lecture wherein Sa'adeh again presented his own side of the story:

> Fayez Sayegh's case surfaced not after I returned [from exile] but before I did when I received, for the first time, the first and second issues of the "Department of Culture Bulletin". Two matters quickly caught my attention in the first issue: (1) the violation of the Party's constitutional laws, and (2) the digression from all the ideological and spiritual mainstays of the Social Nationalist movement.
>
> When I read the following statements in the editorial section of the Bulletin ("To the reader") published by the Department of Culture and Fine Arts – "This Bulletin is issued under the supervision of the Dean of Culture": that the Dean "was the final editor-in-charge of it"; that the Bulletin is "subject to the (unconstitutional) policy of the Dean, rather than to the policy of the Party's leader [i.e. Sa'adeh], as stipulated in the Party's constitution; and that the Department has a cultural function of its own independent from the cultural tasks of the Social National movement - and noticed the individualist arbitrariness and irregularity involved, I asked myself: what is the real motive for declaring the Dean's authority [over the Bulletin] as "final", which effectively means that neither

the Party's higher councils nor the leader himself has any right to intervene? I considered this behavior a serious breach of the Party's constitution and institutions and of everything that may affect the unity of its aims: an egocentric tendency leaning strongly towards selfishness, and an ugly individualistic autocracy that pays no heed to either general will or legal constitution.

Then I read what Fayez Sayegh called "The Basic Declaration of the Bureau of Culture and Fine Arts" published in the first issue of the Bulletin: particularly what he labeled as "the fundamental principles of the Bureau's policy" in the so-called "Declaration". It quickly appeared to me that there was a serious digression from the Movement's outlook, cause, and principles and from the aim of the Syrian Social National Party in that, by his action, Sayegh had divested "culture" of its social national connotation and its attributes and had instead rendered it a "free and independent personal" matter. What's more, his action stripped the Bureau of any accountability to the Syrian Social Nationalist teachings and made it accountable to "high values" that only the Dean had the right to fathom.[23]

After this lecture on January 7, 1948, the affair petered out and the parties withdrew into their own worlds. Fayez went on to complete his PhD in the United States and Sa'adeh continued to lead the Party uncontested. By all accounts, many members were saddened by Fayez's departure. They lamented his parting as a serious loss to the Party and to the national cause to which he had given so much of his time and effort. However, ultimately, the power of Sa'adeh's constructive reasoning proved more than equal to Fayez's challenge, just as it did with the other "transgressors" before him.

---

23 See the first lecture in A. Sa'adeh, *The Ten Lectures*. (Beirut, 1950).

The Fall of Fayez Sayegh from the SSNP

Perspective

The Fayez saga may not have received the attention it deserved, but it was an important episode for all the parties concerned. From the Party's standpoint, the saga led to the irreplaceable loss of a unique person whose defining qualities were widely admired and who touched many lives. Apart from his outstanding record as a prolific writer and a great orator, Fayez was popular, energetic, versatile, and a talented performer – just the kind of person that every political party with a national agenda would want. This explains why Sa'adeh was eager to retain Fayez, and why Fayez, keenly aware of his skills and experience, stood his ground and would not be moved.

For Fayez, the saga was a clustered mess that brought about the meteoric demise of his career as a Party cadre. His almost nine years of dedicated service to the SSNP, during which he rose to pinnacles of power and fame in the Party, were wiped out in less than nine weeks. After this, Fayez faded into oblivion as far as SSNP was concerned. His friends and comrades from the Party continued to remember him as a proud and intelligent man, but they never forgave him for his stubbornness and unexpected recalcitrance. Between loyalty to Fayez and loyalty to the Party, the great majority opted for the Party. Given the knowledge and firm belief in the power of ideology he professed, Fayez should have expected no other result.

The story of the dramatic struggle and ideological conflict between Fayez and Sa'adeh would remain incomplete without a conceptual analysis of the contentious points that divided them. Drawing on both Sa'adeh's writings and Fayez's final word on the dispute, *Whither To?*, an attempt to locate those points and to examine their intricate details will now be made, bearing in mind that ideological differences, by nature, are relative rather than absolute.

4

Disagreement with Sa'adeh

In ideological or political disputes, the contenders normally slant the facts in their direction or concentrate on details that best serve their ends. They engage in tactics of diversion and encirclement to avoid running into a vulnerable position whereby they can be manipulated easily and portrayed as the villain. Sometimes, the chasm between the contenders may emerge as a result of a misunderstanding of the issues involved, of the incommensurable nature of different moral positions, or simply because the arguments and conclusions are based upon different premises. Specifically, ideological

> ... disputes are only able to be settled where there are appropriate criteria that can be brought to bear. [In] disputes between members of the same ideology and in disputes between different ideologies, there are no such criteria.[1]

In the Sa'adeh-Fayez case, the impulse to appeal to Party members played an important part in how Fayez and Sa'adeh framed their arguments. Each side attempted to steer the dispute toward the issues that mattered to them or were deemed important for the Party's future. This created two conflicting perspectives with Sa'adeh locating the substantive core of the dispute in Fayez's loop for existentialist philosophy and Fayez locating it in Sa'adeh's tilt towards a totalitarian position. Both arguments are important and complement each other. One cannot look exclusively or even mainly at one and not the other for an explanation.

---

1   Alistair Grimes, "Ideological Disputes." (*New Blackfriars*, vol. 63, no. 740, February 1982): 90.

This chapter is divided into two parts: (1) a reconstruction of Fayez's perspective on the encounter based largely on the account and analysis set out in *Whither To?*[2] and (2) the precise content and actual arguments Fayez deployed, especially the charges of "transgressions" leveled against Sa'adeh in his account. In the process, fundamental issues associated with the SSNP in general and with the affinity between ideology and philosophy in particular will be discussed to determine who was at fault.

Fayez's Perception of the Dispute

Fayez located the source of the dispute with Sa'adeh in the cornerstone principle on which Sa'adeh's leadership had been built. For him, the root problem lay with Sa'adeh's monopoly on power and the autocratic "abuse" of his constitutional rights. This is the principal argument of *Whither To?* It is set out in dramatic fashion to convey a sense of urgency and concern about the importance of the matter at the centre of the dispute. Fayez states his point clearly at the start of the tract:

> The issue ... pertains to the fate and dignity of the nation, in the face of history and eternity. It is concerned with the future of man before his conscience, freedom, and dignity. It is a matter of life and death for the nation, for us, we its sons who forever are seeking its welfare and prosperity.[3]

In other words, Fayez saw the dispute from a much broader and deeper perspective than Sa'adeh did. For him, the disagreement was not over some minor point, but over fundamental issues that went beyond the Party's purpose and strategy to the very core of human values and worldviews. He portrays it as a decisive conflict between two irreconcilable perspectives: totalitarianism versus constitutional accountability. Moreover, its causes are laid at Sa'adeh's doorstep in a bold attempt to make him the

---

2 F. Sayegh, *Ila Ayn? (Whither To?).* (Beirut, Dar al-Kitab, 1947).
3 *Ibid.*

real initiator of the dispute. In the process, several grievances concerning Sa'adeh's style of leadership are documented and brought to our attention.

According to Fayez, the dispute arose because Sa'adeh did not respect his constitutional and leadership prerogatives. He claimed that, by violating his prerogatives, Sa'adeh tended to a totalitarian cult with all the threatening excesses such a cult is known to invite. To prove this, Fayez delved into Sa'adeh's leadership history to illustrate how it morphed into a dictatorial entity.

The analysis of this history is divided into three distinct but overlapping stages. The first stage stretches from 1932 (the year of the Party's founding) to the end of World War II and this period is described as the highlight of Sa'adeh's leadership. He is hailed as a true leader who served the Party with grace and distinction and who did everything according to its constitution and the oath of leadership. Moreover, he is acclaimed as a shining example of the kind of authoritarian charismatic that is often inevitable in crisis-stricken societies seeking to revive amid hostile forces. Behind all this lay a compelling argument toward which Fayez was intentionally gravitating: Sa'adeh was able to perform his duties diligently and with the unflinching backing and respect of the entire Party because he remained within the parameters that defined his leadership:

1. The "contract" according to which the Party was founded.

2. The Party's Constitution, which vested Sa'adeh with legislative and executive powers subject to the terms of the "contract".

3. The national cause as spelled out and expounded in the Party's Aim and Program.

According to Fayez, Sa'adeh's powers and prerogatives started and ended at these limits. Everything else that lay beyond these limits was non-obligatory. Fayez maintained that (1) Sa'adeh had neither the right nor the power to impose his personal views on Party members and (2) Party members had both the right and the power to accept or reject his personal views. Like everyone else in society, they were entitled to think as freely as they pleased beyond the bounds of the Party's ideology. This spanned the entire spectrum of intellectual, cultural, philosophical, and personal pursuits. Fayez framed his point as:

> In all his research and discussions with the members, especially during the founding stage of the Party, Sa'adeh used to confine his discussion to the principles. He would ask members no more than to believe in these principles and to take them as guidelines in their social, political, and economic thinking and national work. It must be emphasized, though, that, in his capacity as initiator of a comprehensive national renaissance, Sa'adeh took keen interest in intellectual revival, cultural activities, and vital artistic intellectual pursuits. However, this interest did not contain any form of coercion, imposition, or intimidation and, certainly, any element of a comprehensive holistic outlook on life, the universe, and art.[4]

The second stage of Sa'adeh's leadership history is the interval between 1945 and 1947 described as the period of inevitable change due to the new political climate created by World War II and the Party's inability to achieve a breakthrough on both the political and the formal state level. Both factors made a lasting impression on Sa'adeh and forced him to revise some of his perceptions and expectations. According to Fayez, Sa'adeh was also subjected to unexpected turns of events inside the Party that bore even more directly on him and altered his style of thinking. The case of Fakhri Maluf is cited as the trigger in his transformation.[5] A high profile Party member respected

---

4   Fayez Sayegh, *Whither To?*

5   On Fakhri Maluf see John Dayeh, Sa'adeh wa mafakiru an-nahda: Tajribat Fakhri Maluf (Sa'adeh and the Nahda thinkers: The Case of Fakhri Maluf). Beirut: Dar Nelson, 2008). See also, Adel Beshara, "A Great Man Has Died: Fakhri Maluf (Brother Francis Maluf) 1913-2009." (*Al-Mashriq: A Quarterly*

for his balanced philosophical mind and high integrity, Maluf left the Party in 1944 after converting to Catholicism. He cited irreconcilable differences between his new religious faith and the Party's secular view of life as the reason for his departure. Through a series of correspondences, Sa'adeh tried to dissuade Maluf from leaving. He pledged and reminded him that the Party does not interfere with religious beliefs or prevent members from practicing religion provided they keep it to themselves. When all efforts failed, Sa'adeh expelled Maluf and quickly filed a detailed report to the Party's Supreme Council to avert any potential backlash or misunderstanding. In an adjunct to the report, Sa'adeh wrote:

> One of the indications of Maluf's proclivity for deviation is that he was fond of an idea that always tickled his fancies. On many occasions and letters, he repeatedly stated that he would formulate the theological framework of the Syrian Social National doctrine, or the like. In reality, there was and still is an urgent need for many more philosophical and scientific investigation to clarify the depth of the Social National ideology and the robustness of the construction it is erecting with all its facility, beauty, coherency, and high demand.[6]

Fayez seized on this passage. He believed it contained a vital clue to Sa'adeh's subsequent change of mind, and he saw it as furnishing some suggestion or proof that Sa'adeh had decided to pick up where Maluf had left off and formulate the theological framework Maluf contemplated:

> It appears from this paragraph that the idea that was intriguing Maluf was starting to intrigue Sa'adeh as well. If Sa'adeh had succeeded in defeating Maluf constitutionally and organizationally ... Maluf had succeeded in defeating

---

6   A. Sa'adeh, *Complete Works*, Vol. 13, 1946.

Sa'adeh philosophically, in Sa'adeh's soul, forcing him to move towards devising the philosophical (theological) basis for the principles of the Party, and to regard this basis as an integral part of the Party's ideology and, by extension, to consider the "Party's ideology", in its new form, both inclusive and indivisible, thus abandoning the distinction that he (i.e., Sa'adeh) had admitted during discussions between the [Party's] principles and the private philosophy of each nationalist, including himself.[7]

Tapping into Sa'adeh's frame of mind, Fayez concluded that his former leader must have experienced some agonizing moments thinking about the philosophical void created by Maluf's departure. At the minimum, he added, it convinced him of the need to anchor the Party's ideology in a comprehensive philosophical system and compelled him to start working on this system immediately. Fayez also noticed that, as Sa'adeh gradually moved closer to this aim, his toleration for "freedom of opinion" shrunk to religion: the right to believe in God, Resurrection, and other matters of the afterlife.[8] This represented a fundamental break from the previous position when that right extended across the spiritual, literary, and philosophical spectrum.

Taking the analysis to a higher level, Fayez contended that Sa'adeh changed after realizing that other spiritual and philosophical currents, comparable to that of the Maluf case, existed elsewhere in the Party. The matter came to his attention in 1946 after an exchange of letters with his liaison officer, Ghassan Tueini, during which fundamental philosophical issues were raised and debated. In Fayez's view, these communications opened Sa'adeh's eyes to the state of philosophical thinking inside the Party and expedited his ambition to contrive a specific philosophy based on his own personal and private philosophical convictions. Sa'adeh, we are told, proceeded to set out to purify the Party of philosophical diversity and hasten internal

---

7 Sayegh, *Whither To?*
8 *Ibid.*

philosophical uniformity to avoid further disagreements. For the philosophical-minded Fayez, this entailed not only a stranglehold on freedom of opinion but also an unconditional surrender to a single philosophical outlook.

To prove his point and allow the reader to see the issue comprehensively, Fayez mentioned a letter that Sa'adeh had written at the start of 1947, just prior to his return from exile. Fayez extracted some passages from the letter:

> Despite all the great tribulations we have endured over the long years, our faith in each other has remained as strong as ever. You have believed in me as the teacher and guide of the nation and mankind, the planner and builder of the new society and the commander of the new rising forces marching to victory in the name of the teachings (i.e. his teachings) and high ideals. In addition, I believe in you, O ideal nation! You are the teacher and guide of all nations, the builder of the new human society, the leader of the forces of human progress in the name of the new teachings whose life-giving warmth and shining light you bear to all the nations of the world. This light calls on them to discard the doctrine that regards Spirit as the only motor of human progress or Matter as the fundamental basis of human development. It calls them to give up once and for all the idea that the world is by necessity in a state of war in which spiritual forces are continuously fighting with material forces. Finally, it calls them to admit with us that the basis of human development is spiritual-materialist and that superior humanity recognizes this basis and builds the edifice of its future on it. Neither can those who boast about materialistic philosophies dispense with the spirit and its philosophy, nor can those who boast about spiritualistic philosophies dispense with the matter and its philosophy.
>
> The world has come to realize, especially after the last World War, the magnitude of devastation visited upon it by

the partial philosophies and one-dimensional ideologies that flourish on sabotage - the philosophy of stifling Capitalism and the philosophy of unruly Marxism that eventually united with its twin, the materialistic Capitalism, in a drive to negate spirit from the world, and the Fascist philosophy of the spirit and its twin, National Socialism, that monopolized the spirit and aimed at the total control of the world nations and their affairs.

Today, the world is in need of a new social philosophy that can save it from the arbitrariness and error of these ideologies. The philosophy that the world needs is a philosophy of interaction that unites and combines the entire forces of human society. It is the philosophy that your renaissance offers.[9]

Thus, according to Fayez, Sa'adeh's transformation from a national leader to a totalitarian leader was complete. Knowingly or unknowingly, he had detoured the Party on a totalitarian path that imposed severe constraints on the enjoyment of basic rights:

[With this letter] the conversion of Sa'adeh [was] attained. His new philosophy had taken formal shape. In his view at least, his new philosophy (*al-madrahiyyah*) had become part of his Party's ideology just as Marxism, Fascism and National Socialism had contrived philosophical systems and embedded them into their ideologies. This philosophy (*al-madrahiyyah*) and the "Social National ideology", thus, became Sa'adeh's rallying cry to his Party, his Party's rallying cry to his nation, and his nation's rallying cry to the world.[10]

Fayez edges even closer to the key idea towards which he had been proposing and navigating the reader. He states that, by

---

9   SSNP, *Nashrat Imdat al-Iza'a*. (Beirut: 1947).

10 Sayegh, *Whither to?*

marrying his "personal" philosophy with the Party's ideology, Sa'adeh had created an earthly religion that shares much common ground with religious worship and other forms of political religion. Fayez buttresses his argument by invoking a passage from Sa'adeh's return speech on March 2, 1947:

> After fifteen years of disciplined struggle, unparalleled anywhere else in the world, we stand today as a living nation victorious over all the foreign designs which aimed to keep this nation fragmented into contending denominations and sects, all of which have an equal heavenly origin, and to which our social nationalist teachings came offering a single unified religion designed to raise this nation to their level, to find in them its long-term guidance.[11]

For Fayez, the unveiling of this "single unified religion" under the appellation of "Social Nationalism" as the official philosophy of the Party marked the beginning of the third and final stage in Sa'adeh's total transformation. Describing it as a "coup" (*inqilab*), he argued that Sa'adeh completed the full circle by the single act of "imposing" his vision on the Party in a "revised edition" of its Aim and Program. Fayez invoked the notion of a coup deliberately to convey a sense of "break from" as opposed to "adjustment of" an existing condition. He probably also utilized it to depict the act as a coup in the real sense of the word since it was executed during his absence in the Gold Coast (Ghana). Certainly, Fayez purposely characterized the act as a "coup" to exacerbate the range and magnitude of the changes it occasioned:

> It is a fundamental coup that altered the face of the Syrian National Party, its aim and some of its principles, and the significance of its meaning in Sa'adeh's mind and that of its members. The result was the "Syrian Social National Party" - a new party in every sense of the word: new in its aim and objectives; new in its inception and its legal

---
11 *Ibid.*

and constitutional forms; and new in encompassing a total philosophy, an outlook on life, the universe and art, and a specific religious doctrine. It is the philosophy and outlook of Antun Sa'adeh himself, which he had decided to impose on the members of the Party without informing them about the nature of this coup and without alerting them to its occurrence! He did not even bother to explain to them in detail the substance of this outlook, philosophy, and new religion![12]

Apart from the problem of magnitude, Fayez also raised the question of the legality or non-legality of the "changes" introduced by Sa'adeh:

[At the end of the day] what matters to me is that an amendment had been made and that this amendment was instigated unilaterally by one of the parties to the "contract" and that this party then proceeded to enforce it on the other party by an unconstitutional decree.[13]

Fayez claimed Sa'adeh had broken faith with the members and ignored the partnership on which the Party was founded:

The leader had deviated from the principles, plan, and aim of his party. He introduced the amendments at his own discretion and without consulting the members whose view and opinions are a real will and not a shadow of his will. They are a legal will too. The constitutional authority of the leader has no value if he does not respect this will.[14]

Very rarely had anyone, either inside and outside the Party, dared to call Sa'adeh's integrity and reputation into question. Even Sa'adeh's political detractors were careful not to do that.

---

12   Ibid.
13   Ibid.
14   Ibid.

Disagreement with Sa'adeh

Why did Fayez think of doing something so risky? His emotions may have got the better of him or perhaps it was a consequence of abundant pride and arrogance.

As Fayez continues his narrative description of the "coup" (*inqilab*), we learn that, in addition to imposing his "personal" philosophy on the Party, Sa'adeh revamped the Party's administration and machinery (especially the Department of Information and the Department of Culture, which were under Fayez's control for some years) and reworked the Party's publications to align them with his philosophical thinking. For Fayez, this was the capping climax of the "coup". Apart from subordinating the Party's institutional agencies to a single philosophy based entirely on "Sa'adeh's own outlook on life, universe, and the art", Fayez viewed it as the beginning of the end to philosophical freedom inside the Party. For him, it amounted to an absolute surrender to an exact philosophy under which members had no right to think freely, hold alternative philosophical views, or question key features.

The thought regimentation implied by this surrender seemed too problematic or unnerving for Fayez. Addressing himself directly to Sa'adeh, he wrote:

> A person who respects the group for which he is responsible is one who seeks to protect the ability of each member to think freely and absolutely. He presents his theory for the members to discuss and understand and grants every member the right to accept or reject whatever they want. And he who has a sense of respect for his outlook on life, the universe, and the art, and is confident of its validity and accuracy, is not one who tries to imprison his followers in a mental cage. He does not prevent them from exploring any other outlook and he does not preclude any intellectual dialogue between his outlook and other outlooks. On the contrary, he would welcome such a dialogue.[15]

---
15   *Ibid.*

What mattered even more for Fayez was the dictatorial hegemony that Sa'adeh obtained from all this. By imposing his personal philosophy on the Party, Sa'adeh could now not only suppress any intellectual dissent at his own discretion, but also create a condition whereby any philosophical disagreement with him could be construed as a disagreement with the Party itself. Hence, philosophical difference at the personal or individual level was unthinkable. Any disagreement became a disagreement not with Sa'adeh, but with the Party's ideology, and thus, between the member and the Party. The implications of such an analogy are obvious.

AN ANALYSIS OF FAYEZ'S ACCOUNT

Clearly, Fayez harbored some pent up frustrations and petulance well before his public confrontation with Sa'adeh. The intensity and gravity of his allegations clearly attest to this. No less important was Fayez's intentness to blame the dispute entirely on Sa'adeh instead of taking some responsibility for his own actions. He dodges the charge of ideological deviation leveled against him and raises new issues that were not part of the original disagreement. Veering the row in a different direction may have been the motive. Depending on one's perspective, this could be a sign of weakness stemming from an inability to cope with the core issue or the mark of a deliberate tactic to push Sa'adeh into a defensive position.

More significantly, the intellectual substance of Fayez's response raised (or was thought to raise by some) fundamental issues that struck at the core of the Party's outlook. For the sake of manageability, these issues are set out and analyzed under five headings:

1. BREACH OF THE "CONTRACT"

The first fundamental issue was breach of the "contract". Before we discuss this issue, we must observe that the

Disagreement with Sa'adeh

SSNP was founded based on a contract between its founder, Antun Sa'adeh, and the members who accepted his call. The terms of this contract are stated explicitly in the preamble of the Party's constitution:

> The SSNP is founded on the basis of a contract between the legislator (*al-shari'*), who originated the idea of Syrian social nationalism and all those who have accepted it, on condition that the formulator of the principles of the Syrian social nationalist renaissance shall be the leader of the of the Party for life, and that all those who believe in its principles and mission shall therefore become members of the Party, defend its cause, and give absolute support and allegiance to the leader, his legislations and constitutional administration.

No other political party in the Arab World, and perhaps in the entire world, has been founded on a contract of this kind. Even totalitarian parties are not exempt from this criterion since absolute power in those parties is often the product of strength, fear, and sheer force or the subtler forms of deception, cronyism, and persuasion. With the SSNP, members were *invited* to join the party based on a written "contract" that clearly and unequivocally defined exactly what they were expected to do and where their loyalty must lie. No hidden clauses, small print, or catches were involved, and the members were notified of the terms and meaning of the "contract" before joining. The rationale behind the contract was to ensure strict conformity to the Party's ideology as defined by its originator (i.e. Sa'adeh), and by extension, impede anyone from changing or tampering with its principles.

One of Fayez's major grievances enunciated in *Whither To?* is that Sa'adeh had committed a breach that went to the root of the "contract" by "changing" the Party's ideology without the consent of the members. Fayez classified this as an act of gross misconduct and dishonesty:

[The changes] amount to an application in our country of the principle of breaching of treaties and contracts at the discretion of the individual, without any justifications or legal rights ... It is a replication of the actions of recent tyrants. What Sa'adeh did does not, in any sense, flow from the Syrian heritage, which was, in its finest manifestations, a heritage based on legality and legitimacy.[16]

A breach of contract is a serious matter. Morally reprehensible, it could set a bad precedent if left unchallenged: especially when a psychological element is involved and the contract is not about only promising but about the expectations of the parties of one another in a mutually beneficial deal.[17] This is commonly referred to in the legal and political realms as a "psychological contract" whereby the parties understand their contractual obligations to encompass general moral and social norms of reciprocity and trustworthiness.[18] The psychological contract is, by definition, subjective, and its terms do not depend on actual or even constructive mutual agreement.

Fayez's allegation of breach of contract against Sa'adeh would be completely justified if not for his narrow and somewhat lopsided interpretation of the "contract". For some reason, or by mistake, he saw the "contract" primarily in commercial terms as a negotiated deal between two parties (Sa'adeh and the Party members), and thus subject to the elementary process of making a contract: offer, acceptance, consideration, and a mutual intent to be bound. This is not how the "contract" with Sa'adeh was formed. The fundamental character of the "contract" is a moral psychological one based on normative notions: trust, faith, support, mutual respect, and obligation. It is not based on an

---

16 Ibid.
17 Tess Wilkinson-Ryan, "Legal Promise And Psychological Contract." (*Wake Forest Law Review*, vol. 47, 2012): 847.
18 Stewart Macaulay, "Non-Contractual Relations in Business: A Preliminary Study." (*American Sociological Review*, vol. 55, 1963): 55-67.

exchange economy of give and take. Although it is intended to guide both the conduct of the ruler (Sa'adeh) and the relations that ought to exist between him and the ruled (members), it is not a "political contract" in the traditional sense of the word. In terms of actual governing, a political contract, which is an actual contract, "is what is immediately required to keep the governor in check".[19] In the present case, the purpose of the contract was to keep the governed in check versus the governor. This priority reversal stemmed from the well-founded fear that the Party's ideology had to be protected from potential saboteurs and that the only way of doing this was binding the members directly to its originator. It was assumed, logically, that the originator of a new idea is likely to be more faithful and concerned for its safety than any other person.

The contention that Sa'adeh's unilateral "changes" to the Party's ideology amounted to a breach of faith is hard to sustain. The allegation might hold if the "contract" had been of the common kind, and thus would have proscribed any party from changing the terms of the agreement without the consent of the other party or parties. In this case, however, the contract contained no prohibition clause. It was not even implied in its concise text. The terms of the contract were framed purposely in a way that gave one side a clear advantage over the other. As such, it should be treated for what it is: a unilateral contract whereby, at the point of its forming, one party was expected to perform certain acts in the pursuit of a particular aim created and specified to it by the other party. Moreover, since no formal negotiations between the two parties were involved, the contract automatically put the onus of responsibility on the accepting (members) rather than on the offering party (Sa'adeh).

Fayez pointed out with perfect justification that, if Sa'adeh could breach the contractual agreement with such ease and simplicity, what guarantee was there that he would not do it again? At stake

---

19 Kwame Gyekye, *Tradition and Modernity: Philosophical Reflections on the African Experience.* (New York: Oxford University Press, 1997): 126.

was not only Sa'adeh's right to "tamper" with the contract, but also whether members were entitled to challenge him. This valid question needs to be addressed carefully. The answer is simple. Under the terms of the contract, Sa'adeh was obligated strictly to the criterion of his offer: "the idea of Syrian social nationalism". Provided he adhered to this criterion, he was legally and morally responsible. The point Fayez missed is that the contract did not state, explicitly or implicitly, that Sa'adeh could not alter or modify the "details" or contents of this criterion. As the formulator of the idea, he was, ethically speaking, entitled to develop and re-shape it as he saw fit provided he stayed within the parameters of its core framework. He could meddle with the "offer", but he could not change or negate it. The right to meddle arises from his status as the legislator (*shari'*) of the offer. Divesting Sa'adeh of this right, as Fayez attempted to do, (1) reduced Sa'adeh's legislative prerogative in the "contract" to almost non-existent and (2) rendered the "offer" virtually static and impossible to modify by its originator. Thus, practically, according to Fayez, Sa'adeh had no right to modify the particulars of the offer even if the modification was necessary and did not bear on the offer's core substance. It also meant that Sa'adeh could exercise his legislative right under the contract only and strictly with the approval of the members even though no such condition was stipulated in it.

Fayez's insistence on consultation with the members was both impractical and unfair. It was impractical because the members, having originally played no part in the making of the offer, were not entitled to negotiate something they did not negotiate in the first place. Giving them a negotiating role after accepting the contract would also have invited opportunists and interlopers to steer the offer in a different direction from that intended by its originator, and thus, annul the original purpose of the contract. It was unfair because it effectively put the members on an equal par with Sa'adeh even though the basic idea on which the offer was predicated (i.e. Syrian social nationalism) was solely and entirely Sa'adeh's.

This brings us to the final point: did members have rights under the contract, and, if so, when and how? As stated above, the contract was framed deliberately in Sa'adeh's favor to protect the idea-offer from the tampering and modification of others. Under its terms, the burden of performance lay mainly with the members, but this did not necessarily render them completely helpless. Members were entitled to break the contract if Sa'adeh "changed" (as opposed to modify) the offer without their consent or if he reneged on his promise to dedicate himself to the Party's cause. Moreover, if any member was not satisfied with modifications to the contract, he could choose to opt out. Fayez described the "opt out" option as a "mockery" that reduced the member to a mere "puppet in Sa'adeh's hands".[20] Sa'adeh did not respond to this allegation, as overall, he considered the integrity of the Party's ideology more important than the contribution and services of any individual member.

2. Amendment of the Ideology

The second major reservation raised by Fayez relates to the actual amendments or "changes" to the Party's ideology. As indicated above, Fayez regarded those "changes" as a "coup" that transformed the SSNP into a new entity with a different character and identity. The expression "coup" was used to convey a sense of sharp break from a past or an existing condition to another. For Fayez, it differed from evolution:

It is axiomatic that evolution occurs when the seeds for all subsequent phases exist in the previous phases. As for "emergent evolution", during which entirely new properties, features and phenomena not included in the previous phases emerge at certain critical stages or levels in the course of evolution, is not an evolution at all but a coup in every sense of the word. And if, in the final stages, something contradicts with the essence of the first stages, then it is a complete coup as sharp as the

---

20   Sayegh, *Whither To?*

contradiction itself.[21]

According to Fayez, the "coup" occurred at various levels of the Party's program and ideology. It involved:

1. A change to the explanation of the Party's Program.
2. A change to the Fifth Fundamental Principle to incorporate Iraq in the east and Cyprus in the West within Syria's national frontiers.
3. A change to the Seventh Fundamental Principle with the adding of a "cultural" element.
4. A change to the Eighth Fundamental Principle with the adding a new sentence.

Does the above actually amount to a coup? Let us examine the facts. Concerning the Party's Program, the original explanation stated:

> The central theme in the program of the Syrian Social Nationalist Party is national revival, which includes guaranteeing the life of the Syrian nation and the creation of the conditions necessary for its progress and unity...

The new explanation:

> The central theme in the program of the Syrian Social Nationalist Party is national revival, which includes *laying down the foundations of the concept of nationhood in Syria* and the guaranteeing of the life of the Syrian nation and the creation of the conditions necessary for its progress and unity...

Why Fayez considered the add-on "lying down the foundations of the concept of nationhood in Syria" a drastic change is bewildering. Was the SSNP not a nationalist movement? Was

---
21 *Ibid.*

the concept of nationhood not at the essence of its revival program? Did Sa'adeh not write a book specifically on the concept of the nation (*The Rise of Nations*) because its meaning in Syria was ambiguous? The additional sentence merely reaffirmed something that already existed. It did not affect the essence of the Party's program or change its meaning. Only if the Party was not "nationalist" and had suddenly decided to become nationalist could we call it a coup. In that case, it would constitute a paradigm shift in the sense laid down by Thomas Kuhn:[22] a different mental outlook of the world.

Except for one amendment discussed below, all the other amendments to the Party's principles involved minor, scattered sentence adjustments. It would be tedious to reproduce all of them here. However, as an example, we will consider the amendment to the Seventh Fundamental Principle. The original wording of that Principle was:

> The Syrian Social Nationalist movement derives its inspiration from the talents of the Syrian nation and its political national history.

In 1947, Sa'adeh "changed" it to:

> The Syrian Social Nationalist movement derives its inspiration from the talents of the Syrian nation and its *cultural* political national history.

Fayez expressed vigorous objection to the inclusion of "cultural" in the Principle's text. He regarded it as a suffocating restriction on members' right to cultural freedom and as an attempt to impose a single cultural outlook on the nation. Why he would infer that is both baffling and bizarre. Sa'adeh added "cultural" to highlight Syria's rich cultural heritage and to stimulate greater interest into the country's cultural roots. The amendment was

---

22 An American physicist, historian and philosopher of science whose controversial 1962 book *The Structure of Scientific Revolutions* was influential in both academic and popular circles, introducing the term paradigm shift, which has since become an English-language idiom.

the product of an exhaustive study[23] on Syria's intellectual and cultural history that Sa'adeh had undertaken during his Argentine exile. It was not a spur-of-the-moment decision. Even if it were a spontaneous decision, what harm could be done in demanding cultural recognition or in directing the eyes of the country's intellectuals toward the nation's culture? Is culture not an intrinsic part of national life? Is it practical to speak of national revival without reference to culture? The irony is that, on various occasions, Fayez had produced material on Syria's cultural past and took great pride in it.[24]

To the extent that the amendment in question did not change the meaning of the Principle or alter its purpose and general function, it cannot be classified as a complete change. This applies also to the perfunctory adjustments made to the other Principles.

One amendment deserves special attention: the enlargement of Syria's national frontiers. This amendment can easily be construed as a breach to the "contract" if the background details are not clearly known.

Until 1947, Sa'adeh had defined Syria under the Fifth Fundamental Principle as

> ...geographic territory in which the Syrian nation was formed. It has geographical boundaries rendering Syria a country distinctly separate and independent from any other country. It extends from the Taurus Range in the north to the Suez Canal in the south including the Sinai Peninsula and the Gulf of Aqaba, and from the Syrian [Mediterranean] Sea in the west to the desert in the east until its junction with the Tigris.

This definition, which is really an extension of the *Bilad as-Sham*

---

23 Sa'adeh, *Intellectual Struggle in Syrian Literature.* (Buenos Aires, n. p. 1941).
24 Fayez's essay on Lucian of Samosata is a clear example. The essay was found among his archival papers.

concept that early Arab geographers formulated,[25] was widely accepted in the social and literary milieu in which Sa'adeh was born and raised. Even so, in the 1940s, Sa'adeh began to question its validity and authenticity. While the northern and western boundaries were more or less definite and clear, the southern and eastern frontiers varied from one author to another. The final line of demarcation depended on the political arrangements that prevailed in Syria and on the movements of the nomadic peoples living in these parts of the country.[26] Sa'adeh, who was anchored in the search for national clarity, regarded this discrepancy as more than a problem of intellectual inconsistency: it was a dilemma of national proportion.

Consequently, he embarked on a long investigation into the issue, which he described as "almost equivalent to an exploration into historical archaeology ... [and] a kind of search through the layers of history as painstaking as that which the archaeologist conducts when he searches through the strata of the earth".[27] He did not elaborate fully on the scope and character of his investigation. Nor did he reveal precisely when and where it was undertaken. Nevertheless, a shift in his thinking style is discernible as early as 1942.[28] Upon the completion of his investigation, Sa'adeh proclaimed a second definition: Syria's new boundaries now coincided with those of the Fertile Crescent. Thereby, *Bilad al-Sham* and Mesopotamia were merged into a single nation. This meant that Iraq was no longer a politically separate entity from Syria but part of it. The incorporation of the eastern part of the Fertile Crescent also brought the regions of Kuwait and Shat-al-

---

25 The line seemed to move eastward when order and civilised life prevailed and vice versa. Sa'adeh later recorded in the *Ten Lectures* (75) that "If we browse through works of the historians of the world we will find that, except in rare cases, there is not one single definition for a single territory called Syria."

26 *Ibid*, p. 75.

27 In that year he claimed that the existing definition of Syria's boundaries was inadequate because it was extracted from foreign sources which had been written within the context of their own self-interest.

28 *Ibid*, p. 75.

Arab into the Syrian orbit. The other significant change was the incorporation of Cyprus in the west.

Sa'adeh justified those modifications on sociological and geographical grounds. Sociologically, the Fertile Crescent was perceived as a single organic unit: a community of people without any great variation in their physical or psychological make-up. He considered this a new actuality arising from a single social interaction process and a common sense of belonging. In other words, social assimilation in the Fertile Crescent was never limited to one part to the exclusion of the other. There was always contact between the groups that lived in the area, and there were often conflicts because of the attempts of these groups to establish control over the others. To exclude the Chaldaeans and the Assyrians, from whom the name "Syria" probably derives, would be a grave error, and to regard the Chaldaeans and the Aramaeans as two separate people was illogical because, in essence, "they were, in origin and speech, one people".[29]

Sa'adeh conceded that warfare was a common denominator in the relationship between the groups that settled in the Fertile Crescent. He observed, however, that such warfare never assumed a "national" character. Rather, "they were internal wars, a struggle for supremacy among the powerful tribes and dynasties within the one nation which was in the making and which later attained maturity".[30] Each community strove to extend its control over the entire region and to establish its own hegemony, though few succeeded. This led to civil strife between the groups and conflict within the one community. For Sa'adeh, the political development of Syria had not always been stable and various centers of power had emerged not because of separate national loyalties, but because of lust for power.

This infighting, which Sa'adeh likened to the inter city-state conflicts of Italy, corresponded to the divisions of the diverse

---

29   *Ibid*, p. 76.

30   *Ibid*, p. 79.

environment of the Fertile Crescent. Every part of that region pursued its own political aims because communication was difficult and the thinness of population aroused social suspicion. This situation was compounded by Syria's geographical location as the frontier and meeting-point of the Near East and the West. Because of this, Syria has rarely known security. It has seldom had a central state of its own and its history has enjoyed only brief moments of independence.

Geographically, Sa'adeh regarded the Fertile Crescent as a single continuous plateau unimpeded by any significant internal barriers. He emphasized the two principal rivers that flow from the Armenian highlands: the Tigris and the Euphrates:

> The rivers that flow forth from the arch of the northern mountains, in particular the two major rivers, the Tigris and Euphrates, in the big arc lying between the Taurus and Zagros, and from the mountains of Lebanon, render the valleys and plains situated between these mountains, seas and desert a fertile area abound in milk and honey.[31]

The "twin rivers" are but fifteen miles apart in their sources but soon diverge and pursue devious courses. The plain they enclose when they leave the mountain region is one of the most richly fertile plains on the earth. In Sa'adeh's reasoning, the physical geography of the Fertile Crescent is largely dependent upon these two rivers: a view also shared by two contemporary historians of Iraq.

These twin rivers and the elaborate irrigation network which over many centuries has grown up around them, allow the designation "Fertile Crescent" to be extended from the Mediterranean coastal areas to include the Mesopotamian plains as well, notwithstanding the great expanse of desert that lies between the eastern and western segments of the Fertile Crescent.[32]

---

31 Edith & E. F. Penrose, *Iraq: International Relations and National Development*. (London: Ernest Benn, 1978): 2.

32 The view that soil degradation in the Syrian Desert is the result of the combined pressure of adverse and fluctuating climate and excessive exploitation is

Sa'adeh also conjured up a wholly different version of the Syrian Desert and its place in Syria. The Syrian Desert, he claimed, is not a "mere desert", but an area of settled cultivation desolated by the incursion of the Arabian Desert upon the lower arch of the Fertile Crescent. This incursion, which bears a striking resemblance to the current situation in North Africa, is attributed to human negligence and poor management of the natural resources. In turn, these are related to factors such as poverty, ignorance, misguided government policies, foreign invasions, and uncontrolled decline in population.[33] Sa'adeh regarded this incursion as a cumulative historical problem and cautioned against its spread into other areas in Syria.[34]

While this new pattern of thinking might have surprised both sceptics and devoted nationalists, it should not have surprised those with some understanding of the region. Christina Phelps advanced a similar view independently in a separate study of the Syrian Desert. She noted:

> The aspects of the Syrian Desert is a great surprise to many travelers; because the word desert is apt to conjure up a picture of golden sands blown into dunes, only less mobile

---

questionable, because the population in the Syrian *Badiya* was diminutive and the climate in the Middle East did not witness significant changes in the last 5000 years. See A. Leroi-Gourhan, "Vegetational history in SW Syria and Lebanon during the upper Quaternary," *Sahi Institute of Paleobotany*, special publication No. 5 (1974).

33 Historically, the hills overlooking the Mediterranean were once covered with evergreen forests from sea to mountain tops, but large-scale felling left them barren and covered by a degraded drought-resistant scrubby vegetation called *maquis*. Similarly, Upper Mesopotamia once had a complex system of irrigation that allowed almost the entire region to be cultivated in the third century AD until it started to break down owing to lack of attention and a plummeting population. See Fouad Abo, "Desertification and Water Management: The Challenge in the Middle East," Paper presented at the AMESA 12th Annual Conference, Deakin University (Melbourne 1993). Also Eyre, S.R. (1986), *Vegetation and Soils: A World Picture* (London: Edward Arnold, 1975).

34 Grant P. Christina, *The Syrian Desert: Caravans, Travel and Exploration* (London: A & C Black Ltd, 1937), p. 6.

than the sea. Whereas the traversable part of this particular desert is flat in appearance, like a vast undulating plain, and its color astonishes even those who have become accustomed to their variety. The plain is in part gravel-strewn; in part sand covered; and in part hard caked with whitish, glittering dried mud.[35]

Phelps concluded that, while some deserts divide countries and civilizations, others unite them: "The Syrian Desert is one of those which unites adjacent lands".[36]

Sa'adeh highlighted the early history of the Syrian Desert and its physical variety, which, from early times, had allowed enterprising people to build towns and civilizations across its wide landscape.[37] These towns served as halting-places for caravans travelling between the Mediterranean and Mesopotamia.[38] Similarly, the remains of watercourses and cisterns in certain parts of the Syrian Desert provide evidence of the former existence of a great system of artificial irrigation.[39] A nineteenth-century Christian missionary wrote:

---

35 *Ibid*, p. 1.

36 Neolithic materials recently extracted from the Syrian desert indicate that prehistoric villages had flourished in it as early as the seventh millennium B.C. See A. Bounni & K. Al-As'ad K, *Palmyra: History, Monuments and Museum*, 2nd ed. (Damascus; n.p., 1988).

37 A typical example is Tadmor itself. Once a great seat of commerce and arts and a marvellous oasis with sources of fertility, Tadmor furnished a resting place between Mesopotamia and *Bilad as-Sham* and was a primary stop for caravans moving between the Gulf, Persia, and the Mediterranean. But the great "city of the East" has fallen, no more to rise. From an outlying military station of the Roman Empire, it has sunk into an "obscure town, a trifling fortress, and at length a miserable village." See Samuel G. Green, *Bible Lands* (London: The Religious Tract Society, 1879).

38 The agrarian system of ancient civilisations (Sumerian, Assyrian, and Babylonian) provided, for over 2,000 years, an efficient technique in water management, siltation, clogging and soil salinization in Mesopotamia and its adjacent areas. See Fouad Abo, *op.cit.*

39 Quoted in Samuel G. Green, *Bible Lands*, p. 46.

The ground [of the Syrian Desert] is covered with small fragments of flint and limestone, through which a sickly grass tuft or half-withered weed here and there springs up. Not a tree, not a green shrub appears within the range of vision, and animal life is equally rare, for except chance throws in our way a troop of gazelles or a band of Bedawin, we travel for hours without seeing a living creature. Yet, desolate as the country is, we see traces of an ancient road, and at every few miles are the ruins of castles or caravanserais.[40]

Indeed, many Christian travelers' notions of the Syrian Desert were modified considerably in the course of their journey across it.[41]

Ahead of his time, Sa'adeh called for the re-development of the Syrian Desert through a Syria-wide soil control strategy. He hoped that, with the application of new methods in land use rehabilitation, expanded local awareness and the creation of reliable institutions monitoring population growth and ecology would cause the wilderness to thrive again. Such a strategy, which depends almost entirely upon the supply of water (hence the need for the twin rivers), highlights the level and complexity of the environmental problem in the Fertile Crescent which, after many years of human neglect, has made the whole region look like a useless stretch of land without any purpose or historical significance.

On the western frontiers, the demarcation lines were extended to include the island of Cyprus. Cyprus was incorporated for historical and strategic reasons as well as for its expediency

---

40 *Ibid.* Many Western missionaries ventured into the Syrian Desert expecting two days' dreary ride over arid sands, but were astonished to find, in the very midst of their route, a long grass that came up to their horses' stirrups for many a mile.

41 Cyprus has been a valuable military station for Western powers, particularly Great Britain since the inter-war period. It was used as a launching pad for the attack against Egypt during the 1956 Suez Crisis.

as a source of military and security strength.[42] Any foreign control of it was deemed as a threat to Syria. Sa'adeh's interest in Cyprus, though, was not purely because of its military value to Syria. In contrast, he spoke highly of the island and valued its people and heritage. He placed it on an equal footing with the states of mainland Syria and afforded it the same privileges and importance. What made Cyprus so vital for Sa'adeh was its close proximity to the mainland: so close that you "could hear the cry of a bird" from both ends of the coast.

In a way, Sa'adeh's claim on Cyprus is similar to China's demand over Taiwan. One could object to this analogy because China and Taiwan share a common language and were united at one stage, whereas Syria and Cyprus were a world apart in many different respects. However, on the other hand, just as China and Taiwan had a common history, the history of Cyprus and Syria are intertwined intrinsically. According to Stavros Panteli, historically, the Syrians had shown a definite interest in the Island (mainly for economic and security reasons).[43] Another historian of Cyprus, Stanley Casson, remarked that a re-reading of Homeric history and the revelations of the Hittite texts from Boghaz Keui published in 1924 suggest that Cyprus was a secondary centre of Myceneaen development and a place of concentration for enterprises in Anatolia and Syria.[44]

According to Sa'adeh, the division of the Fertile Crescent into two separate parts, Mesopotamia and *Bilad al-Sham*, occurred during the Perso-Byzantine period of occupation. When a decisive victory for either side proved infeasible, the Byzantines extended their rule over the western part of the Crescent, which they continued to call "Syria", while the Persians dominated the eastern part (Mesopotamia, or the land of Assyria and

---

42　Stavros Panteli, *A New History of Cyprus: From the Earliest Times to the Present Day.* (London: East-West Publications, 1984): 8.

43　Stanley Casson, *Ancient Cyprus: Its Art and Archaeology.* (London: Methuen & Co. Ltd, 1937): 18.

44　Sa'adeh, *The Ten Lectures*, p. 94.

ancient Babylon) which they called "Irah". This term was later Arabicized into Iraq.[45] Naturally, this division retarded the evolution of a single Syrian personality for a long period, but it did not wholly efface it.

Fayez failed to see that the original text of Syria's frontiers included part of Mesopotamia, but the borders west of it had not been clearly defined. He may not have known that Sa'adeh had been aware of this imperfection and that he postponed his investigation into it due to political pressure. The evidence suggests that Fayez was informed about the matter in 1947 during his long discussions with Sa'adeh. Two other factors should be mentioned: (1) Sa'adeh was under no obligation under the "contract" to confer with members over any amendment provided he did not tamper with the fundamentals of the Party's ideology; and (2) the amendment did not breach the terms of the "contract" because it remained within the parameters of the original offer. Concerning this point, Sa'adeh noted:

Any comparison between the reviewed text and the original one will show that the social nationalist cause and its teachings remained basically unchanged and that the revision completed the truth and saved it from sectional defects, which it did not escape in the first two editions because of my haste and the pressure from circumstances.[46]

It is very likely that Sayegh, who had been a particularly outspoken critic of impulsive union initiatives, such as King Abdullah's Greater Syria Scheme and Nuri al-Said's Fertile

---

45 According to Francis Godolphin, the whole study of archaeology was certainly unknown to the Greek historians. Much of the material for the knowledge of pre-history was more accessible then than it is now, yet the Greeks were content to rely on folk-tales and poetic accounts of earlier history. "For the majority of the Greeks, indeed, the myth was history. They never bothered to find evidence of living conditions, religious customs, and artistic development..." See *The Greek Historians: The Complete and Unabridged Historical Works of Herodotus* (New York: Random House 1942), xvi.

46 Sa'adeh, *Complete Works*, vols. 15 and 16.

Crescent Plan, rejected Sa'adeh's explanation because the amendments appeared to mimic these initiatives. Already, there were talks going around that the "idea of a Fertile Crescent union [popularized by Nuri al-Said's Fertile Crescent Plan] appealed to Sa'adeh ... as a slogan that could rally to the SSNP those elements which heretofore had resisted the party and its national doctrine".[47] Having dismissed King Abdullah's Greater Syria Scheme and Nuri al-Said's Fertile Crescent Plan as products of Hashemite intrigues motivated by territorial aggrandizement and hegemonic aspirations involving a tacit endorsement of British and Zionist interests in the region,[48] Sayegh probably judged the 'amendments' as a step in the same direction. From a personal perspective, the revised definition of Syria's borders was a blow to his credibility because, to some degree, it contradicted his own prior assessments and debunked his assumptions and alarmism.

All things considered, Fayez's reservations concerning the amendments of 1947 do not stand up to close scrutiny. Most of the amendments were superficial. They either reaffirmed something that already existed or brought some aspects into greater focus and clarity. Their classification by Fayez as a "coup" is an exaggeration. The edition of the Party's Aim and Program in which the amendments first appeared (and which Fayez himself drew on in writing *Whither To?*) was a fourth edition. This suggests that (1) the "Aim and Program" had been modified at least twice before and (2) its content was not static, as Fayez had assumed, but subject to review and revision. Naturally, the person who was responsible for this was Sa'adeh: its creator and sole reference.

An alternative way of looking at it is to imagine Fayez as a

---

47 Labib Y. Zuwiyya, *The Syrian Social Nationalist Party: An Ideological Analysis*. (Harvard University Press, 1966): 86.

48 Importantly, both projects had given little, if any thought, to the question of legitimacy or credence. As Sonoko Sunayama remarked, the underlying interest behind them was largely regime consolidation and the desire for a weaker neighbour. See Sonoko Sunayama, *Syria And Saudi Arabia: Collaboration and Conflicts in the Oil Era*. (London: Tauris Academic Studies, 2007).

member of a Communist Party and Sa'adeh as Karl Marx: would Fayez have been entitled to object if Marx had suddenly decided to revise the Communist Manifesto because new facts had become known? Would Marx have first consulted with fellow Communists before conducting any revision? Surely not! Just as the Communist Manifesto belongs exclusively to Marx, likewise the doctrine of Syrian Social Nationalism belongs exclusively to Sa'adeh. Moreover, just as the right to adapt and adjust the Communist Manifesto belongs exclusively to Marx, likewise the right to adapt and adjust the doctrine of Syrian Social Nationalism belongs exclusively to Sa'adeh. As for the followers, they were free to accept the revised changes and stay put or to reject them and opt out.

(3) The Party's Name

Then there is the matter of the Party's amended name, which Fayez inflated out of proportion:

> It is an amendment that goes to the essence of the Party. It ... places at the heart of the party's name its new philosophical conception, which is now part of its ideology and principles.

At least two issues are involved here: (1) the actual change of the Party's name and (2) the implications implicit in the amended name. Concerning the first point, adding the word "Social" to the Party's name can hardly be classified as a "coup", because all it did was clarify the Party's position along the philosophical spectrum. The "social" dimension added to the Party's name was inherent in the Party's ideology from the outset, but it was taken for granted rather than stated explicitly. Fayez's mistake was assuming that this dimension, of which he was clearly aware, did not constitute a foundation for a philosophical system that ultimately involved a new outlook on life. Regarding the implications of the amended name, it had to do largely with the fact that adding "Social" formerly consecrated "social nationalism" as the official philosophy of the Party. Fayez resented deeply this prospect on the ground that marrying ideology with philosophy would create a totalitarian nightmare with little room for individual and philosophical freedom inside the Party. He may have inferred this from the havoc wreaked by single philosophy parties during World War II. However, for all its realism, Fayez's contention is only partly convincing. It assumes that every ideological party that subscribes to a specific philosophy will develop signs and symptoms of totalitarian behavior or that every totalitarian party is, by necessity, grounded in a single philosophy or inimical to philosophical diversity. This is not necessarily the case. Most ideological parties avow themselves to a particular philosophy not for the purpose of totalitarian control or out of disrespect for philosophical freedom, but for the sake of internal unity.

If, on the other hand, Fayez's objection to "Social" was because it constitutes a name change in itself, then why did Fayez not remonstrate in 1945 when the Party's name was amended from the "Syrian Social Nationalist Party" to the "National Party"? Dropping "Syrian" from the Party's name is more significant than adding "Social" to it. The appellation "Syrian" represents an important distinction: it is the incipiency of the Party and the mark of its character and identity.

(4) Totalitarianism

One of Fayez's oft-repeated claims in *Whither To?* represents the third fundamental issue. Fayez stated that Sa'adeh, consciously or unconsciously, edged toward a totalitarian position by imposing his "personal philosophy" on the Party. Perhaps the most serious allegation of all, it is also the most simplistic. The allegation, at its most mature, involved a chain of inferences and assumptions informed by recent trends in contemporary Western theories on political leadership and control and by the harsh realities of European totalitarianism. Undoubtedly, Fayez's exposure at the personal level to existential philosophy also played a significant part in shaping his attitude.

Fayez's allegation centered on the perception that a totalitarian mindset would result if the Party's ideology were predicated on a specific philosophy, let alone on the personal and private philosophy of its founder. He maintained that, since the Party did not adhere to a philosophical position from the beginning, embracing an exclusive philosophy now constituted another breach of the contract on which it was founded.

Technically, Fayez was right. At its founding, the Party did not lean toward any particular philosophy or espouse a world view. Its fundamental pillars rested on a sketchy ideology, organization, and politics rather than on philosophy. That much is true. However, a counter explanation to this should not be discounted hastily.

First, concerning the issue of "breach", there is nothing in the "contract" that precludes the Party from formulating its own philosophy or from opening up to a new outlook on life. It is admissible as long as the adopted or formulated philosophy does not conflict with the central doctrine of the Party or contradict any part of its stated principles. The key to the legitimacy of the act rests not on the act itself but on the nature of the philosophy: that is, on whether or not it agrees with the Party's vision as defined in its ideology. For example, let us assume that Sa'adeh had decided to enthrone National Socialism as the official philosophy of the Party. In this case, we can safely say that a "coup" and a "breach" had occurred because the contradictions with National Socialism, especially on the racial level, are too obvious to discount. The same principle would apply with any worldview incongruous with the Party's outlook, whether it is Communism, Conservatism, Existentialism, or any other philosophy. The fact that Sa'adeh determined to ground the Party's philosophy in the Party's ideology renders Fayez's claim even more inherently unreasonable.

Second, Fayez's assumption that the Party lacked a philosophical outlook until Sa'adeh proclaimed one in 1947 is not entirely accurate. While it is true that the Party did not champion an exclusive philosophy at the beginning, its principles contained the seeds of a philosophical system based on the fullness of society. Eventually, Sa'adeh developed and accentuated this system in his speeches and writings: defining not only its views on society and the individual, but also its position on an array of issues pertaining to religion, culture, literature, values, epistemology, and the high ideals of good, truth, and beauty. In *Whither To?*, Fayez conceded that snippets of Sa'adeh's philosophical explications had reached him, but he continued to make the absurd claim that he considered them articulations of Sa'adeh's personal views rather than a statement of an official attitude!

Third, Fayez's allegation that Sa'adeh had imposed his own "personal" philosophy on the Party is fatally defective. A cursory review of Sa'adeh's philosophical views, developed and expounded at different stages after 1938, reveals a position of total commitment to the central cause of the Party as the sole compass for his opinions and judgments. Every philosophical perspective Sa'adeh engaged in was related intimately to the Party's ideology or forged into something palatable to it. As any individual, Sa'adeh had certain "personal" preferences in life, but no evidence suggests that he tried to impose them on the Party. For example, Sa'adeh was very fond of Beethoven and other classical composers, but he did not force this fondness on the Party. Likewise, he had definite views on love and marriage, but he kept them to himself. Fayez's shortcoming was that he judged Sa'adeh's philosophical views prematurely before subjecting them to close scrutiny. By doing so, not only did he make the mistake of unfairly accusing Sa'adeh of forcing his personal views on the Party, but also of jumping to the wrong conclusions. Nothing is more revealing regarding this than his claim that Sa'adeh's foray into philosophy came about because of his philosophical altercations with party members, beginning with Fawzi Maluf in 1944. This is not only inaccurate, but also misleading. Sa'adeh's involvement with philosophical issues began well before the Maluf case. It formed an essential part of his ideological discourse as early as 1934.

Finally, there is the contention, so crucial to Fayez, that philosophical diversity, and by extension, freedom of philosophical thinking, would evaporate from confining the Party to an exclusive philosophy. As an avid thinker and an ardent believer in philosophical freedom, Fayez cannot be blamed for taking a reserved attitude towards philosophical uniformity. Subordinating philosophy to ideological interests and imperatives can be fatal if it is not properly managed or if taken to hyperbolic extremes. It has the potential to falsify the essential functions of philosophy in national development and to produce non-philosophical devaluation of philosophy. However, for all its benefits and charms, philosophical diversity is not always practical or even desirable. This is especially the case when a national revival is being attempted and every atom of the nation's energy and creativity is required. Under such circumstances, only philosophy located in the specific realities of a specific society can inspire, inform, and guide real change. During a deep and profound national crisis, the focus of attention is on the effort to establish practical philosophical principles that help the nation transcend parochial and usually discriminative and narrow interests rather than on maintaining philosophical diversity amid the divisions, biases, and adulteration of the existing society. Anyway, the principle of philosophical diversity, as Fayez prescribed, cannot be accommodated practically by comprehensive or ideological parties concerned with society. It is imaginable and desirable in parties organized around specific demands or specific issues, such as single-issue parties, but with comprehensive parties, the pressing weight of reality can outweigh the desire for philosophical diversity. In many cases, restrictions on the dissemination of and engagement with different voices and perspectives inside these parties are introduced to maintain ideological consistency or to avoid derailing conflicts. Without these restrictions, the comprehensive party will become a center of information for diverse philosophical views and forfeit the ideological and spiritual unity required for effective action. Moreover, contrary to Fayez's contention, the subordination of philosophical dictates to ideological imperatives, at least during the transitional phases of a national or social revival, does not necessarily lead to philosophical fossilization. Providing the human mind is recognized as the supreme and autonomous master of everything, which was the view held by Sa'adeh, there is very little risk of that occurring. Philosophical ossification can also be avoided with practical measures. Creating a philosophical platform for the continuous refinement of methods and ideas, for example, can foster a climate conducive to the development of new ideas and hence to the advancement of knowledge even within the framework of a uniform philosophy.

Fayez assumed that all philosophical uniformity is evil and all philosophical diversity is good. This is not necessarily the case. Philosophical diversity within a fractured national context can be as harmful as philosophical uniformity within a stable national context. Each functions better in some situations than others. For example, philosophical uniformity in universities and colleges would fly in the face of academic excellence and progress. Likewise, philosophical diversity during a hard and painstaking revival may not be sensible or practical. It is all relative to circumstances and choices. A nation on the rise is likely to be less tolerant of philosophical diversity than a nation that has arisen. Similarly, a political party on the move is likely to be less accommodating of philosophical diversity than the one in power, or vice versa.

The point is that philosophical uniformity is not always inimical to philosophical inquiry, as Fayez seemed to assume. Sa'adeh's assertion in his last letter to Fayez indicates that he was interested more in developing a unifying national philosophy than in imposing a one-sided totalitarian philosophy. Sa'adeh stated, "There may be nothing objectionable about translating the Berdyaev-Kierkegaard perspective into Arabic and familiarizing the Syrian thought with it." For someone with an acute sense of history and a deep appreciation of the need for internal unity, Fayez's reaction was unusual. Either he completely misread Sa'adeh's intention or the aspect of a national philosophy did not occupy a central place in his philosophical thinking.

(5) Intellectual Diversity

Finally, *Whither To?* culminates in a series of damning judgments. The most pathetic example is:

> In the name of my nation and its dignity in the face of history, and in the name of the citizen in my nation, and in the name of my nation's past, present, and future, I declare Sa'adeh, the suffocator of intellectual and spiritual freedom, an oppressive tyrant, and opponent of the Syrian nation.[49]

It is hard to comprehend that a condemnation of such proportion could flow from Fayez's pen after all the praises he had heaped on Sa'adeh, such as:

> Sa'adeh represents a live embodiment of the strengths and values of life that are latent in each of our souls but are ready to burst and take control of our entity. He represents a set of noble virtues, values, characteristics, and strengths that exist inside every person in a default dormant state and are sometimes visible in some people. In Sa'adeh, they have crystallized and coalesced. Thus, although they remain dormant and inherent in each of us, they are conspicuously, clearly, coherently, and supremely visible in Sa'adeh's character.[50]

What occasioned Fayez's remarkable about-face, and to what extent is it justified?

---

49 Sayegh, *Whither To?*
50 *Sada an-Nahda*, 2 March, 1947.

According to Fayez, the unforgivable sin that Sa'adeh committed and that made him a "tyrant" was his violation of the principle of intellectual diversity. By imposing a "personal" philosophy on the Party and demanding unquestioning commitment to it, Sa'adeh, so the argument goes, created a climate that stifled free thought and individuality and entrapped the members in a mind-numbing stupor. For Fayez, this represented a complete reversal in the breadth of Sa'adeh's tolerance of intellectual diversity inside the Party and a hellish descent into a kind of intellectual moribundity. Repeatedly, he invokes the following statement of Sa'adeh in self-defense: "I have no desire to erase intellectual diversity in our movement. Rather, I want to preserve it and develop it, because it is necessary for our work and success."

Plausible as it may sound, the argument does not have much to be said for it. Its premise depends almost entirely on the "personal philosophy" assumption. In fact, the aspect of "personal philosophy" is so crucial to it that it is repeated almost as a mantra. Yet, for all its preponderance, Fayez does not offer a succinct explanation. He does not discuss what "personal philosophy" is or does not prove that Sa'adeh had a "personal philosophy." He does not reveal the constituents of that philosophy, assuming it existed in the first place. He makes the claim but does not elaborate. Consequently, we are left with a rudimentary observation with little else to go on. This is hardly surprising since Fayez, by his own admission, did not consider Sa'adeh's "speeches and statements as having any kind of official status that obliges party members to accept and submit to them".[51] The inadequacy of this assessment is too obvious to require further comment.

Of far greater significance was the matter of intellectual diversity itself. On this level, too, Fayez's performance was confusing and somewhat of a letdown. He presented himself as a defender of intellectual diversity, but apart from pointing at its inherent value to human progress, he did not successfully explain how it could

---

51 Sayegh, *Whither To?*

possibly work in the framework of an ideological party. Rather, he seemed interested in pursuing diversity in its most full, extreme form. However, diversity is never understood as mere variety for its own sake but as something that facilitates other things: the advancement of knowledge, social equality, fairness, openness to others, etc. Like everything else, intellectual diversity has its limitations even in the context of society or in academic settings where it is supposed to function at its highest level. When the matter involves a political party based on a specific ideology, the limitations take on a completely new dimension. Simply stated, ideological parties are ill-disposed to intellectual diversity in the absolute sense advocated by Fayez. Any political party established on a set of beliefs anchored on a worldview regarding reality, life, meaning, and purpose would expect, if not demand, its members to adhere to its teachings and to strive for ideological unity. Conformity in this context is not necessarily inimical to free thought or intellectual diversity. Members can still discuss and debate different intellectual currents and express their opinions freely, but logically, they cannot use the party to promote the perspectives of another ideology or the tenets of another intellectual current within the party. From this practical standpoint, Sa'adeh contemplated and responded to Fayez:

> [Ideological consolidation] does not conflict with the principle of freedom, whose terms of reference acknowledge the right of all advocates of an ideology to stand side by side in their quest to achieve the key aspect of their beliefs. Also, it does not in any way acknowledge the right of an advocate to work within the framework of a particular ideology for the success of another ideology opposed or detrimental to it.[52]

Sa'adeh was frank and honest with Fayez. He told him: "You failed to realize that it is the natural duty of this movement to consolidate its ideology and to strive for victory just like

---

52 SSNP, *Al-Nashrah al-Rasmiyah lil Harakat al-Qawmiyyah al-Ijtimae'yah.* (Beirut: Vol. 1, No. 2, December 1947).

every movement in the world founded on basic teachings."[53] Astonishingly, Fayez did not pay adequate attention to the rationale behind this observation. He responded with a confusing and hard-to-follow remark: "The principle of free thought permits the followers of a particular faith to hold conflicting views on life, the universe, and art within the framework of full respect for their common faith."[54]

It is difficult to imagine how this can be practical in an ideologically charged institution, be it political, religious, or economic. It is like saying, for example, that members of the Catholic faith are entitled to practice the worldview of their choice (Islam, Buddhism, Judaism, or Protestantism) within the Catholic Church even if it runs contrary to Catholic teachings. If the Catholic Church were to allow this, the result would be total chaos and rampant disorder. Conversely, what the Catholic Church cannot do (and what would be morally wrong if it were to) is to prohibit its members from studying or discussing other religions or from interacting with other members of other religious orders. Nonetheless, the Church may still introduce restrictions if it feels the integrity and unity of its faith is being undermined. The same principle applies to ideological political movements. In this case, the relationship between free thought and faith is much more convoluted due to the nature of political work and its intense competition and rivalry. Here, more than in any other collective institution, the margin for intellectual diversity is very tight. Tolerance for rival ideologies is usually nominal, and the focus of the work is on building and consolidating the worldview of the movement. As Dean of Information and Culture in the Syrian Social Nationalist Party, whose duty and primary task was to protect the Party's ideology from the intrusion of other currents and worldviews, Fayez would have known this.

As Fayez proposed, intellectual diversity can easily become a means of smuggling certain unspoken values into a political

---

53   *Ibid.*
54   Sayegh, *Whither To?*

party. This form of chaotic freedom is capable of ripping the most robust of parties apart and derailing them completely. An ideological party (as distinct from a one-issue party) is like a motor vehicle programmed for a specific journey. The driver is the leader and the passengers are the members. If everyone inside the vehicle understands the purpose of the journey and where they are going, the group will have a better chance of arriving at the designated destination than if the members are divided and quarrelsome. The vehicle is unlikely to make it at all if each passenger wants it to veer in the direction of his or her personal choice. Likewise, an ideological movement cannot function, let alone achieve its objectives, if the members are allowed to engage in or advocate for diverse intellectual currents inside it. It is a recipe for disaster.

Fayez might have responded that philosophical diversity is in a category of its own, because philosophy is basically a theoretical enquiry into the knowledge of truth. But this only presupposes a total break between ideology and philosophy when, in fact, they sometimes overlap. As Barry Cooper has shown, philosophy, taken independently of power interests, is unable to achieve effective truth. There is, as it were, a co-penetration of power and logos.[55] Whatever philosophy may invoke – metaphysics, natural law, divine purposes – it includes the activity of ... a critical assessment of the assumptions and ideas involved in various spheres of human thought and action; of description, explanation, argument and judgment, and other kinds of purposeful behavior.[56]

Ideology requires a constant assessment and interpretation of

---

[55] Barry Cooper, "Ideology and Technology, Truth and Power." In Frederick Copleston and Anthony Parel, *Ideology, Philosophy and Politics* (Waterloo: Wilfrid Laurier University Press for the Calgary Institute for the Humanities, 2008): 93-111.

[56] John Plamenatz, "The Philosophical Element in Social Theory and Practice." In Frederick Copleston and Anthony Parel, *Ideology, Philosophy and Politics*. (Waterloo: Wilfrid Laurier University Press for the Calgary Institute for the Humanities, 2008): 65.

human behavior and of the assumptions, methods, and ideas involved in political activity. As such, some mental activity is involved in this process and this "mental activity seems closer to being philosophical than anything else".[57] Even if philosophy and ideology can be shown to be distinct modes of discourse, and they are in certain respects, it still would not justify philosophical diversity within the context of a single political ideology.

In fairness to Fayez, he does advance a more prudent argument toward the end of *Whither To?*. He maintains that it was wrong of Sa'adeh to suppress philosophical diversity inside the Party if the different views are "consistent with the [Party's] creed". This is a reasonable observation, but Fayez does not elaborate on it. He provides no explanation as to how this diversity might work with the movement's ideology or which philosophical views, aside from Sa'adeh's, might be consistent with it. Perhaps what Fayez had in mind was the freedom to explore different philosophical perspectives to identify the one most adaptable to the Party's ideology than to accept the Sa'adeh perspective as final. This is not implausible, but it requires the recognition of a self-contained worldview as a feature of the Party's ideology, which is a condition that Fayez was not prepared to acknowledge.

For this reason, Fayez's characterization of Sa'adeh as a "tyrant" was ignored. It failed to resonate even with the handful of intellectuals who sided with him. Of the few responses he attracted, the one by his student and strong admirer at the time, Labib Yamak Zuwiyya, was perhaps the most caustic:

> It never occurred to me that you would descend so low as to ascribe intellectual sterility to a leader who showed you the way and lit before you the darkness of the past, and made you aware of all that you possess of true values and errors! It never occurred to me that one day you would be so ungrateful

---

57 Frederick Copleston and Anthony Parel, *Ideology, Philosophy and Politics*. (Waterloo: Wilfrid Laurier University Press for the Calgary Institute for the Humanities, 2008): 9.

and so denying of favor. But you are indeed an ingrate, and your ingratitude implies selfishness that only those who were closely associated with you would know of.[58]

It was both selfish and absurd of Fayez to call Sa'adeh a tyrant after all the open and frank discussions they had had on philosophical issues. The accusation may have been warranted if Fayez had come forward with a philosophy equally or more consistent with the Party's ideology than Sa'adeh's, and Sa'adeh had decided to turn it down for no apparent reason. Since nothing of the sort happened, or seemingly was likely to happen, the accusation is baseless.

CONCLUSION

In presenting his side of the dispute, Fayez raised some interesting points. He addressed fundamental issues and trends that are unique to collective ideological movements and he was bold and outspoken. Yet, his bluntness, tactlessness, and impatience with others come across clearly. He did not seem to mind what others might think or who might get hurt. This suggests strong idiosyncrasies in personality that are sometimes hard to deal with.

With Fayez, we encounter a bleak exposé that depicts Sa'adeh as an originator of a mystical and religious vision of nationhood in which his person attains a sacred aura: a despot who sought to impose his own world view with complete disregard for others; and of all things, an avowed enemy of Syria:

> In the name of Syria's interest, which Sa'adeh taught me during the first stages of his struggle to work for and sacrifice any other interest for it, I declare Sa'adeh in the last stage a destructive factor and a danger to my Syrian nation![59]

---

58 SSNP, *Al-Nashrah al-Rasmiyah lil Harakat al-Qawmiyyah al-Ijtimae'yah.* (Beirut: Vol. 1, No. 2, December 1947).

59 Sayegh, *Whither To?*

Yet, for all his hyperbolic rhetoric, Fayez failed to address the most important issue in the dispute with Sa'adeh: the attachment he harbored for existential philosophy. It is hardly mentioned in *Whither To?* or rebutted despite the extensive space allocated for philosophy in the tract. This is both disappointing and unhelpful. Existential philosophy was the primary factor that shaped Fayez's attitude, response and the extremity of that response. His failure to deal with it reflected badly on him. It caused the issue to fester and grow, solidified the suspicion that he was an existentialist propagator, and enabled Sa'adeh to land the final blow with effortless ease. The role of existential philosophy in the Fayez-Sa'adeh encounter is the topic of the next chapter.

5

The Question of Existentialism

One of the most peculiar and interesting aspects in the Sa'adeh-Fayez encounter is the conflicting perspective that developed after the initial explosion. Both Sa'adeh and Fayez characterized their disagreement as intellectual, but they differed on the substance and nature of the issues involved. The role of Existential philosophy is one example. While Sa'adeh had isolated the source of the disagreement to Sayegh's leaning towards existentialism, Sayegh regarded the existential dimension as a negligible factor in the overall scale of things. His two letters in reply to Sa'adeh in December 1947 and his statement to *an-Nahar* in that month made no mention (or hardly any mention) of existentialism. Likewise, his monograph on the dispute *Whither To?* contained only a brief and passing remark on the subject.

Sayegh's blink at the "Existential issue" in his encounter with Sa'adeh is bewildering. Not only did a very clear focus on Existentialist themes permeate most of his literary works after 1945, the year he completed his Master's thesis on "Personal Existence" but evidence also exists that these themes extended to his Party writings as well. The stamp of existentialism is evident from the "personalist" spirit that pervaded Sayegh's approach to nationalism after 1945 and from the increasing use of "existentialist" terminologies in his analyses and speeches. This seems to have been altruistically driven more to salvage the war-battered image of nationalism from further disfigurement than an attempt to undermine nationalism itself.

Naturally, this raises several questions concerning the role of Existential philosophy in the Sa'adeh-Sayegh clash:

1. Why did Sayegh veer toward existentialism?

2. Did Sayegh attempt to promote existentialist themes inside the Party? If so, when, where and to what extent?

3. Why did Sayegh undervalue the role of existentialism in his dispute with Sa'adeh?

4. Why did Sa'adeh regard the existentialist world view as irreconcilable with his doctrine of social nationalism?

5. Did Fayez harbor a hidden agenda or was he simply misinformed?

A brief outline of some of the key ideas and concepts of the existentialist worldview will help us toward the answers to these questions.

THE EXISTENTIALIST PERSPECTIVE

Existentialism originated from the nineteenth century philosophers Søren Kierkegaard, Friedrich Nietzsche, and Fyodor Dostoyevsky (1821-1881), whose 1864 novella *Notes from Underground* is considered one of the first works of existentialist literature.[1] In the 1940s and 1950s, it experienced a revival through the French existentialist writers Jean-Paul Sartre, Albert Camus (1913-1960), and Simone de Beauvoir (1908-1986), who wrote several scholarly and fictional works with existential themes (dread, boredom, alienation, the absurd, freedom, commitment, and nothingness). Other notable existentialist thinkers of that period include the Russian religious and political philosopher, Nikolai Berdyaev (1874–1948), the German thinker Martin Heidegger (1889-1976), and the Swiss psychiatrist Karl Jaspers (1883–1969).

Conceptually, existentialism is anchored on the belief that

---

[1] See Bernard Paris, *Dostoevsky's Greatest Characters: A New Approach to Notes from Underground, Crime and Punishment, and the Brothers Karamazov.* (New York: Palgrave Macmillan, 2008).

philosophical thinking begins with the human subject: not merely the thinking subject, but the acting, feeling, living human individual. According to this outlook, humans define their own meaning in life and try to make rational decisions despite existing in an irrational universe. Existentialism focuses on the question of human existence and the feeling that there is no purpose or explanation at the core of existence. It holds that, as there is no God or any other transcendent force,[2] the only way to counter this nothingness (and hence to find meaning in life) is by embracing existence:

> Thus, the first effect of existentialism is that it puts every man in possession of himself as he is, and it places the entire responsibility for his existence squarely upon his own shoulders. When we say that man is responsible for himself, we do not mean that he is responsible only for his own individuality, but that he is responsible for all men.[3]

From this duality between existence and the individual person, several essential and basic beliefs, shared by most existentialists, have emerged:

- Each individual—not society or religion—is solely responsible for giving meaning to life and living it passionately and sincerely or "authentically".

- There is no common human nature. The basic given of the human predicament is that we are forced to choose what we will become and to define ourselves by our choice of action: all that is given is that we are, not what we are.

---

[2] Not all existentialists are atheists. There is, in fact, a branch in existential philosophy called Christian existentialism. Often traced back to the work of Søren Kierkegaard, Christian existentialism is a theo-philosophical movement that takes an existentialist approach to Christian theology. See Jacques Maritain, *Existence and the Existent: An Essay on Christian Existentialism* (*Court traité de l'existence et de l'existent*), translated by Lewis Galantière and Gerald B. Phelan. (New York: Pantheon Books, 1948).

[3] Jean-Paul Sartre, "Existentialism is a Humanism" (lecture given in 1946). In *Existentialism from Dostoyevsky to Sartre*, ed. Walter Kaufman. (Meridian Publishing Company, 1989).

- Human choice is the central factor in the creation of all values. Despite the absence of pre-established objective values, we are entirely responsible for what we become, and this puts the future of humanity in our own hands.

- Freedom is autonomous. That is to say, freedom, rather than being random or arbitrary, consists in the binding of oneself to a law, but a law that is given by the self in recognition of its responsibilities.

- Existence precedes essence, which means that the most important consideration for individuals is that they are individuals—independently acting and responsible, conscious beings ("existence")—rather than what labels, roles, stereotypes, definitions, or other preconceived categories the individuals fit ("essence").

- Pro-active: Man must not be indifferent to his surroundings. He must take a stand, make choices, commit himself to his beliefs, and create meaning through action.

To be an existentialist, then, it is to assume that people and things in general exist, but that things have no meaning for us except as individuals and that we create meaning only through acting upon them. Thus, we are the only ones who can decide what our life purpose is. No other being or force can decide for us: we are free individual agents. As Jean-Paul Sartre would say:

> Man can will nothing unless he has first understood that he must count on no one but himself; that he is alone, abandoned on earth in the midst of his infinite responsibilities, without help, with no other aim than the one he sets himself, with no other destiny than the one he forges for himself on this earth.[4]

If "existence" is the real frame of reference, then human reality or human subjectivity is the foundation of all thought and action.

---

4   *Ibid.*

Man first exists. Then he encounters himself, surges up in the world, and consequently defines himself. In the course of this, each individual has not only the right to choice, but also "the duty to choose". What he chooses is what gives life meaning, not *vice versa*. Hence, the responsibility of building ones future is in one's hands, but because the future is uncertain, one cannot escape from anxiety and despair:

> We are always under the shadow of anxiety; higher responsibility leads to higher anxiety. The pursuit of being leads to an awareness of nothingness, nothingness to an awareness of freedom, freedom to bad faith and bad faith to the being of consciousness, which provides the condition for its own possibility.[5]

Fayez, the Party and Existentialism

As indicated earlier, Fayez and Sa'adeh attached varying importance to the issue of existentialism during their dispute. Sa'adeh maintained that Fayez's endeavour to promote existentialist ideas inside the SSNP precipitated the dispute. In his December 1, 1947 letter to Fayez, Sa'adeh wrote:

> After I sensed a possible resolution of the dispute with the government, I examined the events that transpired in the movement during my absence or in the literature circulating inside it, including new trends of thought and literary works. In the process, I read your book *Al-Baath al-Qawmi* (*National Resurrection*). To my astonishment, I found that, except for (1) the chapter "The Nation, its essence, its constituents, and its characteristics," which is based on *Nushu' al-Umam* (The Rise of Nations), (2) the chapter "The New Order - The New Society" which is consistent with the orientations of the social nationalist movement, and (3) some snippets in other chapters that

---

5 D. R. Bhandari, "Existentialist Perception of the Human Condition: With Special Reference to Sartre" (unpublished lecture at Proceedings of the 20th World Congress of Philosophy, Boston, 1998).

are likewise consistent, the main chapters dealing with the ideological and social principles and the philosophy of the Social National movement and its basic teachings are predicated on an ideology that is totally at variance with it. These chapters and the general orientation of your literary and cultural activities are infused entirely with the outlook of Berdyaev and Kierkegaard on man and human affairs. This individualist personalistic outlook of Berdyaev and Kierkegaard, which regards individual personalism as the essence and end, is totally inconsistent with [the] outlook on which the Social National movement was created. In the chapter "The Objective," you quote directly when you say "The personality of man (the individual) and its development is the ultimate objective of society" (meaning that society is nothing but a means to this end). You also state that it is wrong to speak of society as having a unique character because society is "only the sum of its individuals."[6]

It troubled Sa'adeh that Fayez had been using "the Party's propagating agencies to disseminate [existentialist] ideas and views instead of the teachings of the movement for which these agencies were specifically created, and which, in every respect, revolve around society and not the individual or the individual personality."[7] The claim is serious and worth detailed investigation to determine its validity. As well as personifying Fayez as an ideological renegade, it makes him the real abuser of his powers and privileges: enough to render any person an object of detestation.

Rather than engage Sa'adeh in a serious discussion over the matter, Fayez took the shortest shortcut: he denied the allegation in a brief two-sentence statement without elaborating or providing evidence. But a shortcut, to repeat one of Charles Issawi's pungent aphorisms, is not only the longest distance

---

6   Reproduced in full in the section "Letters" at the end of this book.

7   *Ibid.*

between two points: it is quite often the most perilous route.[8] Fayez took the shortcut either because he regarded the allegation as unimportant or because the allegation represented a demand that Fayez was either reluctant to confront or unable to defend. The weight of evidence overwhelmingly favors the second possibility: Fayez deliberately tried to dodge the existentialist allegation raised against him because it was indefensible.

No concrete evidence exists of Fayez altering any part of the SSNP's national doctrine. He did not quote directly or synopsize excerpts from existentialist writings and insert them into the Party's literature. However, strong evidence exists to condemn him on the lesser charge of trying to instill an existentialist spirit in the Party or seeking to bend its outlook towards an existentialist direction. The evolving and shifting focus of his party writings between 1938 and 1947 clearly attest to this. Until 1944, the trajectory of his writings adhered strictly to the Party's guidelines and principles. It exhibited all the marks of its ideological imperatives, utilized its distinctive vocabulary and expressions, and extracted heavily from Sa'adeh's writings. After 1944, we discern the gradual unfolding of an existentialist dimension emphasizing moral choices like self-responsibility, integrity of character, personal development, self-awareness, individual freedom, and the inauthenticity of human life. Fayez does not extract from extant existentialist writings or mention an existentialist thinker by name. He simply attempts to recast the Party's doctrines in an existentialist light or give them a subtle existentialist flavor. He shows this in four passages.

The first passage, from a study on human currents and their impact on the Party's concept of national revival, contains specific and basic existentialist themes applied within a nationalist context:

> [The] process of refining or upbringing [is] a process of building a human being completely developed in talents,

---

[8] Quoted in Samir Khallaf, *Lebanon's Predicament*. (Columbia University Press, 1987): 19.

fully open to and connected with values, and fully expressive in his different activities of all human aspects. It seeks this perfection (fulfillment) as a human objective and produces a person who sees a painful manifestation of his deficient humanity and limited nature in the urgency to focus on various aspects of his entity. This attitude aspires to build individuals who appreciate all these aspects in their human entity and yearn to express them fully in their life. It regards the building of people of this kind, who appreciate values and attune their lives to them, as the aim of refinement. It aims to develop their sense of responsibility and enable them to accommodate values and make crucial decisions inspired by their human dignity.[9]

The second passage comes from a 1944 lecture to the Party's student branch in Beirut. In it, Fayez introduces, perhaps for the first time, the concept of the "human person". He emphasizes its significance, uniqueness, and inviolability as well as the person's essentially relational or communitarian dimension:

A society as that of ours, in the condition it is in, before it is in need of political freedom, or economic prosperity, or military power, or mechanical civilization, is in dire need – a need that propels him to cry from the depth of his being and places him between life and death – to "persons" … The "person," in the plenitude of his being, is behind every apparatus and system … The "person," in the plenitude of his being, is the sole guarantee that economic prosperity would remain a subordinate to the values of life, not its master, and a means for man to use and not an idol for him to worship. The "person," in the plenitude of his being, is the solitary justification for the mechanical civilization … The "person," in the plenitude of his being, is the sole potential for the evolution of a sound cycle of social life,

---

9   From an unpublished essay found among Sayegh's papers at the University of Utah's J. Willard Marriott Library (http://cdmbuntu.lib.utah.edu/cdm/landingpage/collection/uu-fasc) Translated and reproduced below.

free of maltreatment and antagonisms in society.[10]

While showing no desire to abandon the nationalist mantle, Fayez continued to inject the Party with existentialist concepts blended cleverly to maintain a balance with its ideology. The third passage exemplifies this:

> The problem of national crisis is not a theoretical problem detached from our ordinary personal life so that we can neglect the need to address it or postpone our response to it until further notice: both neglect and postponement, in themselves, are specific responses to the problem. The problem of our national crisis, then, is a category of "existential" problems that strikes at the core of our inner self...[11]

The fourth passage is even more ambiguous. Only the most observant existentialists can decipher its esoteric existentialist texture:

> Our national revival is established on the principle of respect for man as he is. It develops man in a way that coheres with his real nature. It thus declares that man in this country will "be"! ... Our nation, standing as it is at a crossroads today, finds in our national revival a decisive decision that we will be a human society, that we will have human spiritual courage, and that from the heart of this nation, real humans will emerge instead of deformed creatures who have decided to eliminate their own humanity.[12]

The frequency of Fayez's application of existentialist concepts tended to rise progressively. The more enamored he became

---

10 Fayez Sayegh, *al-Baath al-Qawmi*. Second Edition. (Beirut: Dar Fikr, n.d.): 197-98.

11 *Ibid*, p. 130.

12 *Ibid*.

of existentialism, the more enthusiastic he became about existentialist idioms and phrases. This is understandable given that Fayez was preparing his Master's thesis on existentialism.[13]

However, the problem is deeper and much more involved than merely transmitting existentialist ideas. New evidence discovered in Fayez's archives at the University of Utah implicates him of deliberately and stealthily seeking to remold the SSNP on existentialist lines in collaboration with other like-minded party cadres. This evidence is found in a private letter from Fayez to Ghassan Tueini, an SSNP cadre. Like Fayez, Tueini was a pupil of the existentialist Charles Malik. Although he was acting as liaison officer between the Party's HQ in Beirut and the exiled Sa'adeh, Tueini kept the dialogue with Fayez secret. He did not disclose any details to Sa'adeh or warn him of Fayez's intentions.

Embedded in this dialogue was the question of whether the Party (referred to as the "institution") should remain a centralized unit floating in a world of abstract rhetoric and bound to the whims and fancies of an undisputed leader or if it should democratize and become more flexible and open to different possibilities. Fayez has no doubt about which possibility to start with:

> I do not believe that compromise is possible in this matter. The institution can be either of two; an institution of individuals that respects and advances the individual, considering the entire social life and pertinent benefits as a tool whereby to reflect his rich entity and his fertile personality, in faith, love, and cultural production, or an institution of slaves and machines that exploits them for its own general "good" and its "teacher," being "above" the individuals! ... As an active member of the Party, I work despite this contradiction. My sole objective is to purge the Party that I love, the nation that I serve, and the comrades with whom I work and struggle—I wish to rid them all

---

13 Fayez Sayegh, "Personal existence: An Essay." (an unpublished Thesis: American University of Beirut, 1945).

of my slavery to impersonal considerations, which are the same exact "vague abstract considerations" — to cite Karim Azkoul — not the practical tangible considerations![14]

After stating his preference for existential individualism, Fayez declares his readiness to take on any potential opposition. His tone is unmistakably existentialist and his intention is clearly to refashion the Party's system:

> I am aware that I am in a grave situation that is fraught with risk-taking, given the contradiction between the nature of the Party system and the essence of "nationalism" as understood by many on one hand and not just individualism as a school of thought but, rather, the entity of the individual and its realization on the other... I am even aware that this risk-taking will lead one day to an inevitable conflict with the representatives of the non-individualistic outlook and interests in our institution. However, I will not retreat, nor will I shy away from the battle. Moreover, if I do enter the battle, it would be from the inside not the outside, and I will declare the enemies of individualism in the Party to be enemies of the Party in the true sense of the word... In other words, I am adamant that my conflict will not be like that of Fakhri (i.e. not in a manner that destroys the possibility of fulfilling his duty towards the Party and compels the loyal Party members to take a non-neutral stance towards him, given the nonconformist nature of his work). In contrast, I will fight, within the party the tendencies which I believe contribute to the Party's decline and demise, and which are even at work to transform the Party into an "accursed" movement that is detrimental to individual values and human dignity![15]

If any doubt remains about Fayez's existentialist intentions and

---

14 Fayez A. Sayegh Collection at the University of Utah: (http://cdmbuntu.lib.utah.edu/cdm/search/collection/)

15 *Ibid.*

plans for the Party, a paragraph from the same letter clears that up:

> I am speaking of this conflict as if it is underway... and perhaps it is indeed underway, but "its execution is deferred," for the two tendencies are effective, and strongly so... They are effective in the subconscious of members, fueled by the values harbored by the individual members who represent these two tendencies... I am confident that, despite the simplicity of the other tendency and its conformity with the mentality of the masses and with Information clichés and the mysticism of the nationalist struggle, the elite members have started to develop a feeling of their value as humans and their dignity as humans, and a feeling that followers, politics, and economy, are manifestations of their collective human lives and, thus, they must not be a master, a nightmare, and a restraint of their individual humanity... The publication of *Umdat al-Thaqafah*, *al-Hadaf*, and *al-Ba'th al-Qawmi*, the lectures that I delivered this year in many places especially in the Student Executive Branch, the orientation of the newspaper, and my personal communications, all had a great impact in reviving the individual human tendency within the national revival, and in ridding the Party of the idol of nationalism (at least in the psyche of its intelligentsia). Do not forget that my role – as Dean of Culture and Information and editor in chief of the newspaper - as well as my clean partisan slate unblemished by any scorch (I say this in all honesty, and you know that my intention is not to boast), all of this supports the mission that we fulfill within the Party so that the Party would fulfill it to the nation...[16]

Fayez then drops a bombshell concerning his first published existentialist work *A Call from the Depths: Reflections on Man and Existence*. Long considered "an agonized response"

---

16 *Ibid.*

to a personal crisis arising from the tragedy of Palestine,[17] he actually wrote the work to veer the national movement along a new trajectory:

> I am fully engaged this fortnight in writing a book that will be a landmark in the history of this struggle within the national revival. If this book, entitled *Nida' al-A'amaq* (*A Call from the Depth*) finds its way to intellectual nationalists, I will be confident about the future of freedom and spirit in the national revival.[18]

The concluding paragraph of the letter is especially revealing, blunt and vocal:

> By the way, did you notice in the nationalist writings you read these days the abundant "spontaneous" emphasis on values, freedom, individualism, spirit, and the depths of the human being, etc.? Compare this to the past emphasis on idolizing the nation, regarding it as a physical entity, and the idolization of the system, etc.![19]

Evidently, from the tone of this letter and the new direction that subsequently appeared in Fayez's Party writings, Fayez did not disclose the full truth about his existentialist activities. He clearly strove to inculcate an existentialist perspective on the Party without explicitly seeking to change or modify its national doctrine. The inculcation occurred at the interpretive rather than at the textual level, which means that Fayez did not target the SSNP doctrine *per se*, but that he merely sought to impart an existential interpretation to it. He sought to reconcile the national doctrine of the SSNP to an existential outlook by

---

17 Habib C. Malik, "The Reception of Kierkegaard in the Arab World." In Jon Stewart (ed.), *Kierkegaard's International Reception: The Near East, Asia, Australia, and the Americas*. (London: Ashgate Publishing Limited, 1989): 76.

18 Fayez A. Sayegh Collection at the University of Utah: (http://cdmbuntu.lib.utah.edu/cdm/search/collection/) 14 September, 2017

19 *Ibid.*

carving out a common ground between them based on certain ideas or values that served as an anchor for him. Anyone agonizingly caught between two different currents that both appeal to his intellectual senses and pride was liable to fall into this trap. The painful irony of Fayez's predicament is that both nationalism and existentialism appealed to him proportionately. Nationalism appealed to his patriotic and political aspirations while existentialism appealed to his gentle human nature and free spirit.

The allegation that Fayez utilized his senior Party posts to promote an existentialist outlook is also true. An unpublished essay found in his archival records suggests that his existentialist coaching inside the Party began in 1945 upon the creation of a cultural department in the SSNP. As noted earlier, this department was placed under his personal direction. The essay strikes an unmistakably existentialist note. In it, Fayez takes the first tentative step toward the fusion of SSNP national doctrine with existentialism:

> "By instituting a Department for Culture and Fine Arts, at this point in its history, our revival has taken a decisive step toward acknowledging its unequivocal embracing of [that] current" that values human life above abstract ideas. He then discusses how social manifestations serve as an avenue available for man to

> ... redress his personal deficiencies and individual limits and to cooperate with other humans to express his own entity. This avenue is available for one to return from within this rich human life to himself at moments of seclusion and to attain within his innermost being a connection with the spiritual entity existing in the depth of the universe (i.e. the ultimate reality connected to the depths of human character).[20]

---

20 *Ibid.*

The Question of Existentialism

Fayez continued to utilize the nationalist vocabularies of the SSNP as he veered toward existentialism. However, he seemed to be more comfortable with himself imparting to these vocabularies a "human" touch and a "moral" range rather than adhering to them as mere nationalist slogans. He begins to tap into a vision of nationalism that mediates between individual and nation and hews closer to the spirit of personal freedom as a national objective. A novel idea in its time and place, this idea was already attracting attention in Western scholarship, particularly at the hands of American political scientist, Hans Morgenthau.[21] Morgenthau wrote:

> Nationalism as a political phenomenon must be understood as the aspirations for two freedoms (one collective, the other individual): the freedom of a nation from domination by another nation and the freedom of the individual to join the nation of his choice.[22]

Since nationalism arose in opposition to state oppression of the individual, then, in Morgenthau's opinion, it represents a triumph for individual liberty and collective security combined.

Especially striking is the subtle and unannounced manner with which Fayez pursued his objective. Only a select few like-minded existentialist party cadres were privy to his intentions. They remained tight-lipped on the subject or surreptitiously encouraged him to follow his ideas without considering the repercussions too much. The rest of the Party had almost no grasp

---

21 Hans Joachim Morgenthau (1904–1980) was one of the major twentieth-century figures in the study of international politics. Morgenthau's works belong to the tradition of Realism in international-relations theory, and he is usually considered, along with George F. Kennan and Reinhold Niebuhr, one of the three leading American realists of the post-World War II period. Morgenthau made landmark contributions to the theory of international relations and the study of international law. His *Politics Among Nations*, first published in 1948, went through five editions during his lifetime.

22 Hans J. Morgenthau, "The Paradoxes of Nationalism". (*The Yale Review*, XLVI, 1957): 481.

of existential philosophy to understand what was happening or to question his intentions. Anyway, the reverberation of the Party's slogans in Fayez's fiery speeches and the extraordinary reticence shown by his seniors served as an adequate tranquilizer.

EXISTENTIAL NATIONALISM

The 1940s was a period of great uncertainty and drastic change. The scale of human misery and destruction during the World War II, the tragedies of human suffering, the atrocious and unprecedented loss of life, and the unspeakable crimes that were committed did more than change the political landscape: it left many people stunned and looking for answers. Both thinking and practice changed radically because of the conflict. The war riveted the eyes of the intellectuals on questions of human life and dignity. It kindled renewed interest in practical moral issues and raised questions of great philosophical importance into existing assumptions, claims, concepts, and methods.[23] Totalitarian ideologies were particularly targeted: absolute uniformity, single mass party, centrally managed networks and systems, undisputed leadership, economic regimentation, national pride, and political terror. The consensus that emerged, at least among the philosophers and intellectuals of the day, can be summarized in two points:

1. The lion's share of the blame for the human atrocities of the war rested squarely on the shoulders of totalitarian regimes on both sides of the political spectrum.

2. Totalitarian ideologies are innately and functionally inimical with the cherished values and dignity of human life.

Existentialism arose from the chaos of this disillusioned world. It

---

23   See A. W. Purdue, The Transformative Impact of World War II, in: *European History Online* (EGO), published by the Leibniz Institute of European History (IEG), Mainz 2016-04-18. URL: http://www.ieg-ego.eu/purduea-2016-en URN: urn:nbn:de:0159-2016041204 [2017-10-12].

took a bleak yet powerful stance of integrity that some began to fear but others admired. Existentialists acknowledged what they saw, but they refused to romanticize or mythologize it. They admitted that life was absurd, but not humankind. Once man comes to grips with the absurdity of life, he can choose to bring meaning into his life. He just needs to step forward and make choices that make life meaningful. This panacea to avoid mental, emotional, and spiritual conformity allows totalitarianism to take control.

As an active member of a political party founded on a comprehensive ideology, Fayez felt the full brunt of this new climate. Two circumstances fed its impact on him: (1) the exposure of the American University of Beirut where he was studying to the anti-collectivism spirit and the new intellectual emphasis on individual freedom as an empirical point of reference, and (2) the subjection of the students to a tirade of verbal criticism of militant nationalism and institutional collectivism.

One active person on this front was Charles Malik, Fayez's philosophy teacher. An admirer of German philosophy who studied under Heidegger in Freiberg under "the suffocating environment created by Nazism in the mid-1930s,"[24] Malik made no secret of his fondness for existential philosophy and his disdain for collective ideologies. In the process, nationalism received a fair share of criticism.[25] The basic message was that nationalism, like all other 'isms' binds us to a sense of determinism or false security that ultimately deters our better natures. Its emphasis on conformity can be just as stifling to our autonomy and personal integrity as any social concentrated system. Even when it is not anti-individualism, nationalism's collective pursuits can reduce the individual in us to the passive status of a participant subject.

---

[24] Habib C. Malik, "The Reception of Kierkegaard in the Arab World." In Jon Stewart (ed.), *Kierkegaard's International Reception: The Near East, Asia, Australia, and the Americas.* (London: Ashgate Publishing Limited, 1989): 69.

[25] Quoted in Fayez Sayegh, *al-Baath al-Qawmi.* (Beirut: Dar Fikr, 2nd ed. n.d.): 74.

The ever-alert Fayez quickly picked up the message. His familiarity with existentialism and its contemporary relevance and place within philosophical schools of thought gave him an advantage over other members of Malik's audience. Also, having studied under Malik, he understood his teacher's intentions very clearly. At the first opportunity, he published a modest rebuttal in which he took issue with Malik's singular depiction of nationalism as a collective thought-form that skewers the meaning and identity of man. Drawing on an existential approach, Malik had classified nationalism as a worldview that recognizes only the "national" in the being and everything else as worthless. The hardcore nationalist Fayez rejoined with an equally existential argument that the nationalist worldview regards man first as a "social being" and then as a "national being" at an elevated stage in human development. Furthermore, as a "social being", Fayez asserted that a nationalist is not necessarily a robot of the collective will, as Malik had claimed, but a dynamic factor and a prime mover in the formation and advancement of that will:

> My relationship to my group ... is a relationship between a human being (who could not be if not for the group that contributed to what he is) and a group (which could not be if not for the individuals who formed it). The reality, then, is not one of a group whose interests do not intermix with those of the individuals who constitute it, and not one of an individual insubordinate and holding off everything from the group including his being. Rather, it is a group and an individual that complement each other and neither can exist without the other.[26]

Nonetheless, Malik's pitiable assessment of nationalism spurred Fayez into brainstorming. Around this time, he started to infuse the national doctrine with healthy doses of moral clarity, ethics, and practical human wisdom in an attempt to counter the rising climate of anti-nationalism.[27] He found everything he needed

---

26   *Al-Baath al-Qawmi*, p. 75.
27   Sayegh's method should not be confused with earlier existentialist-centered

to make his vision alive in the fundamental realities of human life of existential philosophy itself: dignity, self-identity, human choices, ethical existence, will, freedom, heroism, and a range of other moral values and principles. Despite what most people thought, Fayez did not see nationalism and existentialism as mutually exclusive or as two sides of a coin. He determined that an existential nationalism existed and could be proved through common logic.

First, however, Fayez had to demonstrate, in the way of theoretical justification, that:

1. An intellectual synthesis exists between nationalism and existentialism.

2. Despite its apparent "collective" nature, nationalism is an ideology of concrete lived experience that does not detract from the importance of "individuality" or the "personal".

Fayez addressed both requirements with existentialist logic. He argued that, just as the individual is imbued with a sense of morality and quest for existential meaning, the nation is involved in a quest for existential self-actualization and fulfillment. With a clever manipulation of existential jargons, he underscored the presence of existentialist themes at the centre of the national project, especially the notions of "self-liberation", "citizen", "freedom", "individual dignity" and "heroism".[28] His procedure does not entirely negate the "collective" character of nationalism, but it modifies the order of its priorities. Nationalism ceases to be a drive for collective life and becomes a collective instrument for creating a society in which individual choices and freedom are paramount to its prosperity. Fayez then enumerated five

---

approaches that accentuated the "individualist" tendencies of nationalism. See Jacob Golomb and Robert S. Wistrich, (Ed.) *Nietzsche, Godfather of Fascism?: On the Uses and Abuses of a Philosophy.* (Princeton: Princeton University Press, 2002): 274-75.

28 It is worth noting that these themes permeated his Master's thesis and first written work on Existentialism, *Personal Existence.*

conditions that must exist for nationalism to fit into an existential framework:

1. It is not jingoistic patronizing;

2. It looks critically at the illusions of politics and commercialism that would enslave us;

3. It is dynamic and enterprising, because no power enslaves human life more forcefully than disinterestedness and lack of effort;

4. It is liberating whether from outside forces or from internal burdens; and

5. It encourages people to think for themselves, question the status quo, and look for real virtue in the only place it can be found, inside "ourselves".

The existential value of nationalism, then, is that it seeks to answer the question of meaningful personal existence through participation in a collective national meaning.[29]

Thus, nationalism is only what we choose to make of it. Unless we allow it, it is not bound to any sense of determinism. How it turns out depends entirely on the trajectory we choose for it, who we are and aspire to be, and the method we adopt in our national pursuits. That choice, and the freedom it posits, determines whether nationalism will be totalitarian or democratic. A narrow jingoistic nationalism may foster the mass conformity on which totalitarianism thrives. Alternatively, when nationalism is based on conscience and logic, it precludes the kind of radical behavior that would result in hedonism. It would be free and moral at the same time.

The French existential philosopher, Jean-Paul Sartre, once declared that we are completely responsible not only for who we are, but also for who we plan to be:

---

29 Bruce P. Rittenhouse, *Shopping for Meaningful Lives: The Religious Motive of Consumerism*. (Eugene: Wipf & Stock Publishers, 2013): 12.

>...existentialism's first move is to make every man aware of what he is and to make the full responsibility of his existence rest on him. When we say that a man is responsible for himself, we do not only mean that he is responsible for his own individuality, but that he is responsible for all men.[30]

Fayez also attempted to follow this line of reasoning: that with nationalism, as with every major human project, an incredible amount of responsibility falls on man himself, on the purposes he pursues, and on the "choices" he makes in life. Ultimately, man alone is responsible for creating a meaningful life in an absurd and unfair world. He can choose whether nationalism will be bad or good, excessive or benign, aggressive or passive. It boils down to his ability to make informed personal choices. The pendulum is in his hand. He can swing it towards a nationalism that subdues individual identity and freedom for the group or towards a nationalism that promotes a more balanced approach in life. But what if man cannot choose or is deprived of the freedom to choose? The existential Fayez would reply that the blame would rest primarily with man for allowing such a situation to arise in the first place.

By "man", Fayez meant the individual person in line with the existential tradition of Nikolai Berdyaev. A devoted Russian Orthodox Christian, Berdyaev introduced the concept of "personalism" as an existential notion positing "the primacy of freedom over existence, of Spirit over nature, subject over object, personality over the universal, creativeness over evolution, dualism over monism, love over law".[31] For Berdyaev, "personality" is a whole, a unity of multiplicity, changing and affirming itself as a primal unity. It is creative, independent, and a living, concrete, dynamic quality. Unlike the individual who

---

30 Jean-Paul Sartre, "Existentialism is a Humanism" (lecture given in 1946). In *Existentialism from Dostoyevsky to Sartre*, ed. Walter Kaufman. (Meridian Publishing Company, 1989).

31 Nicolas Berdyaev, *Slavery and Freedom*. (Semantron Press; 2nd edition, 2009): 10.

... is a naturalistic category, biological and sociological, and it appertains to the natural world ... Person realizes itself in social and cosmic life, but it can do this only because that within it ... is independent from nature and from the principle of society.[32]

Personalism stands at the opposite end of collectivism. It emphasizes the human personality over collectives like the society, nation, or state, and it regards the self-worth of every human being and his or her right to the fullness of life as an end in itself. Personality is a "whole" and everything else is "parts". Personality for Berdyaev

... comprises body, soul, and spirit [and] comes from God and not from one's parents. It has character, which is power over oneself and a victory over slavery to oneself, making possible a conquest of the environment and achievement of independence.[33]

Fayez adopted Berdyaev's theory almost verbatim and then overlaid nationalism with it. He began to represent nationalism as a means to the fulfillment of individual personal welfare and human freedom. Consciously or unconsciously, he moved away from the primacy of society without renouncing it or denying its value. In the process, he metamorphosed the central ideals of Social Nationalism of "truth, goodness and beauty" to the personal level.

Fayez succeeded not only in offloading the responsibility of nationalism onto the individual, but also in angling it in a "personalist" direction. This completes the transition to an existential nationalism. Presently, nationalism ceases to be a strictly collective enterprise and becomes a project in which our

---

32 N. A. Berdyaev, "The Problem of Man," http://www.berdyaev.com/berdiaev/berd_lib/1936_408.html [16 July 2014].

33 Richard A. Hughes, "Nikolai Berdyaev's Personalism." (*International Journal of Orthodox Theology* 6:3, 2015): 69.

mission is to attain meaning by embracing those activities that generate a sense of universal purpose and value in our personal lives. How we go about this depends on the basic approach we choose. An approach based on logical reasoning is bound to yield a different result from one based on blind faith or misguided idealism. The choice we make and the trajectory we pursue ultimately determine if nationalism will be a desirable aesthetic value or just another absurd charade.

Fayez versus Sa'adeh

In marrying nationalism to existentialism, Fayez mirrored a topical trend in nascent "Arab existentialism" of blending local and existential themes together. The Egyptian philosopher Abd al-Rahman Badawi (1917-2002) set the pace for this blending with a "major project ... aimed at achieving an intellectual synthesis between Sufism and existential philosophy".[34] Badawi maintained:

> The idea of the perfect man creates the union between Sufism and Existentialism on the basis of the humanist trend. Indeed we found in it the strongest assertion of this humanist trend since it harbours the deification of man. But existentialism places human existence in lieu and in the place of divine existence.

Badawi proceeded to demonstrate how certain notions, such as "anguish" and the "perfect man", are central in both existential and Sufi thoughts:

> Between these two trends, existentialism and Sufism (mysticism), there are deep links at the levels of the principles, the method and the targeted aim... the Sufi trend is based on the doctrine of subjectivism, that is it

---

[34] Yoav Di-Capua, "Arab Existentialism: An Invisible Chapter in the Intellectual History of Decolonization." (*American Historical Review* 117(4), 2012): 1061-91.

does not recognize any other true existence outside the individual subject.

Similarly, Fayez sought to fuse the national with the existential to create an "existential nationalism". His thinking

1. Predicated nationalism on individual subjectivity.

2. Presented nationalism as a quest for meaning and identity.

3. Placed man (the 'Person') at the centre of all things.

This did not represent a complete break with the national ideological doctrine of the SSNP. Many aspects of that doctrine can be easily construed as existential. The "Doctrine" (*al-aqidah*) itself was largely composed as a written response to a people seeking to define not only what it means to be "national" but also what it means to exist. Its first criterion and starting point is the existential question "who are we?",[35] and its essence, though contextually national, covers issues of broad human and existential concern:

> Since antiquity, our nation has faced a number of critical issues that require sincere answers. These are:
>
> • Are we a living nation?
>
> • Are we a society with a goal in life?

---

[35] In Sa'adeh's words: "The question ... "who are we?" means the beginning of the investigation into what our reality connotes. It is the starting point of any human thinking endeavouring to understand its reality, environment, and intentions in life and the world around it. It marks the beginning of serious thinking into the very meaning of human community, like ours, and into the supreme goals that give expression to our reality, our existence and our essence. All of this means that the principles of thought upon which our national renaissance was born and for which the Syrian Social National Party strives, are deep philosophical principles concerned with the crucial issues as distinct from others that appertain to a specific time, and thus pass from existence with that period, or to some incidental form. Rather, they are universal and permanent principles or, philosophically speaking, principles that cannot be ascribed to some momentary specific time or situation, disappearing when these conditions have ceased to exist." (Extracted from *The Ten Lectures*).

- Are we a people with high ideals?
- Are we a nation with a single will?
- Are we a group of people who realize the importance of methodical action?[36]

These questions represent an aspect of existentialism. They mark, on a philosophical level, "the beginning of serious thinking into the very meaning of human community, like ours, and into the supreme goals that give expression to our reality, our existence, and our essence".[37] Hence, existence in the Sa'adeh perspective is not subject to fate or some type of determinism. It depends on the power of the human mind, the value and limitations of our rational nature, and especially, on the realization that life is defined continually by our actions and choices. This demonstrates a clear connection with existentialism, because it places man ('society' and not 'person') at the center of national existence and existence at the heart of human concern.

Also, both existential philosophy and Social Nationalism exhibit strong interest in existence as a fact subject to human knowledge:

> We cannot envisage existence without knowledge. Indeed, we cannot claim that any supposed existence that cannot be recognized through knowledge has the same value as a fact, because a fact is a human psychological value, and only man is capable of differentiating between truth and falsehood through knowledge.[38]

Like existentialism, Social Nationalism is unconcerned with the metaphysical world. Its frame of reference is strictly

---

36 *Ibid.*
37 *Ibid.*
38 *Ibid.* In his PhD thesis, Fayez wrote: "Existential knowledge is knowledge of or about existence, that is knowledge of or about the existence of an existent." Fayez Abdullah Sayegh, *Existential Philosophy, a Formal Examination* (unpublished PhD dissertation, Georgetown University, 1950): 16.

human existence from a secular ethical perspective. Neither existentialism nor Social Nationalism accepts the dependence of the individual or the group on supernatural forces or other forces uncontrolled by man. Neither assents to quietism or inaction nor declares that there is no reality except in action. Furthermore, neither subscribes to a pessimistic view of life. According to Sartre, existentialism is a humanism because it reminds "man that there is no legislator but himself".[39] Social Nationalism is "a humanism", also, because it regards the human mind as the "supreme legislator".[40]

If the affinities between existentialism and Social Nationalism are that strong, why did Sa'adeh rebuke Fayez so sternly over his existentialism? In answering this question, fairness to both Sa'adeh and Fayez must be a basic consideration. By all accounts, Sa'adeh did not ask Fayez to abandon his existentialist views or to abstain from studying or probing its philosophical tenets. He merely instructed Fayez to desist from infusing the Party's "Doctrine" with explicit existentialist notions and to stop using the Party's agencies to promote an existential perspective acquired from external sources. As the Party's founder, it was his moral duty to protect the Party from any initiative that might compromise the integrity of its "Doctrine" or undermine its independence. The truth of any doctrine depends, not on the capability of human reason to reconcile it with external opinions and views, but on the credibility and unity of the message it communicates. Once the message is doctored to convey other than the "truth" it represents, its vitality and coherence suffer and it disintegrates into an arena for conflicting ideas and opinions.

---

39   Jean-Paul Sartre, "Existentialism is a Humanism", *ibid*.

40   "The human intellect is the supreme and fundamental source of legislation. It is the supreme gift of man and the means to distinguish categories in life. If principles and procedures are imposed that destroy this capacity to distinguish and perceive they negate the rational mind. This intrinsic feature of man would be annulled and man would cease to be human and fall to the level of beasts that are made to roam around without intelligence or sense of direction." (Extracted from *The Ten Lectures*).

The Question of Existentialism

From this context, Sa'adeh articulated his response to Fayez. The alarming factor for him was not so much Fayez's foray into existentialism, but Fayez's sloppy adaptation of existentialist notions that prioritized the individual person over the group. This was both disquieting and intimidating for Sa'adeh, because it negated the social foundations of his own doctrine. Naturally, once the foundations are destabilized, there is no telling what can happen to the structure.

Fayez misinterpreted Sa'adeh's response as an infringement on his personal freedom and right to subscribe to the philosophy of his choice. He argued that a Party member could be faithful and true to the "Doctrine" regardless of their philosophical position. The rationale he gave for this contention was simple and direct: one can still believe in "Syria for the Syrians" or in the "independence of the Syrian cause" or in the "separation of religion from the state" – all aspects of the "Doctrine" - without having to adhere to any specific philosophy. Ultimately, what counts is the commitment and not the philosophizing. If Sa'adeh had no hesitation in rejecting this explanation, it is because it suffered from serious shortcomings that cannot be overlooked casually or carelessly:

1. It is self-contradictory to suppose that one can simultaneously partake in a collective national cause and cling to an individualist personalist posture. This is tantamount to conducting a war with an army of undisciplined soldiers who regard themselves as separate beings neither attached nor dependent on one another. A national cause, by necessity, is a collective enterprise. As such, it is subject to the criteria of collectivism not individualism.

2. It is problematic to claim that a person can concurrently adhere to a national political "Doctrine" framed in collective terms and still be able to follow an independent philosophical path in the personal life. Asking an existential individualist to accept that "The national

interest supersedes any other interest" (a principle in the "Doctrine") is equivalent to asking a religious orthodox person to endorse the "separation of religion from the state" (another principle) or a Communist to acknowledge the nation is more important than class.

3. It divests the "Doctrine" of its social philosophical texture and renders it purely political. Fayez's mistake was that he understood the "Doctrine" as a rigid set of beliefs and dogmas rather than as a philosophical statement about life told from a nationalist perspective. The "Doctrine" appeared to him as a guideline for political independence and social political reforms. However, behind its political veneer, there was a comprehensive outlook lay life and a full-fledged worldview on human ethics, aesthetics, religion, culture, epistemology, existence, identity, dignity, etc. Fayez was acutely aware of the existence of this outlook as evidenced by his constant evocation of its distinctive expressions "al-insan al-jadid" (the new man), "al-nazrah al-jadidah lil hayat" (the new outlook on life), "al-muthul al-ulia" (the high ideals), and "haq, kheir, wa jamal" (truth, goodness, and beauty).

4. It is both practically and conceptually unreasonable to assume that a political party can function, let alone achieve its objectives, without some form of internal philosophical uniformity. Generally, political party members would either be required to adhere to the party's philosophy, if it has one, or to follow a philosophical outlook that bears strong compatibility with its stated aim. Political parties based on comprehensive social national agendas, such as the SSNP, are particularly subject to this rule.

5. It is an obvious recipe for chaos and self-destruction. One can only imagine the disintegration that would stem from allowing members to practice and preach divergent and conflicting philosophies inside a political party while purporting to be pursuing a common political agenda. It is sufficient to transform any political party into an arena for rivalry and dueling currents.

A second and perhaps more important reason why Sa'adeh rejected Fayez's existentialism relates to Berdyaev's notion of personalism. A cursory glance at Berdyaev's *Slavery and Freedom* was sufficient for Sa'adeh to formulate a negative assessment of that notion. The absolute value attributed to personality in Berdyaev's philosophy, which Fayez embraced almost unconditionally, appeared fundamentally anarchic to Sa'adeh:

> Every aberration is admissible and commendable under such a dazzling anarchy. Every desire, every lust, and every recalcitrance is an exigency of "freedom." There can be no other way to realize individual personality except through such anarchy. For individual personality cannot self-construct except through deviance, objection, insubordination, lawlessness, and being at cross-purposes with the world. Any intellect or thought that restrains the "freedom" of a person is not a fitting "condition" for individual personality.[41]

Equally troubling was Berdyaev's characterization of personalism as "a defiance of the cosmic harmony".[42] For Sa'adeh, it amounted to insubordination bordering on total anarchy:

> Personalism is a very subjective doctrine, a perpetual revolt that propels the person to object and rebel in order to assert his personality, and for fear that acceptance of any thought or judgment or convention may be understood as implying acquiescing in a decision stemming from society or the state or God. Disobey and gain! This is the trademark of individual personalism! Disobey and gain; disobey relentlessly to gain even more! It is the golden rule of this unusual creed.

---

41 A. Sa'adeh, "The School of Selfishness." (In *al-Nashrah al-Rasmiyyah lil Harakah al-Qawmiyyah al-Ijtima'eyah*, vol. 1, No. 3, 1948).

42 N. Berdyaev, *Essai de Métaphysique eschatologique*. (Aubier, Paris, 1941): 159-160.

However, the primary source of concern for Sa'adeh was personalism's clear and visible opposition to society:

> Even though the principle of individual personalism does recognize the existence of society, it does so for the sole purpose of objectifying personalism ... Accordingly, society has no jurisdiction over the individual. Rather, the individual has exclusive jurisdiction over society. Individual personality can hold society accountable, but society cannot hold individual personality accountable![43]

Sa'adeh's final judgment of personalism was "A doctrine of anarchic selfishness".[44]

Such circumstances, in outline, prompted Sa'adeh to rebuke Fayez over existentialism. Several claims and counter-claims were made during the clash that almost veered the discussion between the two men towards an unpleasant course. At one point, Fayez justifiably argued that, until their clash in 1947, Sa'adeh had never plainly stated that the SSNP was committed to a particular philosophy. While initially insisting he would not be drawn into a personal slanging match, Sa'adeh responded to this claim with alacrity. He told Fayez that had Fayez attempted to study the Party's principles more thoroughly, he would have discovered the marks of a self-contained philosophical system in them without a statement of declaration.

Actually, Fayez's claim was misplaced because, even if it was valid, it did not give Fayez the moral or legal right to promote a philosophical vision in the Party without first consulting with Sa'adeh. As Fayez knew, the Party's constitution clearly and

---

43 A. Sa'adeh, "The School of Selfishness."
44 *Ibid.* Some observers believe existentialism forms a philosophical ground for anarchism. Anarchist historian Peter Marshall claims, "there is a close link between the existentialists' stress on the individual, free choice, and moral responsibility and the main tenets of anarchism" in Peter Marshall, *Demanding the Impossible: A History of Anarchism* (London: Harper Collins, 1992): 580.

exclusively reserved that right to Sa'adeh. Inflexible and unwilling to bend, Fayez then took the unusual step of accusing Sa'adeh of seeking to purge the Party of philosophical diversity in order to impose his own personal philosophy on it. The accusation did not stick. Neither Sa'adeh nor the Party took it seriously.

Did Fayez Harbor A Hidden Agenda?

Based on the available evidence, there does not appear to have been a hidden agenda or a sinister reason behind Fayez's behavior. Fayez was fundamentally motivated by a sort of professional pride or desire to demonstrate that nationalism, for all its abuses and misuses, has a rational and moral compass if it is adhered to and correctly applied. Whether the result turns out to be good or bad is determined almost entirely by the trajectory that its advocates choose to pursue and the meaning they impart to life. Hence, it is all about our choices. What this means is that nationalism *per se* is not flawed, but the potential for flaw exists from the way we frame our actions and decisions.

Secondly, Fayez was driven by a personal desire to extricate the nationalist discourse from the clutches of xenophobic politics. He wanted to raise nationalism to a level of parity with modern rationalism after the havoc and destruction of the Second World War. Conjoining the national idea with a popular and fast-spreading philosophical approach like existentialism seemed like a great idea. Apart from the theoretical challenge it entailed, the blending of nationalism with existentialism had several advantages:

- It deflects popular and intellectual attention away from the ugly facets of excessive nationalism;
- It injects new concepts, ideas, and thought-patterns into the nationalist ideology;
- It steers discussions in a new direction and opens up new possibilities and insights into the nature of nationalism;

- It expands the nationalist perspective beyond the narrow one-dimensional thought and behavioral pattern prevalent at the time; and
- It imparts a direct human and moral character to nationalism.

Finally, the desire to steer the Party away from the path of collectivism may have impelled Fayez. With so much negative energy coming from Europe, following a disastrous experience in collective ideologies, the appeal of existentialism as a philosophy of moral striving was too strong to resist. Existentialism stood at the opposite end of collective chauvinism. As such, it served as a useful tool against jingoistic and personality-killing totalitarian tendencies. Fayez probably introduced existentialist notions into the SSNP to counter-check any existing or prospective tendencies of the same sort inside its institutions: idolization of the nation, leader, or party. All forms of idolization were deemed evil or conduits to the evilness of collectivism. Not even society was exempted from this rule:

> The acceptability of the myth that society has a super-personal existence, which can be abstracted from, and which transcends, in time and in existence, the individual persons who alone are real ... [gives rise] to a hierarchy of values ... in which Society is at the top, and personality lower down in the scale. With this movement performed, the impersonality of society reaches its culminating point: its danger becomes more apparent. A series of confusions sustaining one another, thus gradually lead to the postulation of a self-sustaining, permanent social entity, apart from, outside, and above the individual personalities, and superior to them in worth. Collectivism, with all its horrors, both theoretical and practical, is established as a result.[45]

Fayez utilized an existential perspective partly to prevent the Party from sliding into collectivism through the veneration of

---

45 F. Sayegh, *Personal Existence*, p. 124.

the nation or its leader by its members. His letter to Ghassan Tueini, from which several passages are quoted above, attests to the veracity of this assumption. Similarly, existentialism served as a means to rid the Party of what Fayez perceived as a glaring "impersonal character" and disposition toward outward appearances as opposed to spiritual essence and the values of true moral existence.

Based on these considerations, it would be a grave mistake to label Fayez as a Party conspirator. His record of accomplishment in the Party between 1944 and 1947, the period of his most extensive involvement with existentialism, attests to an unmatched devotion and enthusiasm for the national doctrine. He certainly had enough quality work behind him not to be dismissed as a pretender or a villain. Despite their differences, at no point did Sa'adeh characterize Fayez or his existential experiment as an act of treachery or disloyalty: he merely refused to entertain the thought of remodeling the Party's ideology after Fayez's ideas, and simultaneously, after Fayez's personal inclinations.

Conclusion

Despite his fondness for existential philosophy, Fayez took great pride and pleasure in the SSNP's national doctrine. For the duration of his active life in the Party, he remained deeply committed to its reform program and attuned to its national message. At times, his spirit and energy for the Party verged on pure evangelism, evidenced by a passage from one of his many speeches in 1946:

> At a time when politicians were trying to attract great masses, enticing them, and begging for their applause, the Social Nationalist Party was working hard to build the new individual: the conscious and mature person who is prepared to volunteer as a soldier in the salvation movement and who expects no reward save sacrifices and difficulties. These new virtues of struggle, which manifested themselves in the

> National Revival (thus forming a unique new phenomenon in the history of the nation), are our joy and the source of our pride. They are the testimony of history to the eternity of our cause and the integrity of our movement. We present them to you as proof of the values that define the Social Nationalist Party.[46]

Fayez lived by the standards of absolute faith. He executed his tasks with the utmost devotion of a Party propagandist and often spoke about a vision of the future that brimmed with the optimism and aesthetics of a glorious past:

> The Party is not a mere political alliance or an organization that indulges in superficialities, styles, formal uniforms, ranks, and Information. Nay! The Party is the conscience of a nation that has awakened, and the spirit of a people that has rebelled in pursuit of glories. The National Party embodies this awakening of the consciences of the faithful aroused by the memories of ancient glories and stirred by the belief that the nation can be and will be as glorious as it was in the past.[47]

However, for all its emotional and dramatic power, Fayez's enthusiasm was tempered by scepticism and anxieties. He led a double life: a public one as the Party's voice and vehicle to the people and a private one as a rising existentialist keenly aware of, and engaged in, the task of self-definition and trying to find meaning in a broken world. Fayez was comfortable with this duality as long as no one suspected anything or attempted to interfere with him. For almost three years, until Sa'adeh stepped in and brought him back to reality in 1947, no one dared to draw his attention to the potential conflict of interest in his double-life. This fact fuelled Fayez's ego and sense of self-importance even more. One cannot be without ego and self-pride. Yet these

---

[46] F. Sayegh, "The National Party Appears Barefaced." *An-Nahda*, (Beirut, 1946).

[47] F. Sayegh, "Reform in National Life" in *al-Baath al-Qawmi*.

attributes must be tempered by perspective, logic, and a sense of loyalty and direction. If one is in a position of leadership and authority, as Fayez was, an inflated ego can be dangerous and tragic to both one's self and others.

Precisely and literally, this is what happened to Fayez. With Sa'adeh absent and the Party's local leadership beguiled by the temptations of petty politics, he was left alone to do as he pleased. This untamed freedom, coupled with the pleasure of holding several senior posts and an almost exclusive public representation of the Party, instilled a sense of invincibility and independence in Fayez. He certainly felt independent enough to interfere with the Party's doctrine without consulting anyone. Hence, his endeavor to marry nationalism and existentialism arose. It was an exercise in futility and frustration, but it had seemed like a great idea at the time, at least from Fayez's perspective. However, it was never more than a marriage of convenience arranged by Fayez for an existential crisis he was having within himself. Regrettably, he did not have the courage to admit this and Sa'adeh did not have the data to judge it as such.

Conclusion

The story of Sayegh's "Party Years" is a neglected period in an eventful life. It is worth telling and knowing if we are to understand Sayegh's character and convictions. The roots of Sayegh's subsequent life and thinking are planted firmly in that period. His hardline opposition to Zionism, pragmatic attitude toward pan-Arabism, advocacy for positive nationalism, acrimony for Communism, and affection for Existentialism are grounded in his early years when he engaged in a broad range of academic and political inquiries and debates as a student at the American University of Beirut and as a pupil in the national ideological school of Antun Sa'adeh. After 1950, Sayegh built on this dual exposure: perfecting certain things and discarding others, yet never breaking completely or even partially from it.

I

Three distinctive features mark Sayegh's character and the course of his Party years. The first is his exceptional intelligence and oratory skills. He was a magnificent speaker. His ability to present logical and coordinated arguments in a pleasing manner and to display an elocutionary style of delivery common to great speakers earned him the respect and admiration of superiors and peers alike. No less important was Sayegh's encyclopedic knowledge, which he used efficiently and effectively to convey his message with logical proof. His audience was often captivated by his ability to improvise with thoroughness and incisiveness and to speak on a wide variety of subjects with almost flawless grammar. Sayegh was a gifted orator by instinct, but this gift may have remained dormant or marginal if not for his exposure to nationalism, which depends on oratory power or ensnarement by a political party that valued and encouraged oratory and public debate. The Syrian National Party provided Sayegh with both the opportunity to develop his oratory skills and a stable platform from which he displayed his speaking power.

The second feature to be considered is Sayegh's activism and advocacy. The period of 1938-1947 was the most intense phase in Sayegh's lengthy career as an activist. During those years, he established himself as a campaigner for social and political reform, an advocate for national unity, and a crusader against Zionism and Communism. Inspired by Sa'adeh's exemplary leadership and selfless devotion, Sayegh became a senior leader in Sa'adeh's Party. His meteoric rise to occupy important positions in two of its most vital departments, culture and information, gave him control over party publications, including its newspaper *an-Nahda*, access to its varied resources, and the opportunity to act as its primary spokesman on public issues. His record and performance were impeccable. Despite the war, the overbearing control of the French, and mounting academic commitments, Sayegh remained active on several fronts. He was both outspoken and passionate about the principles and key message he was assigned to convey. The breadth and depth of his political and social activism were so intense that his presence was felt well beyond the parameters of the Party.

The third feature is the asymmetrical trajectory that Sayegh's intellectual development assumed between 1938 and 1947. This asymmetry is evident in his determination to pursue and attempt to reconcile between two conflicting currents: (1) a society-first nationalism and (2) an individual-foremost existentialism. The two currents had some points of similarity with each other, but also several noteworthy points of departure. That Sayegh would endeavor to strike a balance between them indicates that he found each current agreeable, in one way or another, with some aspects of his personal convictions and ingrained values. His insatiable desire for national unity was interpolated with an inner yearning for moral and individual self-perfection in an act of delicate balancing. However, the contradictions proved insurmountable and eventually caught up with him. He found himself on a collision course with Sa'adeh, who balked at the idea of subordinating society to existential and individual self-perfection. During the course of their confrontation, the two men discussed and debated many issues relating to ideology, freedom, and the final aim of human existence, but the disagreement proved more intractable than anyone could have imagined. When given an ultimatum to toe the Party's line or leave, Sayegh elected to leave despite some hesitation and reluctance. His ejection from the Party in December 1947 ended almost a decade of accomplishments, but much more remained to be accomplished without the SSNP.

II

Sayegh's rise and fall from the SSNP evoke several intriguing questions:

1. Where do individual rights inside political parties start and end?

2. To what extent do personality differences influence internal party disputes?

3. Is absolute leadership sometimes inevitable, and if so, under what circumstances?

4. What kind of relationship should exist between the individual and society?

5. Is freedom of thought more important than the general/public interest?

6. How does ideology relate to philosophy?

These and other questions, which are debated extensively to this day, emerged patently during the course of Sayegh's disagreement with Sa'adeh. The two men discussed and debated them in a succession of private meetings. To make sense of this disagreement, it is important to identify and understand the factors that influenced Sayegh's thinking and the context in which he formulated his responses. Five factors stand out:

1. *Sa'adeh's absence*: The first and perhaps most important factor was Sa'adeh's absence during Sayegh's Party years. This absence, due to a forced exile, (a) deprived Sayegh of the opportunity to master the Party under Sa'adeh's close supervision and (b) gave Sayegh power and free rein before he had gained sufficient grasp of the national ideology. Consequently, Sayegh formed a conception of the Party that fell below, or did not meet, Sa'adeh's expectations. He was left to his own devices for far too long and fell under the influence of two unpropitious currents: (a) an internal current that metamorphosed the Party into a parochial agenda, and (b) an external current that frowned at collective ideologies and promoted a mostly individualist perspective.

Such a situation would not likely have arisen if Sa'adeh had been around to advise Sayegh or to identify the potential problems associated with both currents for him. No doubt, an intimate introduction to Sa'adeh's philosophical views would have allowed Sayegh to arrive at a more balanced perspective than the one he did.

2. *The Second World War*: The new climate of opinion and resurgent spirit of anti-nationalism and anti-collectivism generated by the Second World War bore directly on Sayegh either through his academic pursuits or through his personal interest in moral philosophy. Exposure to a dramatic change of perspectives can be both mentally and emotionally draining. It often puts an intellectual in a predicament that involves the reassessment of values and propositions. Some intellectuals may weather the storm, while others may not.

In the case of Sayegh, it perched on a fragile balance. Although he did not cave in to the new climate and continued to associate

Conclusion

with the SSNP, his perception of the Party's national doctrine underwent a series of rapid metamorphosis. The notion of "positive nationalism" began to creep into his nationalist discourse coupled with new concepts and moral values congenial to the post-World War climate. Also, his previous politically charged method gradually tapered off to make way for a more human-centered approach grounded in universal norms and principles.

3. *Existential philosophy*: Sayegh's brush with this philosophy reinvented by the War while Sa'adeh was absent, contributed vastly to his disagreement with his idol and leader. It is claimed that the irresistible attraction of Existentialism is such that, once a person finds a way into its labyrinth, it is difficult to find a way out. Its accent on freedom, individuality, free choice, and personal will is a powerful and binding force that cannot be easily shaken off. For those seeking an exit from the woes of reality, it can be a life-changing experience from which it is hard to turn back or stop believing in it. This seemed to be clearly the case with Sayegh, and thus, it should not be overlooked or underestimated. However, contrary to established beliefs, its significance in his disagreement with Sa'adeh lay not in the ideological dimension, but in the psychological dimension. For even if Sayegh had acquiesced to Sa'adeh's demand to desist from Existentialist assertions inside the Party, their disagreement would not have dissipated because Existentialism exercised such a psychological hold on Sayegh that it would have resurfaced. In other words, the new perspective on the world that Sayegh had obtained from Existentialism rendered his clash with Sa'adeh both inevitable and insurmountable.

4. *Sayegh's academic stature*. Academics generally approach political party work differently from ordinary members. They can be more "deviant" and sharper than others and prone to express their personal views on party political matters. Academics are likely to ask difficult questions, broach complex issues, and be eclectic about answers.

They are inclined, by training and practice, to demand greater freedom, resist authoritarian directives, and be more attuned to political perspectives and realities. Their priorities and values are also different. Most importantly, academic intellectuals generally do not like to admit defeat or to backtrack. Their sense of pride and self-worth can sometimes be a source of irritation and make them fiercely competitive. These features cannot be ignored or masked when pondering Sayegh's disagreement with Sa'adeh.

Not only do we need to consider Sayegh's academic character, but we also need to consider the breadth and aura of his academic achievement and the sense of elation and self-pride he obtained from it. It should be coupled as well with the aspects of Sayegh's personality, which was alarmingly stubborn and very argumentative. These traits, which seemingly made him an excellent speaker and an academic, made him impervious to the authority and power of others.

5. *Sa'adeh's homecoming*: If Sa'adeh's absence was critical, his homecoming on March 2, 1947 was decisive. The reason is fundamental because Sa'adeh's return turned Sayegh's life upside down in a most undermining and unexpected way. Until then, and for almost three years, Sayegh had occupied a central position in the Party. His oratory power and dynamic performance had gained him wide popularity and acclaim at all levels of the Party and beyond. He enjoyed a free hand in all its cultural affairs and the overwhelming support of his superiors in almost all his initiatives.

With Sa'adeh's return, all of this ended abruptly. Sa'adeh eclipsed Sayegh almost instantly starting with his extempore and fiery return speech. His impact was so strong and far-reaching that Sayegh's stature inside the Party dwindled to almost nothing overnight. He faded from the limelight for the rest of 1947. His public appearances and writings were markedly reduced, and with that, the attention and affection he once commanded.

Conclusion

The psychological impact of such a transformation on Sayegh, coupled with the inferiority complex that usually results from it, is a pertinent factor. The loss of authority or strength can lead to an atmosphere of uncertainty and even melancholy. It can breed a sense of meaninglessness, contempt, and grievance and lead to negative and false assumptions. Empirically, it is difficult to establish how much Sayegh was hurt by his dwindling fortunes, but he could not have continued to feel as comfortable and secure as he once did.

By looking at Sayegh's clash with Sa'adeh from this broader perspective, two facts emerge: (1) the clash was not a spur of the moment episode, but the product of cumulative factors that spanned an entire spectrum of psychological, historical and ideological concerns; and (2) the clash was somewhat inevitable given the divergent paths that each man had pursued afar from each other, especially from towards the end of World War II. Even if Sayegh had relented and bowed to Sa'adeh's demands, it would only have deferred the encounter, not averted it. The divide between the two men was so wide it seemed insurmountable. Eventually, their divergent worldviews were bound to clash, as Sayegh reached a point of no return with Existentialism and his perspectives on life underwent a dramatic change.

III

Sayegh's fallout with Sa'adeh, whom he held in the highest regard until their disagreement, transcended the standard boundaries of internal party politics and backroom business. Sayegh pushed Sa'adeh to the limit. He did not accept Sa'adeh's explanations at face value and challenged him with pointed questions and not-so-subtle suggestions about the Party's central vision. During his almost six-month debate with Sa'adeh, he committed to a particular viewpoint and made himself very clear to his leader. Regardless whether he was right or wrong, the fact that he revealed himself to Sa'adeh and took the challenge right up to him attests to his intelligence, strong character, and self-confidence and belief in his views. Despite all this, Sayegh came second while Sa'adeh won the contest decisively. Sa'adeh retained full control of the Party and managed to ostracize Sayegh with the minimum of fuss and repercussions.

Any number of reasons can explain this outcome: not the least of which was Sayegh's intransigence. Contrary to early beliefs, Sayegh, not Sa'adeh, leaned toward a stubborn and rugged position. Sayegh's unbreakable attitude and the relentlessness with which he pursued his views often bordered on obsession. In contrast, Sa'adeh maintained an open mind and paid courteous attention to Sayegh's opinions and feelings. He abstained from dismissing Sayegh until his patience had been exhausted and he could no longer bear Sayegh's obstinacy.

Sayegh's inflexibility, coupled with his refusal to defer the matter, affected his reputation negatively. He came across as a wantonly cruel and capricious villain who placed his own personal views ahead of the Party. This contradicted what he had been preaching about loyalty and commitment. The ferocity of his challenge, hard on the heels of a political confrontation between Sa'adeh and the Lebanese government, did not bode well with members, who expected him to show restraint and dignity rather than defiance and acrimony. Having observed him in action and experienced his enterprising spirit, they were bewildered by his lackluster and casual approach during that confrontation. They felt, not without good reason, that he had let the Party down by not jumping to Sa'adeh's defense or speaking out against the intimidation of the Lebanese regime. Consequently, Sayegh's standing inside the Party declined so dramatically that, when his clash with Sa'adeh became public, members chose Sa'adeh *en masse*.

Another shortcoming was Sayegh's strict and exceedingly academic approach. This problem occurs when academic-minded activists allow their intellectual and scholarly pursuits to interfere with political exigencies. Sayegh's mistake was precisely that: he tried to superimpose on the Party and its issues an overly intellectual academic perspective even when it seemed disproportionate with the Party's national vision and the special and difficult conditions under which it functioned. His approach was awkward, too, especially concerning existentialism and freedom of thought. With existentialism, for example, he drove himself into a vulnerable position by focusing on the "individualist" dimension in Berdyaev's philosophy rather than on its "societalist" underpinnings. Likewise, his approach to the touchy question of freedom of thought verged on a moral utopia and the introduction of values and standards that are incompatible with the pressing demands and circumstances of a national revival. Such a confrontational and abrasive style can only last so long, and eventually, it backfired. Sayegh's style alienated many members and created sympathy for Sa'adeh, whose pragmatic approach was already widely received and appreciated inside the Party.

Additionally, several ambiguities left Sayegh vulnerable to serious criticism. The perceptions and ideas he tried to promote failed to resonate with Party members because they targeted the wrong issues at the wrong time for the wrong reasons. Usually, his views, though intelligent and thought-provoking, appertained to a post-revival stage in national life rather than the stage of actual revival. An example is his stand on "freedom of thought" inside the Party. It has been utilized to depict him as a crusader for individual freedom fighting an unbending perspective of a totalitarian leader, Sa'adeh. If that was the case, why did Sayegh's views receive hardly any support from the Party? The answer is because his views on "freedom of thought," and the fury with which he expressed them, did not reverberate with the Party. Most members unreservedly accepted Sa'adeh's analysis that, during revival, the nation must enlist every atom of its strength and unity and develop into a unified entity with a single outlook on life. This demands not only the subordination of individual freedom to national freedom, but also the formulation of a shared philosophical vision to prevent factionalism and to keep the revival going in the right direction. Sayegh's error was not that he broached the question of "freedom of thought", but that he broached it ahead of its time. This weakened his case against Sa'adeh and cost him the support and admiration of people who could have furthered his cause at the right time.

However, the most important reason for Sayegh's defeat was Sa'adeh himself. Sayegh had miscalculated at two levels: he underestimated Sa'adeh's popularity and competence while overestimating his own popularity and competence. Sa'adeh was a man of tremendous strength of character, unquestioned integrity, and strong intellectual ability. He could respond to philosophical objections with equal force and coherence. He was also very popular with members and widely admired for the dignity and courage with which he led the Party. How Sayegh could have failed to notice the obvious is a mystery. Some say that he was the victim of an over-inflated ego that allowed him to believe that he was permanently invulnerable; others that his existentialist Party colleagues who consoled him during the encounter and urged him not to back down had misled him. Either way, Sayegh only had himself to blame for his defeat. Having witnessed Sa'adeh in action and observing the ease and facility with which he was able to purge the "transgressors" in the Party's senior ranks, just a few months earlier, he should have known better than to challenge a popular leader on his turf of natural advantage.

In short, the complexity of Sayegh's clash with Sa'adeh cannot be reduced to a simple disagreement of views. Clearly, there were psychological factors involved, as there usually are in most personality clashes, as well as topical issues that should be taken into account in the consideration of their discord. Approaching the dispute from this broader perspective enables us to capture the essence of Sayegh's defiance, the watershed moments that shaped his behavior, and the intransigence with which he addressed himself to the challenge. Both his and Sa'adeh's position become more understandable when placed in the context of the two men's value systems and the contemporary developments that took place behind Sa'adeh's back and intrinsically inside Sayegh's world.

CONCLUSION

IV

One of the most puzzling aspects in the Sayegh-Sa'adeh clash is that, after publishing what appears to be a final statement on the encounter (*Whither To?*), Sayegh never returned to it. For over three decades, during which an impressive array of books and articles flowed from his pen, he refrained from mentioning Sa'adeh in any capacity or context. On the single and rare occasion on which he alluded to Sa'adeh, in a private letter to his brother, he desisted from even uttering his name.

This omission, made almost two years after his ejection from the SSNP and in the aftermath of Sa'adeh's execution on July 8, 1949, is indicative of the hurt and anger that Sayegh experienced and was clearly still carrying from the encounter. Conversely, however, it can be perceived as a symptomatic representation of a resentful mind and an egocentricity verging on narcissism. An unmistakable egocentric undertone even runs through Sayegh's "forgiveness" as if he wanted us to believe that not only was he forgiving, but also, he was free of any blame. However, in any dispute or disagreement, usually more than one person is at fault and no one is completely blameless. Anyway, blame is irrelevant or at least peripheral when the crux of the disagreement is largely intellectual or ideological.

From a contemporary perspective, Sayegh's blocking out Sa'adeh completely can be interpreted as meaning one of two things: either Sayegh harbored a strong sense of guilt and regret for having taken a wrong turn and being too proud, could not bring himself to admit this, or he did it to avoid negative backlash from the Party and those who still supported Sa'adeh. After his departure from the SSNP, some reports implicated him in certain unethical acts ranging from colluding with others to delaying Sa'adeh's return to Lebanon in 1947 to failing to hand over the total amount of contributions collected during his Party-sponsored visit to Ghana. He was also accused of siphoning off internal Party papers and documents for personal use and never returning them. Sayegh's self-imposed silence precluded a response to these allegations. In short, Sayegh's willingness to 'forgive' was an admirable act, but he failed to carry it through publicly.

V

Because ideological disagreements can be difficult to resolve, neither all the credit nor all the blame falls on one side. With regard to this investigation, this fact prompts two questions: "Did Sa'adeh contribute to the dispute with Sayegh? And if so, how?".

Outside observers, particularly those who place a premium price on individual freedom, will almost certainly answer affirmatively to the first question. They might even hold Sa'adeh entirely responsible under the principle of "freedom of thought". This is both unfair and manipulative, because it ignores crucial theoretical and practical imperatives associated with political work. Given that Sayegh was committed to a specific national program that involved self-discipline and ideological observances, invoking the principle of "freedom of thought" under such circumstances is not only untenable but a perversion of the truth.

Nevertheless, this does not exonerate Sa'adeh of blame or responsibility. His procrastination in proclaiming the philosophy of the SSNP until the end of 1946 (almost 15 years after its founding) should not be overlooked. A philosophy should embody a coherent position on fundamental problems such as reality, ethics, truth, values, existence, and knowledge before it can be said to exist. Thus, although the Party's ideology contained certain philosophical notions and recognized the natural superiority of society over the individual, it did not form a complete philosophy. The aspects of its position on fundamental problems were either non-existent in the Party's ideology before 1947 or existed randomly in some of Sa'adeh's speeches and writings in exile. By then, Sayegh had already become too infatuated with existential philosophy to discard it and embrace a different worldview whose features were unclear.

Conclusion

Realistically, how was Sayegh to know that the Party's ideology embodied a philosophy when no formal statement had been issued to that effect until 1947? How was he to discern the existence of such a philosophy, let alone configure its vital elements, from intermittent hints Sa'adeh made during regular Party functions abroad or published in Latin American diasporic Syrian newspapers that rarely reached Lebanon? In fairness to Sayegh, prior to the disagreement, he had limited access - or even no access at all - to Sa'adeh's philosophical observations to realize that Sa'adeh was steering the SSNP towards a philosophy of its own.

Sa'adeh may have also contributed to the dispute by taking an emphatic and unbending stand against existential philosophy. It is true that existentialism is individual-centered, but in some vital respects, it is also group-centered. As a way of life, existentialism sees freedom as a guiding principle to realize our potential while acknowledging the challenges we may face. It also provides us with awareness on how genuinely we can "exist as we please" while keeping in mind our responsibility as members of society. Hence, existentialism is not anti-society as such, but rather against the limits that society may attempt to impose on personal freedom through the state. Nonetheless, it is a slippery slope argument, because existentialism, by necessity, is solipsistic.

By taking a very negative and one-sided view of existentialism, Sa'adeh exacerbated his disagreement with Sayegh. Existentialists would almost certainly criticize him for failing to distinguish between "individuality" and "personality" and for taking aim at existential philosophy without differentiating between its diverse schools and approaches. The dispute may not have proceeded as far as it did if Sa'adeh had engaged Sayegh in a philosophical debate on existentialism rather than invoke his powers against Sayegh. While Sa'adeh and Sayegh did hold long discussions during 1947, they centered mainly on amendments to the Party's ideology rather than existentialism.

One could also criticize Sa'adeh for not paying enough attention to Sayegh's state of emotional and psychological agitation. With almost cavalier unconcern, Sa'adeh brushed aside factors of psychological nature such as the impact of World War II, the exposure to and lure of existentialism, the evolution of Sayegh into a philosopher, the sense of personal pride and self-esteem that Sayegh had developed during Sa'adeh's absence, and the loss of independence that Sayegh suffered from Sa'adeh's return in 1947. No doubt Sa'adeh was driven by the need to protect the Party's ideology from external philosophical intrusion, but the strict application of laws without adequate attention to psychological factors can be detrimental. At times, they can even produce results opposite to the original intentions.

If Sa'adeh had proclaimed the SSNP's philosophy earlier or produced even a short document explaining its main elements before proclaiming it, the dispute with Sayegh may not even have surfaced. Such disclosure would at least have provided Sayegh with some material to study the Party's philosophy and to form his own opinion rather than compelling him to accept it without question or objection. The philosophical mind does not function according to rigid party rules and dictates: it must be able to imagine and challenge as freely as possible:

> An individual with a philosophical mind reveals characteristics which we can classify them from three aspects of comprehensiveness, penetration, and flexibility. This individual always makes an attempt to treat their thoughts with exhaustiveness, considers the issues in relation to a vast field which is relevant to the long-term goals, question the truisms and add to his/her chance for a movement beyond the ignorant bigotries, personal prejudices, and the cliché imaginations. Such an individual enjoys a flexibility which is accompanied by innovation, heterodoxy, and creativity and scrutinizes the issues from various aspects and points of view.[1]

---
1   Jafarian Yasar Hamid, Faghihi Alireza, Seifi Mohammad, "Prediction Of The

Sa'adeh could have avoided controversy by preparing the ground for the proclamation of the Party's philosophy. He could have done even better engaging Sayegh in its formulation or by tapping into his philosophical views and opinions. This would have had the double effect of appeasing Sayegh's philosophical ego and resulting in a more peaceful transition.

VI

One last observation is in order. Since his passing in 1980, Sayegh has been chiefly remembered as an "Arab nationalist" who had the interests of the "Arab nation" at heart. The PLO and the Arab Group at the United Nations, for example, described him as "a great man who spent his life defending the issues of his Arab nation and the right of its Palestinian people to liberate its country from the brutal Zionist occupation." Similarly, Sakr Abu Fakhr, in a recent tribute to Sayegh, maintained that Sayegh's parting with the Party in December 1947 marked the beginning of his transition from the idea of "Syrian nationalism" to the idea of "Arab nationalism". Yet, in reality, Sayegh did not completely part intellectually from the SSNP or develop into an Arab nationalist.

A cursory glance at Sayegh's intellectual and political record from 1948 until 1980 reveals a stable pattern, consistent with and complementary to, the core themes he had developed during his Party years. For example, in relation to the Palestine question, the conclusions he reached during his SSNP years were either retained or perfected after 1947. He continued to berate the Zionist project with the same ruthlessness and tenacity as before, and he continued to draw mostly on the same point of view and the same perspective he had procured under Sa'adeh. If there are exceptions, it is because the specter of anti-Semitism was always in the back of his mind. Even so, the idea of a separate Jewish state in Palestine remained off-limit for Sayegh, just as

---

Organizational Effectiveness Of The Primary Level Schools By The Factor Of Philosophical Mindedness Of The Educational Directors." (*IJBPAS*, December, 2015, 4(12), Special Issue): 888-912.

it had been during his time in the ranks of the SSNP. To the very end, he maintained: "Israel is, because Palestine has been made not to be".

Secondly, the anti-Communist and anti-Soviet views that Sayegh developed during his Party interlude continued to resonate with him. The Soviet-Arab entente of the mid-1950s and the subsequent emergence of Nasserist and Arab socialism, which momentarily captured his imagination, failed to change his anti-Communist conviction in any marked way. He remained as decidedly suspicious of Communism and the Soviet Union as he ~~was~~ had been during his time in the SSNP. His 1958 laconic study "Communism in Israel" is a clear case in point. Though written to placate growing American public concern about recent Soviet rapprochement with the Arab World, it contained a damning assessment of Communism and Soviet support for Israel.

Thirdly, for many years after he left the SSNP, Sayegh maintained a basically nationalist discourse in dealing with the major issues of his time. Whether he was advocating for Palestinian rights or promoting Arab unity, he continued to articulate his views according to nationalist percepts: "national self-determination", "national identity", "national belongingness" and "national rights". The omnipresence of these percepts in his writings indicates clearly that he remained a nationalist at heart. During the 1950s, he invoked the theory of "dynamic nationalism" as a healthy reform-craving process and temporarily transposed and applied it to Arab nationalism. He dispensed with the idea when the "Arab resurgence" under Nasser lost its spark and early vibrancy and devolved into an unmitigated disaster. This does not necessarily mean that Sayegh embraced the ideology of Arab nationalism or became an "Arab nationalist" as he is sometimes portrayed. On closer scrutiny of his writings, particularly on the subject of Arab unity, we find that:

1. Sayegh merely described rather than endorsed Arab nationalism.

Conclusion

2. He leaned toward Arab unity in the political sense (along the lines of an Arab league or front) rather than Arab unity in the national meaning of the term "Arab nation".

3. He took up the subject of Arab unity as a matter of convenience rather than conviction almost certainly to appease the Arab League and the Arab regimes (noticeably Yemen and Kuwait) for which he worked as a diplomat at the United Nations.

4. He resorted to pan-Arab terms ("Arabs", "Arab unity", "Arab mind" etc.) mainly out of necessity to fit in, so to speak, with the dominant discourse at the time (both in politics and academia).

5. His flirtation with "Arab nationalism" if it can be proved, was ephemeral at best and precipitated largely, if not wholly, by the atmosphere of optimism inspired by Nasser's rise and soaring popularity inside and outside Egypt.

6. Sayegh did not join a pan-Arab movement or take special interest in the Arab nationalist parties of his time even at the height of pan-Arabism in Syria and Egypt.

It cannot, however, be denied that Sayegh, for all his nationalist posturing, maintained a safe distance from the Syrian nationalism of his early years. He never returned or desired to return to it. Yet, at no point in his post-SSNP life did Sayegh attack or criticize the Syrian national idea or promote Arab nationalism as a better alternative. In contrast, it was usually the concept of Arab unity as perceived in the Arab nationalist discourse that he targeted. His study *Arab Unity: Hope and Fulfillment* is a case in point. He noted: "… three inherent weaknesses of the idea of Arab unity [are apparent]: its vagueness as to form, and its general indifference to instruments and methods; its oblivion to disunifying political forces; and its scorn for utilitarian inducements." Attributing these weaknesses jointly to a psychological-existential attitude and an imbalance in the Arab outlook on socio-political affairs, Sayegh ridiculed the Arab nationalists for failing to take "due cognizance of the real, objective, and stubborn elements of diversity in the Arab World". He added: "If Arab nationalists could not reconcile themselves to the admission that there was real diversity in the Arab situation, it was because the doctrine of an Arab nation-in-being was unduly rigid and static, and because the political philosophy within the context of which that doctrine was formulated was not capable of simple, undifferentiated application to the Arab situation." The correlation between this theory and the SSNP's concept of Arab unity is too obvious to be stated.

VII

Sayegh's Party years constituted one of the cornerstones of his life. It was the soil in which his roots were deeply and firmly embedded and the experimental phase that gave him his first political connections and knowledge. During that time, Sayegh excelled in almost all the assignments and progressive roles he held. He served the Party with diligence, conscience, and profound dedication and left an indelible mark on many lives. Along the way, he made many friends and also many enemies, and he learned and taught a great deal, too. Sayegh loved the Party and delighted in the fellowship of his comrades. They loved him just as much and delighted no less in his presence and oratory power. Those who knew Sayegh privately professed their admiration for his abilities and probably considered him heir apparent to Sa'adeh. They were not overly chimerical either. Sayegh had both the intelligence and the charisma to lead, and he may well have succeeded Sa'adeh had he exercised self-discipline and not allowed his intransigence and hubris to interfere with his Party commitments.

Ultimately, Sayegh gave away his achievements in the SSNP. Everything he had worked hard for fell apart, and he ended up on the outside. For the uninformed observer, his expulsion from the SSNP may seem the price he had to pay for his stubborn defense of the values he cherished: individual rights, freedom of thought, and personal freedom. However, this is both inaccurate and misleading. The hard reality is that Sayegh wanted out at the first opportunity because, after Sa'adeh's return in 1947, he found himself unable to perform with the same freedom, ease, and unaccountability. Sa'adeh's presence had robbed him not only of the limelight, but also of the prestige and aura he had once enjoyed both inside and outside the Party. The impact of such a transformation on Sayegh's ego and pride can only be imagined.

The question arises, why didn't Sayegh just resign? There is no clear-cut answer to this question. One possible reason is that 'resignation' is not something that a stubborn and defiant personality as that of Sayegh's would consider. Apart from the blow to his fighting spirit, resignation had the potential to project him as the loser in the confrontation and Sa'adeh as the winner, exactly the outcome that Sayegh did not want. Another possible reason is that Sayegh decided to persevere rather than resign to appease his followers and admirers in the Party who urged him on and pledged to support him in any potential showdown with Sa'adeh.

Ten years is a long time in anyone's life, but it can seem like a lifetime when much work and dedication has gone into it. Sayegh's experience is a clear case in point.

Appendix

1

THE SYRIAN NATIONAL PARTY QUESTIONS AND ANSWERS

Question: What was the motivation for the founding of the Syrian Social Nationalist Party?

Answer: The Syrian Social Nationalist Party was established by Mr. Antun Sa'adeh in 1932 as a clandestine party. It was discovered only after it had spread throughout the country and attracted thousands of members. The best way to respond to the question of what motivated Sa'adeh to establish the Party is to refer to his improvised defense on the first day of his trial on January 24, 1936:

> The practical motivations that led me to establish the Party were: to end the chaos of existing nationalist beliefs in society and to achieve their unification into a single ideology centered around its entity and interests; to direct it away from sterile illusions and toward practical thinking and work; to train the young generation in particular in the exercise of national rights and the virtues that unify society and elevate its outlooks and systems; and to instill discipline into the rising generation and train them to use their talents for the sake of both advancing their nation and understanding their public responsibilities.

Question: What are the broad lines of the Party's platform and principles?

Answer: The Party's principles, platform, and Aim, as elucidated by the Leader, are available in print and published forms. Circulated widely ever since the inception of the Party, the principles can be categorized as:

(a) Outlined in the first article of its constitution, the Party's principal aim is "the creation of a Syrian Social Nationalist renaissance that will restore to the Syrian nation its vitality and strength, and the organization of a movement that would seek the complete independence of the Syrian nation, the vindication of its sovereignty, secure its interests, raise its standard of living, and aspire to create an Arab front." This definition clearly states that the Party's Aim is a comprehensive national one concerned with the nation's life from all aspects and with securing all its interests. For this reason, the Party is not a mere political party; rather, its ideology and "national" principles deal with all the affairs related to the nation's existence, from the economic, to the social, cultural, and political. Based on this, we can define the various principles of the Party in detail within the framework of this comprehensive aim.

(b) The Party's political objectives are: the restoration of national sovereignty to the Syrian nation in a meaningful and real sense that would guarantee the practical independence of Syria; the recovery of Syrian unity after partition had tampered with it for 25 years; and the integration of Syria closely with the Arab family within the framework of an "Arab Front". The Party's plan for an Arab front was practically approved by the Arab leaders who convened in the Alexandria and Cairo conferences and drafted the Alexandria Protocol and the Arab League Charter. In its memorandum to the Alexandria Conference on September 20, 1944, the Party officially defined its objectives concerning the "Arab Front":

1. Developing a program for a system of collective security and joint military defense.

Appendix

2. Unifying external political representation, if possible.

3. Formulating joint economic measures and an economic policy developed by a central economic authority that would develop the main plans for production and distribution in the entire Arab world...

4. From the social and cultural aspect, the Arab nations that are members of the front would participate in orientation programs, which will be unified in their broad outlines but tinted by distinct local features resulting from the discrepancy in levels.

Clearly, from this synopsis, the Party's agenda for Arab cooperation is ambitious. It seeks to enhance Arab ties, overcome narrow-sighted isolationism in the Arab world, and eradicate it from popular life.

Another delicate issue remains: the current existing entities in the Syrian homeland, especially the Lebanese entity. The Party believes that the main problem it has to address is not the current political situation in Lebanon, but rather the general national social situation imposed by certain factors, which, in turn, imposed this isolationist political entity in Lebanon. The former must be addressed before the latter. We also emphasize that Palestine and Alexandretta are two intrinsic issues that we will not balk at or stop pursuing.

> (c) Social objectives: the Party seeks to create a highly advanced civil system free of social injustice, stratification, and social privileges. It strives for the social unification of the people over and above the prevalent social decay that creates conflicting communities within one society and arouses uncharitable and antagonistic sentiments at the expense of the nationalist spirit. Sectarianism, stratification, tribalism, and regionalism are all declared by the Party to be corrupt manifestations completely at odds with the Party's basic national belief: "The Syrian nation is one social community".

(d) Economic objectives: the Party works to redress the problem of economic production, combat the foreign exploitation of the country's resources, eliminate social injustice and inequality between the classes by combating feudalism and building a national economic system that would allow the state to take control of economic affairs, and establish a system of economic life on the basis of production. Consequently, the Party would save workers and farmers from injustice, not by helping them to usurp the rights and wealth of the other classes, but rather by raising the standard of economic life and national production and hedging against exploitation in the distribution of the national wealth.

(e) We should remember the Party's endeavor to "create a strong army that can have an effective weight in determining the fate of the nation and the homeland"; its work to "prevent clerics from interfering in national politics and judiciary"; or its perseverance to connect the immigrant to the nation and bring him/her back to his homeland.

Question 3: To what extent has the Party been able to implement these principles?

Answer: We are weighing a political party, not a government, for its work. The scope of the work of political parties, from a tangible practical perspective, is definitely narrower than the scope of the work of governments. Governments have a grip on the resources of people, hold legislative and executive powers, and control the military forces and financial resources available in the entire state. We should also remember that civil liberties, without which any party cannot fulfill its national duty towards its country, were suppressed and stifled during the era of the mandate. Moreover, the Party does not presently enjoy the freedom it requires to perform its work fully and completely.

Despite these two factors, which impede the Party's ability

APPENDIX

to fulfill its principles, the achievements of the Syrian Social Nationalist Party are:

1. The Party has practically realized the nation's sovereignty in its homeland. Despite the mandate and its restrictions, Party members worked for the interest of their nation – and their nation alone – without recognizing the legitimacy of the mandate or its restrictions. They snatched back their right to productive national work from the hands of the foreign authorities.

2. The Party has practically realized the nation's unity in all regions of the country. Party members are scattered throughout the Syrian statelets and regions despite the artificial boundaries that divides the nation. Consequently, the Party has developed into a single national society within the larger national society, which foreign wills had conspired to divide and destroy its political unity.

3. The Party has proposed a comprehensive national ideology by which all issues facing the nation can be addressed in a thoughtful and correct manner. With this work, the Party has presented a theoretical intellectual framework for the general management of all national affairs.

4. The Party has been a practical school where members have been trained to shoulder responsibilities and exercise discipline in administration and leadership. Such training is of paramount value in a nation that aspires to assume the place it deserves without the help of foreigners, especially since the regimes that reigned in the nation have created a generation oblivious of the meaning of responsibility and untested in the actual exercise of it.

5. The Party has also been a school of life that nurtures the virtues of struggle, sacrifice, sincerity, shouldering difficulties, and persistence in its members in pursuing their national mission despite foreign forces being mobilized to impede their progress and struggle.

6. The Party has worked to enlighten public opinion and

explain to it the reality of the various issues facing the nation. The Party did not let a single major event in the nation's life pass without explaining its nature to the people and outlining the policies required to address it, whether through its periodical announcements or internal missives. For example, the memoranda and statements on the questions of Palestine, Alexandretta, the Alexandria Conference, the Common Interests, the Syrian-French crises, etc.

7. The Party has laid the basis for the close relationship that must exist between immigrants and their homeland by establishing branches in all centers of Syrian immigration and dedicating a central office (the Office for Cross-Border Affairs) for immigrants to look after their affairs and link their respective branches with the Party at home.

8. The Party has established – through the Dean of Culture and Fine Arts – a nucleus for a high Party council to tend to the affairs of public enlightenment and culture; establish offices, clubs, and night schools; issue cultural bulletins; and sponsor authorship, translation, and publishing. With these efforts, the Party has addressed the disgraceful deficiency in the nation's cultural life.

Question 4: What is the Party's attitude toward the status quo?

Answer: If by "status quo" is meant the present situation of the nation, then the answers above more than adequately explain the Party's position. However, if it is in relation to the current "political situation", then the Party declares that the backbone of the present situation is social nationalist and not political, and that all changes in the political system will remain decidedly truncated and incomplete unless they address, primarily, the general social, economic, and national situation. We need to change the foundations of the governmental process before changing the individuals in charge of the government. The coming and going of individuals on the same principles and from the same political school will not result in any change in the status quo.

Appendix

Question 5: What is the Party's attitude toward the other political parties?

Answer: Since the Party works for progress and national unity, it endeavors, and it will always endeavor, for greater cooperation between parties and groups (despite the difference in principles and platforms) and for the mobilization of all efforts in the cause of the general interest rather than for the purpose of inter-party quarrels and hostilities. We believe in the principle of the freedom of political parties, no matter how different their platforms are from ours.

But we also believe that one principal criterion should determine the extent of freedom granted these parties and of our readiness to cooperate with them. This criterion is the degree to which these parties are loyal to the nation's interests above every other interest and above the partial interests of individuals, religious sects, classes, and parties.

Some groups unmistakably operate at the behest of foreign policies and for a foreign interest. We believe that these parties are betraying the nation, and therefore, it is an act of betrayal to cooperate with them or to demand their right to freedom.

The freedom of political parties is provisional. It is contingent on the party's loyalty to the interest of the nation, regardless of differences in programs and methods. Within the confines of this basic condition, we call for the freedom of parties and for cooperation among them.

2

How Do Nationalists Perceive Sa'adeh?

What Does He Mean To Them?

What Is Their Relation To Him?

These three questions sit on the tongue of the cunning, the admirer, the neutral, the member who is at the threshold of Party life, and the member who has scaled to the core of the movement. Today, March 1, on the occasion of his birthday, the eyes of thousands of young people in this nation from north to south and from east to the sea and beyond are fixed on one man: Antun Sa'adeh.

What is the relationship that connects us to Sa'adeh? What dynamic link exists between him and each of us?

1. Sa'adeh represents a live embodiment of the strengths and values of life that are latent in each of our souls but are ready to burst and take control of our entity. He represents a set of noble virtues, values, characteristics, and strengths that exist inside every person in a default dormant state and are sometimes visible in some people. In Sa'adeh, they have crystallized and coalesced. Thus, although they remain dormant and inherent in each of us, they are conspicuously, clearly, coherently, and supremely visible in Sa'adeh's character. This is the first manifestation of our relationship to Sa'adeh. In himself, Sa'adeh represents the "actualization" of the values that our souls aspire for and the "incarnation" of the virtues we are able and eager to embody. He is, in his life and existence, a living fulfillment of the wishes and hopes we harbor. He is, in his "reality", a realization of what we dream to be and aspire to achieve.

Appendix

Sa'adeh represents each one of us in his tendencies and potential. Inside each of us, there is a Sa'adeh ready to emerge.

2. Second, Sa'adeh does not only realize these strengths and values in himself, but he calls us to realize these strengths and values in ourselves. The Nationalist who appreciates Sa'adeh and recognizes his true worth but remains unaffected deep down by Sa'adeh is neither a genuine Nationalist nor a true follower of Sa'adeh. Furthermore, the Nationalist who admires Sa'adeh but is unmotivated to be what Sa'adeh had been is neither a true Nationalist nor a true follower of Sa'adeh.

Indeed, true genuine realization of these inspiring natural values is but a call to the same values to rise from their slumber, to become dynamic and effective, and to crystallize inside every soul that comes in contact with them or with the dynamic current they have generated. If Sa'adeh had fulfilled these values only within himself without calling on those with whom he came in contact to fulfill them in themselves, he would not have truly fulfilled them in himself. Verily, the embodiment of life is forever a call for life!

Nevertheless, Sa'adeh could not have called on anyone to strive for such fulfillment if these values were not latent inside him or her. As I said before, the values that Sa'adeh embodies in himself are values that exist in every soul. If they did not exist in our souls, neither Sa'adeh nor anyone else would be able to invoke them in anyone.

Sa'adeh's true worth is not in inculcating new values in us. Rather, it is in introducing each of us to his real self, in fuelling inside it a new struggle with its existing state, and then in pushing it to realize its genuine nature and replacing its spurious nature with it.

Inside each of us exist the seeds of the values that were fulfilled in Sa'adeh. Had this not been the case, we would not have been able to become like Sa'adeh; and we would not have been able to appreciate or respect him. Did he not say, "There lies in us every science, philosophy, and art in the world"? Did he not say that he predicates his trust in the revival of the nation on his trust in the vitality inherent in the sons of the nation? Did he not also say, "There is strength in you which, if activated, would change the face of history"? Did he not presume, in everything he did or said, the existence of the powers and values that represent the national revival in the soul of each soldier of the revival? From where do we derive our slogan of "Freedom, Duty, Discipline, and Strength" except from ourselves? Where can we find it but in ourselves?

3. The third manifestation of our relationship with Sa'adeh is that Sa'adeh is the source of our trust in the possibility of achieving these values in ourselves. Sa'adeh is a living entity in whom these values have been realized and proof that these values are realizable. An inspired novelist may paint a beautiful portrait that captures all that is in Sa'adeh of life's elements, and this picture may inspire us to bring out these elements in ourselves. However, it cannot generate in us the confidence that we can ever be like the person in the portrait! Sa'adeh is neither the product of myths nor a portrait created by an artist. He is a human being who lived among us. We observed him in trials and tribulations, which stand as conclusive proof of his true nature. Who would dare to say after today that this sacrifice, this firmness, and this sincerity is beyond human reach now that they are crystallized, before our eyes, in a man of flesh and blood?

This is Sa'adeh the man before he became Sa'adeh the Party Leader and a legend shrouded in myths.

3

THE PLACE OF THE WORKER IN THE NATIONAL REVIVAL

Workers, their rights, and their duties are among the fundamental issues in the life of nations, especially in emerging nations that are on the threshold of progress and new advancement. Accordingly, a nation aspiring to a proper life cannot take an oscillating or ambivalent attitude toward this fundamental issue. It cannot take an attitude that is at odds with the principles of truth and justice.

Before we explain the attitude of the National Movement toward this issue, we need to review some of the existing perspectives on it.

THE CAPITALIST PERSPECTIVE

By virtue of its position and interests, the capitalist camp is inclined to take a hostile attitude toward the demands and rights of workers. This perspective is dictated by self-defense and the need to combat labor unions. Any concession the capitalist class makes to the working class is often made in response to the persistent pressure of workers. Therefore, we find that capitalists tend to ignore the pain and poverty of the workers, and the terrible financial, psychological, medical, and cultural conditions in which they languish. The capitalists treat workers with indifference. They do not consider such matters from the standpoint of human rights, justice, or national interests. Rather, they measure all things in terms of their economic interests and labor output.

THE COMMUNIST PERSPECTIVE

In response to this unjust capitalist tenacity and the hostile capitalist attitude toward the workers' cause, some labor groups have taken counter actions bred by their desperation and deteriorating financial and spiritual conditions and stoked by certain anarchical groups adept in the art of Information, incitement, and agitation.

In short, the basis of the Communist perspective is the conglomeration of workers and their quest to apply pressure to have their mounting demands gradually fulfilled. Eventually, they aspire to establish total control by workers over the assets of society, impose a "dictatorship of the working class", eliminate classes and private ownership, and stamp out inheritance rights and private enterprise.

Moreover, the Communist perspective is closely interwoven with an international campaign to bond workers together in international conferences aimed to develop a common policy for workers from across all nations. The campaign aims to mold these workers into a single group committed to reaching out to other working class groups around the world. It gives them more attention and care than it gives its own nation and its progress. Thus, we find that the communist worker is inclined to feel that his immediate interests are more closely linked to those of the worker in another country than to the interests of the nation at large. His loyalty, too, tends to be to the working class around the world rather than to his own nation. Unsurprisingly, then, communist workers often feign to ignore nationalist calls, transcend national interests, and deem themselves above national loyalty. Only recently, we observed the Arab Communist Party in Palestine calling for mutual understanding with communist Jews to combat the Palestinian people in their struggle against the foremost danger facing the nation: the danger of Jewish settlement in Palestine epitomized in the Zionist movement.

THE NATIONAL PERSPECTIVE

Against these two sectional factions, which tend to foster

hostility, injustice, and exploitation in the nation, the National revival takes a counter position that has the capacity to ward off this hostility, surmount exploitation, and achieve social cohesion, national unity, state justice, and harmony among citizens. Let us discuss this perspective both in its fundamental premises and in its details.

1. The Fundamental Premises

1. The national doctrine begins by affirming the value and sanctity of work in the nation's life. It disdains and combats the contempt that aristocratic classes have for work. The national revival considers work a sacred duty in the life of society and measures the value of citizens in proportion to their contribution to national progress. The national revival does not want parasites that live in society on the shoulders of those toiling classes who bear the responsibilities of work and production. Each citizen must work so society can live a happy refined life and the citizen can live a life of dignity and honor.

2. However, work comes in various forms: economic, cultural, political, etc. Economic work falls in various subcategories: the entrepreneur is a worker, the manager is a worker, the technician is a worker, and employees are workers. Each of these categories of workers has rights and duties.

3. The distribution of output, according to the national doctrine, is based on the axiom of production itself. This principle of justice affirms the right of every citizen to free life and the fruits of his labor.

   The national revival is not prepared to relinquish the principle that justice is the basis for the sound distribution of wealth and awarding common producers. Any system that is not based on justice is corrupt at its foundations. Just as capitalist exploitation is inconsistent with social justice, likewise worker domination that seeks to exploit the other classes and deny them their right to life is inconsistent with justice. Hence, under the system of the national state, justice (which recognizes the right of every producer to benefit from the fruits of his work) is fully guaranteed.

4. Finally, the national doctrine insists on achieving the highest standards of living for every member of society, so that no class in society is deprived of life's basic freedoms and rights, as is the case with the working classes in our country.

2. Fair National Policies

Based on this, the sound national state is bound to enact fair policies that seek to preserve the rights of all groups, secure social justice, and foster harmony and mutual understanding instead of decay and division. These policies would define the principles of equitable pay and the conditions of work dismissal, safeguard the workers' right to rest by defining the hours of work they must perform and the time off they are entitled to, cover all the health provisions required to protect the workers' health and cater for their needs in times of disease, disability, old age, and sudden dangers, and secure the workers' right to express their opinions on the actions and procedures relevant to them. These policies must also contain provisions that protect the rights of employers to secure the continuation of work in an atmosphere conducive to national economies. Ensuring that these economies are not impeded and the rights of employers are not trampled is imperative.

3. Sound National Spirit

On its own, however, policy-making is insufficient. It is merely a formal legal expression of the right national spirit and the relationships that must prevail among citizens of all classes and groups. We cannot attain a perfectly good solution for the issues of work and workers except by infusing a national spirit into the people: the spirit of brotherhood, cooperation, mutual concern, and justice. Without this spirit, policy-making is of absolutely no value.

The spread of the national spirit among the ranks of workers and capital owners is the only way to solve work problems and achieve justice and brotherhood. The spirit alone can save society from capitalist exploitation and shield it against the infiltration of the destructive communist spirit of anarchy and demagoguery into the nation.

4

The National Party Appears Barefaced

Joy to the nation that considers the past and sees the likes of Baalbek in its heritage. This eternal legacy has defied an age roaming around in continuous attempts to annihilate it with an insatiable appetite. But woe to the nation that is glued to the past and does not look to the future to build an eternal future worthy of the eternal past!

Joy to the nation that boasts of its past, takes pride in it, and exerts conscious efforts to extricate it from the claws of intentional negligence and motivated forgetfulness. But woe to the nation that confines itself to boasting and accordingly neglects its present reality and its existing debilitating and degrading condition. It ignores its duty toward its future: a duty that is doubly imposed on it by the accumulation of its heritage in the past!

Joy to the nation that has known glories and grandeur, but woe to the nation that forgets that its real glories are only those it succeeds in saving from dissolution and extinction and that builds more glories to exult over. The National Party was founded based on this principle by a group of young people versed in the past of their nation and its achievements and endowed with a faith in their nation inspired by this knowledge. They marched forward to build their new nation in the light of this faith. In other words, a dynamic revival in the form of young people who believe that the nation can be, or rather will be, more than it was in the past.

Based on this principle, the National Party worked and struggled despite insurmountable obstacles to revive the nation it serves and to resurrect the people it loves. The Party's struggle is the most conclusive proof that the vitality of the past in all areas of human activity, which contributed to all the domains of glory, has not ceased to exist. Instead, it remains alive inside the people and is poised to rebound as soon as it receives the true call of duty.

Thus, the National Party was a real embodiment of the longing in the souls of sincere conscious citizens yearning for a new refined life whether or not they knew it. With its ideological cause and a framework that defines this yearning within a comprehensive conception of the meaning of nation and its cause, and with its reform programs, the Party became the ideal course for the people to pursue in their drive to revive the nation, realize its cause, consolidate its independence, and raise it to the peaks of glory. Additionally, with its practical application and the currents of revival emanating from it, the Party became the effective instrument that will ensure the implementation of the required reform.

Yes, indeed! The National Party represents the embodiment of the hopes that lurk within the souls of the people, the wishes that live in their hearts, and the duties that dwell in their consciences. Our eagerness to work for the Party and our belief in the success of its cause were born out of this realization and its commitment to the protection of the vital interests of the nation.

*****

Ladies and Gentlemen,

At one time, the affairs of the country were subject to the wills of its enemies who exercised total control over its resources. It was only natural for these enemies to focus on combating the burgeoning national revival, and simultaneously, actively encouraging all other groups and movements that represented the corruption of the existing order and worked to perpetuate foreign control. They did this instead of rising against corruption and trying to undermine the presence of foreign rule and domination.

The tallest trees bear the brunt of storms. Some of them break and bow down before the crushing power of a storm while others fall as it gradually pulls away. Meanwhile, little shrubs and plants pass through the crisis neither aware of the storm nor noticed by it. Similar to the storms, when popular discontent sets in and a nation rises in revolt, the colonial powers blink at the weak small movements with callous and total disregard to their presence. They mobilize their spies and supporters and all the forces and authority they command to combat the conscious strong fledging movements. Some of these movements yield to pressure and then recoil, while others emerge from under the pressure with their heads held high in might and honor.

The colonial foreigner was wiser than to oppress the national revival in a blunt and direct manner and more shrewd than to fight it for its patriotism in full public view. Therefore, he took a more cunning course: he tried to turn the people and its beguiled groups against the revival through the evil tactics of character assassination, rumor mongering, and fabricated accusations.

Accordingly, the colonizer placed the Party behind a very thick screen, muffled its voice, and chained its hands. He simultaneously devised false accusations against the Party and spread vicious rumors about it to tarnish its reputation and drive a wedge between it and the national population.

The Party sustained this situation. It traversed the campaign of malicious gossip and rumor mongering unaffected and unyielding. It was confident that the truth would inevitably come out. During that time, the rumors and allegations piled up. Some challenged the sincerity of the Party by claiming that it was a treasonous agent of foreign enemies! However, the accusers could not agree on the identity of this foreigner. Some said it was the Germans, Italians, British, French, or Zionists, but time proved them wrong. It proved that the Party is not and can never be a servant to the foreigner.

The sole objective of the Party is to revive the people, rekindle its power and vitality, and resurrect it from its deep slumber by

APPENDIX

relying entirely on the will of the people and their faith. Time proved that the Party that openly fought and is still fighting the foreigner (regardless of his color, format, and status, whether he is a colonialist or a mandated person, or whether he is a seeker of special privileges or a player behind the scenes) does not work behind closed doors to spread the domination and influence of the foreigner. It fought and is still fighting Zionism publicly, legally, politically, and practically. It declares that the Palestinian question is a matter of concern for the Lebanese and not an external problem; and it refuses to believe in Jewish racism and Zionist fossilization and materialism. Such a party cannot derive its inspiration from the Zionist. Time has demonstrated that the foreigner who fabricated this monstrous accusation and tried to prove it is the same foreigner whose prosecutor general once stood before a foreign military tribunal and withdrew from the bill of indictment the accusation against the Party that it cooperated with foreigners.

Others took aim at the Party's aims and principles. Some claimed that the Party is an enemy of the Lebanese entity and strives to undermine its existence. Others alleged that the Party is an enemy of Arab cooperation and seeks to tear it apart. Others still maintained that the Party merely aspires for a political union with adjacent states. The principles of the Party and the statements of its senior leaders have exposed these allegations to be patently false in every aspect, and the work of the Party has all but put them to rest. Indeed, the Party has proved, in both word and deed, that it does not seek a political union, a political merger, or a patch up fusion of states or statelets. Rather, its first and foremost mission is substantive and constructive reform in the realm of societal life. It is a social party versus a political party. It does not interfere in politics except when the nation stands in need of sound policy guidance on the most ideal programs for social reform. The Party has also demonstrated, in word and deed, that it is an enemy to every enemy of the independence and dignity of Lebanon and that it would defend this independence at any cost for the sake of consolidating Lebanon as a fortress for freedom and fundamental spiritual values. Finally, the Party has indicated, both practically and theoretically, that, for Lebanon to lead a safe life, it must not barricade itself behind a steel frame of hostility and constant quarrel with its neighbors. Ideally, a state of cordial political relations should exist between Lebanon and its neighbor states. There should be cooperation in all the domains of life consistent with regional realities and the principle of partnership. In addition, maximum cooperation and friendly relations should exist between Lebanon and all members of the Arab League within the framework of respect for the sovereignty of member states.

Others directed their criticism at the Reform Principles. They alleged that the Party seeks to undermine religion and constrict the work of the clergy by calling for national cohesion, repudiation of sectarian disunity and in-fighting, separation of religion from state, and the prevention of religious clerics from interfering with state and judicial affairs. However, they did not think to mention that the Party has a true and deep respect for religion and calls for the veneration of moral values. They neglected to reveal that it fights sectarianism because sectarianism corrupts religion and fractures the nation. They did not mention that the Party resists the interference of clerics in state affairs because it distracts them from their religious duties and subordinates state affairs to the control of individuals who are not qualified to manage the civil affairs of society.

Still others alleged that the Party was an enemy of feudalists although the Party is only an enemy of feudalism as a system: a bad system that squanders the wealth and resources of vast areas of the homeland and facilitates the creation of unemployed groups that live off the labor of toiling men and women screaming for help.

The accusations kept coming in succession, but the Party, confident that the truth would triumph in the final round, learned to tolerate them. That round has now come, and the light of truth has burst forth. The truth of the Party has become clear to all: its objectives, intentions, and programs. If the era of independence can claim one merit, it is that it has enabled the sincere groups in the country to work freely to demonstrate the reality of their causes. It has enabled them to scale the open podium of life with their true and bare faces and remove the thick screens of suppression and misguidance that had prevented this from happening in the past. Thus, the present era can take pride in the fact that it enabled the first step on the path to true independence.

*****

Ladies and Gentlemen,

I do not intend to explain to you in this address the principles, objectives, and program of the Party. These principles have been amply proclaimed, published, and clarified; and the people have lost faith in mere rhetoric and want deeds and actions. Let us ask then, "What has the Party achieved so far and what is it doing?"

First, the National Party practically managed to restore to the nation its sovereignty and control over its affairs well before it had obtained its political sovereignty and independence. During the colonial era, the Party defied the authority of the ruling colonialist, his Senegalese lances, and his tanks, prisons, detention camps, press campaigns, and speeches. It challenged his will to maintain the status quo as it existed. It stood firm disseminating the call for the nation's cause and preaching the reform principles that lead to the advancement of society. With this, the nation's sovereignty and will were effectively realized.

Second, the Party has practically succeeded in achieving social unity and popular consensus. Instead of a people riven with antagonistic factions, conflicting classes, and warring families, the Party has given rise to a group of young people solely committed to nothing else but their participation in a unified national life, and unwilling to identify with any form of communal solidarity, whether it is sectarian or class or clannish, as elements that divide the people unnecessarily and tear its unity apart.

Third, the Party has truly succeeded in building a new citizen despite the old environment and the currents of backward and spurious life that envelop it. It has liberated him from these forces, aroused in him the sense of responsibility and duty, empowered him with strength and discipline, and launched him into society as an unswayable and loyal soldier shining the light of a new and progressive life on society.

Fourth, the Party has practically succeeded in creating a prototype of the new society to which the nation aspires: a society of modern upright citizens whose new life rotates within the life of the old society as a leaven working to change the old condition in its entirety.

Fifth, the Party has succeeded in steering the nation in the right social direction and in educating the people about the reality of the national issues they are likely to encounter in the course of life. Through its proclamations, statements, bulletins, lectures, and speeches, the Party has provided much needed guidance to the people. It has helped the nation understand its interests by lighting the way before it and clarifying its issues and concerns as they arose. Such a service is of great value in a country whose people are in short supply of rational guidance and sensible leadership.

Sixth, the Party has eliminated the myth that we are people unworthy of life and cannot rely on ourselves. With this, it restored self-confidence to the nation, guided it to areas of strength buried inside it, and rekindled a new faith in a new future.

Seventh, the Party manifested certain fighting virtues and struggle ethics for which the nation was in dire need. It allowed these virtues to blossom over the years bursting with impediments, obstructions, and persecutions. The history of the Party's struggle is ample proof of its sincerity and of the heroism of its members.

Appendix

At a time when loyalty to the nation was an object of ridicule and mockery, reckless allegations by the deceived and misguided, and the recoil of the indifferent, the Nationalists were surging with an incredible faith to defy such a sick spirit. They relished every persecution and endured humiliation for the sake of the nation's life. They affirmed its right to exist, or rather, what is more sublime than existence: its right to freedom, dignity, and progress.

At a time when the public arenas were packed with fakers claiming that the price of struggle and fighting should be awarded to them, the Nationalists were brimming with the resolve of the believer that such a price and the sacrifices that must be endured as a price for victory ought to be borne by him.

At a time when the so-called advocates of patriotism were dispersing and fleeing at the first shock, leaving others to bear its brunt, dodging responsibilities, and being unconcerned except for their own standing and reputation, the Nationalists were dashing to sacrifice (the silent kind of sacrifice). They were fuelled by the insistence that each of them should carry the burden of the entire nation and shoulder the entire shock that strikes the soldiers of reform in the battles of life.

At a time when men lurked in the corners of their homes, satisfied with securing their livelihood and seeking to keep life going, the nationalists were disdaining livelihood and scorning life because they had envisioned something more sublime than life itself: to contribute to the betterment of life, its advancement, and revival anew.

At a time when patriotism was a function of deeply confused and disoriented political work and a parody of vague and resounding slogans, the nationalists were treating their movement as no less than a total revolution spinning inside every soul and penetrating every city, village, and home to shake off the old, destroy the corrupt, and establish the edifice of a new sound life.

At a time when parties and movements were established with meteoric speed only to collapse under the pressure of circumstances or hollow structure or lack of resources, the National Revival was a unique and striking phenomenon in the history of this nation. Its enduring spirit, tenacious struggle, and a firmness that knows no retreat or compromise marked it distinctly from all other movements. It was determined to stay the full course until final destiny.

Finally, at a time when politicians were trying to attract great masses, enticing them, and begging for their applause, the National Party was working hard to build the new individual: a conscious and mature person who is prepared to volunteer as a soldier in the salvation movement and who expects no reward save sacrifices and difficulties.

These new virtues of struggle, which manifested themselves in the National Revival, thus forming a unique new phenomenon in the history of the nation, are our joy and the source of our pride. They are the testimony of history to the eternity of our cause and the integrity of our movement. We present them to you, Ladies and Gentlemen, as proof of the values that define the National Party.

Also, Ladies and Gentlemen, you and the rest of the population are the arbitrators to whom we resort for judgment of our revival and the support on whom we lean in our confidence in the victory of this revival. Our victory is your victory. Our goal is to make the people happy and jubilant. We refuse to derive strength or popularity except through the support of the people, and we refuse to streak to the final victory except by the will of the people.

5

THE NATION IS ONE SOCIAL COMMUNITY

The National Party does not suffice with the political dimension of national life. Nor does it suffice with independence as a political reality to achieve. The Party does not make the error of ascribing the maladies of society to foreign wills. Indeed, internal danger is more serious than external danger. If combating external dangers is a component of treating a disease, then combating internal dangers is a precaution against contracting the disease in the first place.

Moreover, the Party does not regard independence as the pinnacle of national struggle. Instead, it considers independence a starting point in its illustrious journey. Independence is not an end in itself, but a means to attain the primary objective of our nation's ascendancy and dignity. True independence is not mere legal formalities: it is a slow, silent, and endless internal reconstruction process.

Therefore, the Party distinguishes between independence as a mere political concern and true independence that encompasses all aspects of life. It declares that true independence is (a) a perpetual internal struggle; (b) independence from internal corruption, maladies, and the forces of its decadence; and (c) independence from external interests and their objects. At a time when patriotic movements focused on the political aim, confining their efforts to arbitrary activities in pursuit of independence in its narrow political sense, the National Party announced a comprehensive national program of action that transcends politics, extends to all the interests and aspects of life, and expands beyond the narrow political sphere. Hence, the Party was the first national movement to integrate economic, social, cultural, and intellectual affairs in its reform program and to declare that the nation's revival would remain incomplete if it does not occur in each of these fields.

Accordingly, the Party inclines toward the social aspect. It analyzes its weaknesses and presents programs for their treatment. Meanwhile, it has found the primary danger to society's unity and the chief impediment to mobilizing the nation's powers to defend its rights and desire for progress in the nation's disintegration into hostile groups. Consequently, the Party declared that the nation is one social community and set out to proclaim that sectarian divisions, tribal hostilities, class struggle, and all other forms of division in the nation are national dangers that must be mastered and overcome. It also declared an unrelenting war on all aspects of our social lifestyle that are likely to augment the various manifestations of these divisions. Thus, it fought sectarianism in policy-making and spoke against the interference of the clergy in the affairs of the national state and its judiciary. Through this attitude, the Party restored the spiritual relation between man and God. To religion, it restored the holy position that befits it and the respect it deserves when it rises to the center of spiritual power that dwells in souls and deems itself far above being a tool of exploitation or a catalyst for enmity and hate. By combating sectarianism, the Party saved religion and authentic religiosity from the thorns dotted around them.

Some of the results of the basic principle "the Nation is one social community" are:

- The internal unity of society as a condition more desirable than fragmentation and hostility;

- The participation of all citizens in the life of their nation, each within the context of their own class and profession regardless of their sect, region, and family;

- The need to respect the diversity of classes, sects, duties, and professions and to consider this diversity a source of

APPENDIX

enrichment to the national life instead of seeking to suppress it or encouraging conflict between the groups;

- The capacity of every citizen to carry out their vocation in the service of the nation;

- The need to respect the right of every citizen in life and the respect that the citizen must demonstrate for his or her duties toward society.

6

Reform in National Life

Any living being must have justification for its existence. These justifications vary. Some originate from the will of those with concentrated interests clutching to existence, while others originate from the wills of groups that rebel against such interests and rise to destroy them and eliminate them from existence.

What is the justification for the existence of the National Party and its survival and endurance? When foreign imperialism was crouching heavily on our nation's chest, stifling its breath, shackling its hands, sucking its blood, paralyzing its powers, tearing its unity apart, and impeding its development and progress, the semi-partisan political movements and self-styled leaders and pseudo-leaders had no slogan to define themselves and their work except passive patriotism and liberation from the foreigner. But this was a passive slogan: pale and stricken. Indeed, it was a confused and bewildered slogan with no direction.

The patriotic movements would sing the praises of independence, but for them, independence was only a sentimental expression to which the masses were too much inclined and which orators could use to beg for applause. Independence at the time, with its confused meaning and undefined essence, constituted the final stage of national struggle and the point at which all hopes and expectations ended. It was a mere expedient for the self-serving, the seekers of fame, the professional maneuverers, and those who barter with the most sacred sentiments of the people.

In the midst of that emotional exuberance formed of a sound tendency toward a life marred with the passivity of the work for independence as such and misguided by the expediency of opportunistic political corporations, a man as obstinate as conscience, as solid as steel, and as firm in faith as a mountain stood up. An army of vigilant faithful youth stood behind him.

Appendix

He aroused slumbering powers inert in the souls of the nation to gush forth, fiercely and daringly, to rush and crush the obstacles that the colonialist and the dwarves (who found their support in colonialism and in whom colonialism found its best support) had placed in their way. Amid that emotional exuberance, a man stood up and screamed:

Independence in itself is not my nation's ambition. Nor is it the aim of the sacred current that cries out loud deep inside my brothers' thoughts, yearning for a free sublime life. Independence is not an objective where our hopes end and our efforts cease upon attaining it. Independence is not the culminating point of struggle. Rather, true independence is only the curtain raiser for the solemn stage of exalted struggle.

A liberation that suffices with ejecting the foreigner and leaves his legacy of germs and parasites to roam freely and actively in the nation's body is nothing but a superficial, deceptive, and empty liberation. A liberation that does not seek to achieve the objectives that subjugation has prevented us from realizing is, in every respect, subjugation. Our liberation from others, if it does not originate from liberation in ourselves, is baseless.

If we respond to the call for liberation and work for it while we are not free and are not enjoying the blessing of creativity and innovation that lie at the essence of freedom, then the freedom that we demand is a shame on us and a smirch on our history.

If we succeed in saving ourselves from the oppression of the foreigner without saving ourselves from his legacy of diseases, weaknesses, poverty, hunger, chaos, disunity, sterility, indifference and lack of confidence; if we suffice with a ceremonial freedom without freeing ourselves from the nightmare of slavery whose germs have gnawed at the core of our consciences; if we remove the foreigner, but our history remains tied to his whims and dictated by his will and our future remains subservient to currents and circumstances not within our grasp, then we would have done no service to our nation.

The cry of a true national conscience crystalized in a righteous son of this country and resonated in a national revival. It has since been vindicated by the course of events. For, independence did come, and here we are living in its shadow. But is this the ideal outcome we had hoped for? Has sectarianism disappeared; has class discrimination dissipated; has exploitation and monopoly receded; and has chaos and scandals in the administration abated? Are we basking in economic prosperity, security, safety, stability, and freedom of opinion and speech?

I will leave the answer to the conscience of each listener. The answer I might give is likely to be less vicious than the answer your conscience might give.

*****

The National Party's first message is: "Formal independence in itself is not our ultimate aim, but rather the pursuit of a free, advanced, and prosperous life."

The National Party's fundamental aim is: "Our objective is not to work and struggle for the sake of a formal independence that (a) is granted by the foreigner under the pressure of circumstances and the exigencies of international conflict; (b) maintains corruption and iniquities as they are; and (c) sustains the elements of slavery on the inside. Rather, our aim is to work and struggle to build a new nation; to resurrect the national conscience; to define the path to a truly good and correct life, and to uproot the evils and corruption that contribute to our sterility, humiliation, disunity, and our perpetual deterioration."

Additionally, this is the cry of the National Party: "We do not consider the evacuation of foreign armies – officially finalized today from our beloved Lebanon - practically and literally complete until it is paired with the evacuation of all the maladies under which the people groan and is directly coupled with true comprehensive and fundamental reform."

The National Party denotes: "The Party is not a mere political alliance or an organization that indulges in superficialities, styles, formal uniforms, ranks, and Information. Nay! The Party is the conscience of a nation that has awakened, and the spirit of a people that has rebelled in pursuit of glories. The National Party embodies this awakening of the consciences of the faithful aroused by the memories of ancient glories and stirred by the belief that the nation can be and will be as glorious as it was in the past."

The main justification for the existence of the National Party is to work toward:

- resurrecting and reviving the nation,
- liberating it internally,
- building it on sound foundations,
- establishing edifices of justice, love, and solidarity throughout it,
- reviving its confidence in itself, and
- raising it to the summits of glory and to heights where only eagles soar.

Subsequently, if someone asks: "What justification is there for the existence of the National Party now that we have attained independence and the evacuation of all foreign troops is complete?" we answer: "Today – particularly today, and today more than ever – the existence of the National Party is an indispensable necessity in view of its constructive reform commitment."

We are well aware that the reform we desire – a reform that encompasses all aspects of our national life – cannot be attained unless it is comprehensive and unbroken or truncated. It cannot be realized through patchwork but only through basic destruction and reconstruction. It cannot be achieved by treating the effects but by treating the causes. It cannot be embedded into institutions and systems before it is embedded, first, into the ethos of individuals.

Accordingly, the National Party has determined that individual personal reform, as a factor that takes place in the depth of every citizen, is the only key to effective reform, because construction is less concerned with outward appearances, styles, and superficialities and more concerned with foundations, pillars, and mainstays.

The general reform of the nation, which can only be conducted by the will of the nation and which only emerges from the people, pivots around a single axis: the ethos of the citizens. For this reason alone, the National Party managed to carry out its slow and silent work unaffected by the buzz of clamor and undaunted by the ignorance of the uncomprehending except through clamor and commotion.

The Party has done its work well to build the new citizen. This citizen is loyal to his nation; works hard in its cause; is fully aware of the nation's entity, unity, and mission; and is free of the vices of selfishness, greed, and exploitation. The heart of the citizen is full of faith in himself, his cause, and his country. It pulsates with love and cooperation. He is aware of his responsibility and propelled by the power of duty; and he is strong by the power of spirit and faith. One day, this new citizen will be the pillar of the new nation.

Indeed, the National Party has worked hard to build this new citizen. The totality of these citizens, in their interaction in the Party, has formed a new society in the heart of the old and worn-out society: a leaven to resurrect the new nation and disseminate high ideals and new virtues in it. Indeed, the Party has been an enterprise that embodies this new nation and a vanguard of its advent. The Party, thus, has been the conscience of the nation that awakened after a long slumber only to become, in itself, the vanguard of the new nation and its model. The Party has been the living voice of the nation that cries out to the nation so that it can live. It is the echo of this cry and the embodiment of the life of the new nation.

*****

Therefore, we see the Party as a reformist institution that strives for reform and not for any private ambition. We deem the Party above having any interest other than the nation's interest, especially as it teaches its members that: "the nation's interest supersedes every other interest." Far be it that the Party would make itself a barrier between the citizen and serving the nation.

We are not driven by conceit to claim total monopoly on devotion to the nation. Nay! We declare that every individual who works for the good of the nation and seeks its salvation with the right methods is a valued comrade to us, whether or not he joins the Party. To us, the Party is a means and the nationalist, from our standpoint, is a soldier: a silent soldier who works for the good of the nation without ambition for reward.

7

THE PARTY IS A LEAVEN FOR THE NATION'S LIFE

Granted first that "party" is a symbol of the nation's sovereignty and a vehicle for the practical fulfillment of this sovereignty; second that it is an institution to nurture the young generation and to develop and rear citizens; and third that it is a practical system for implementing some reform projects and developing modern institutions, the "party" is an indispensable and vital necessity in the nation's life. The people cannot build an advanced national life and enjoy a life of freedom and prosperity unless the right kind of party rises among them. However, there is a fourth and final purpose for the "party" that is a by-product and the result of the three other purposes. The party, in its members, supporters and advocates, is like a leaven in the nation's body. From it, new virtues, high ideals, and fresh faith penetrate and seep into the ranks of the people.

In the body of an ageing, deteriorating nation lying dormant over its weaknesses, desperate of the possibility of reform, and torn into factions, sects, classes, and clans — in the heart of such a nation, the party is, a new society and a new nation spinning with a new life. A good party represents the nation of tomorrow in the nucleus of the nation of today and yesterday! It represents the embodiment of sound values and sublime ideals and their dynamic implementation in the heart of a weak and backward nation.

Accordingly, a good party evokes conflict between the tendency for renewal that it represents and society's tightly held forces of conservatism and reaction. As the bearer of the banner of liberation in a battle fought inside the soul of each citizen, its echoes reverberate in every sphere of the nation. It is a reservoir of the forces of momentum that stir up revival and liberation, feed it with fuel, and furnish it with firmness, intrepidity, and perseverance. In the course of its life, in the virtues that are embodied in that course, and in the interaction between its members that translates, consequently, into mutual cooperation and collective determination, the party is a perpetual fountain of dynamic vitality in the nation's body: a vitality that seeks to root out its vices and create a new nation.

Therefore, if the party is an institution that embodies the new values and systems, and if it is a source for their conflict with the old values and systems at the core of the nation's entity, then it is a harbinger of the establishment of the new nation. Indeed, it is the rising free new nation in its first incarnation. It is the new nation unveiled at the heart of a nation desperate for renewal. It is the new life taking shape and running in the veins of the present nation to renew its blood, energy, and vitality. It is the virtuous nation we seek, the nation we work to build, which now exists among us and which we have seen in the lives of its children and in their interaction. The party is indeed the nation of tomorrow within the nation of today. The party is an entity that will create a nation in its own image and after its model.

8

NOTE ON THE PALESTINE PROBLEM

SUBMITTED TO THE ANGLO-AMERICAN INQUIRY COMMITTEE PREPARED, ON BEHALF OF THE NATIONAL PARTY

FAYIZ SAYIGH, M. A.

BEIRUT - MARCH 19TH, 1946

Mr. Chairman, Gentlemen of the Committee

It gives me pleasure to express my gratitude for the privilege kindly accorded me of presenting to your honourable Committee the point of view of the National Party, concerning a problem which we consider to be vital and of great significance, and upon the just solution of which peace and security in the Holy Land and in the Near East will depend.

The National Party has, as a matter of fact, hesitated before deciding to present its point of view to your honourable Committee: for our experiences of previous Commissions, that had inquired into the Palestine Problem, and attempted to reach a just solution for it, without avail, are not very encouraging; and national groups, in the Arab World, have developed - not without reason - an attitude of suspicion towards the possibility of arriving at a just solution of the Palestine Problem through Investigation Commissions.

But, in deciding to present its point of view to your honorable Committee, the National Party has given fresh evidence of the deep-rooted confidence which our people have in your sense of justice, as well as in the sincere resolve of the British Government to come at last to a just solution of the Palestine Problem.

Appendix

I. The Right Approach To The Palestine Problem

It behooves us, at this stage, to look back upon the above-mentioned attempts of previous Commissions to offer successful solutions to the Palestine Problem, and to study the causes of the failures of such attempts as such a study may save us from falling again into previous errors. In this spirit and with this objective I beg to digress, at the outset of this Note, into casting a glance at the natural limitations of the methods of inquiry of previous Commissions, and the principles determining their study of the Problem, which could not but render their efforts futile.

1. In the first place, the previous studies of the Problem have all taken their departure from an erroneous starting-point. For it was the promises given by British Officials to Jewish and Arab representatives, and binding the British Government to definite lines of policy, that have been studied; and it is the reconciliation of such conflicting pledges through giving them particular interpretations, that has been attempted. This, however, is considered by us an erroneous starting-point, and an erroneous manner of approach, not only because - empirically - the attempts have proved fruitless, but also because they were *a priori* doomed to failure: for they did not look upon the problem - as they ought to have done - from the standpoint of a judge seeking to redress a grievance, nor from the viewpoint of an arbiter aiming at giving a just solution, but rather from the position of a politician desiring to mitigate an embarrassing perplexing situation, and to disentangle a complex knot, which is rendered all the more intricate by the conflicting pledges that have gone to create it. It is in this very conception of the Problem that the difficulty of reaching a solution for it lies; and it is precisely this conception of the Problem that gives it the character of apparent insolubility which it seems to possess.

In our opinion, such an approach must give way to an alternative approach. The traditional conception of the Palestine Problem as a dilemma with which the Promising Authorities are confronted, due to their simultaneous declaration of contradictory and irreconcilable promises, must be exchanged for the alternative view of the Problem as an injustice which the Palestinians have been made to suffer through the introduction, into their country, of an alien people, ambitious enough to look upon this country as their own, and to seek to transform it into a national home wherein they will be not only the numerical majority, but the ruling power of the state as well! For, indeed, it is this that is the problem; and it is from this angle that it has to be viewed.

If it is true that an erroneous conception of a problem, and a wrong approach to it, inevitably lead to an erroneous solution, and consequently preclude the possibility of finding a real solution at all - it follows that the previous failures of all attempts to solve the Palestine Problem are due less to an intrinsic insolubility than to an unfortunate blunder in the approach to it.

2. Going side by side with this erroneous starting-point, and rendering the problem all the more intricate, was the error of linking up the solution of the world-wide Jewish Problem with the solution of the Palestine Problem. Such an attitude is erroneous not only because the former Problem is extremely complicated, and involves International Jewry on the one hand, and the whole Western World on the other, but also and primarily because, on principle, it links up two independent problems, and suspends the solution of one of them until the other is settled.

In recording this fact, we have the pleasure to record our sincere appreciation of the wise distinction between the two Problems, which has been recognized by your honourable Committee; and we welcome this new approach to the Palestine Problem as a measure that will put your investigations, from the very start, on the right track.

For the truth is that the unfortunate situation of World Jewry (which certainly, provokes our sympathy and the sympathy of all humanitarian people) must not be remedied by any such measures as would involve equal misery to another nation, or would simply pass on the plight of one people to another. If the world-wide Jewish difficulty has to be settled (and the effort to settle it is certainly one upon which we look with sympathy and appreciation), it still must not be settled in such a way as to create a new and equal difficulty to a people which, to say the least, is not responsible for it. To seek to alleviate the sufferings of the Jews, by causing equal sufferings to another people, is not only an unreasonable attempt; nor only a fruitless attempt (seeing that Palestine certainly cannot solve the Jewish Problem); nor only an imprudent attempt (which would create a new problem, while leaving the first unsolved) but also and primarily an unjust attempt, which imposes new miseries upon a people which is by no means responsible for the miseries, the alleviation of which is being sought.

We have no intention, in this Note, to make a study of the Jewish Problem, nor to offer proposals for its settlement: but we insist that the Palestine Problem has been rendered insoluble precisely by this artificial link that has been made between its solution and the solution of the Jewish Problem. And while we assure your honourable Committee of the sympathies which our people have towards the alleviation of all sufferings, and the settlement of the world-wide Jewish Problem, we beg also to emphasize that a continuation of the attempt to make such alleviation and settlement at the expense of the national rights of the Palestinians, is a moral blow to our confidence in the sense of justice that prompts such settlements, and a serious impediment against all good will in the Arab World towards the British Government, as well as against security in the Holy Land and in the Arab World in general.

3. A third confusion that has proved detrimental to the previous attempts to solve the Palestine Problem was the confusion concerning the real objective of the attempts. For, in all such attempts, what has been sought was a compromise rather than a genuine solution - a compromise that has "peace" for its aim

rather than a "justice". In our view, there are situations when peace ought to be sacrificed for justice: and the whole experience of humanity in the last war has been a confirmation of this belief. It is not peace at-all-costs that true peace-lovers work for; but rather a just peace; and even extreme pacifists are at times confronted by situations where a just peace seems unattainable, and where justice is preferred to peace. The Palestine Problem seems to confront its investigators with such a situation; and where the alternatives are either a compromise which sacrifices justice, or a sincere loyalty to justice even at the risk of disorder and unrest, then the moral sense ingrained in the peace-loving conscience ought to suspend its pursuit of peace in the name of its endeavour to achieve justice. In the name of true peace in the Holy Land, we insist that an unjust peace must be abandoned, and justice must be first sought!

It would appear from the above survey that only if the Palestine Problem is looked upon by your honourable Committee as a national problem in the first place, involving the fate of a nation rather than the pledges of a foreign power, and only if the said Problem is distinguished from the Jewish Problem, and its solution is separated from the settlement of the latter; - and only if the solution is sought in the direction of justice rather than in the direction of formal stability resting upon unjust foundations: only then will the Palestine Problem be really understood, and your efforts to find a solution for it prove fruitful. And, when viewed in this light, the solution will not be far to find.

It is from this angle that we shall present to your honourable Committee the grievance of the Palestine People, and describe the nature of the Palestine Problem - confident that the very presentation of the Problem in this light is itself the sure guide to its solution, and the true pathway to the achievement of justice.

APPENDIX

II. THE NATURE OF THE PALESTINE PROBLEM

A. HISTORICAL ORIGIN

It does not require a thorough acquaintance with the history of Palestine to realize that the country is, socially and economically, a part of a wider social unity, a fraction of a national community; and that its isolation and segregation into a political territory is only an arbitrary act, justified by, and depending upon, no natural factors and considerations. As a matter of fact, such isolation, when introduced after the First World War, was not only provocative of serious protests both within and outside Palestine, but also was detrimental to its National, social and economic interests. So, historically, the Palestine problem goes side by side with the creation of Palestine as a political entity, and such a creation is itself part of the problem in its wider aspects.

Social life in Palestine, even before the emergence of nationalism, was part of a wider social life in a community which "developed freely within the boundaries of the Syrian country" immediately, and within the Arab World in general.

Into the territory of which Palestine was a part, hordes of Semitic tribesmen, of various branches, infiltrated, peacefully at times, and warringly at times; and, through the contact and interaction of these various groups, a process of national social blending developed and continued from time immemorial. Within this social context, social, economic and cultural interaction resulted in the amalgamation and fusion of these racial groups, and in the emergence of a national community with a distinctive national character. Arabic groups - among other groups - had infiltrated into the country on various occasions: but by far the most influential movement, both numerically and politically, was the general movement of Arab penetration, after the rise of Islam, which settled in the country (and in neighbouring countries), and interacted with the pre-existing population, and gave the nation its languages. The newcomers interacted also with the pre-existing national culture, thus making of the nation an Arab nation, more strongly akin to its sister-nations than ever before. It follows that the "Arabs of Palestine" of the present day are the descendants of that ancient native stock, living in the country from time immemorial.

Jewish immigration, it goes without saying, was thus not an exceptional movement in the history of the country. But, as is well known, it was predominantly a movement of warfare; and the Hebrews penetrated into the country as conquerors, and established their principalities by the force of arms. Thanks mainly to their deep-rooted Messianism; and their racial belief in their chosenness as a people, and in their ordination for a divine mission appointed to them by God; and their resultant racial exclusiveness, the Hebrews failed to be assimilated within the wider social community, into whose life they had entered as intruders, and in which they maintained their aloofness and segregation. When their defeat at the hands of foreign armies took place, and their dispersion ensued, they left behind them not a home from which they were expatriated, but rather a temporary abode, into which they had entered by warfare, within which they had maintained their precarious rule as victors, and from which they were expelled as a vanquished race.

The subsequent career of the Jews - the intensification of their Messianism, their further crystallization as a defeated and grieved race, their subsequent inner solidarity as an embittered minority, their aspiration for the repetition of a golden age of political dominance and freedom associated with Palestine, their belief in a divine promise to re-assemble in the Holy Land, all these spiritual developments, born of frustration and of hope, are not parts of the history of Palestine, but rather of the racial history of the Jews.

In due course, however, such spiritual feelings and aspirations as the Jews had developed, were passed from one generation of Jews to another, all over the countries of their dispersion; and grew in intensity as time passed on, failing to disappear, due to their religious and literary associations. And instead of the assimilation of the Jews in their new abodes, there arose the unfortunate phenomenon of a racial group, jealous of its internal solidarity, proud of its religious and cultural mission, and ever-aspiring to return to a country it believes to be its own. Such a lack of preparedness on the part of the Jews to be assimilated naturally resulted in a corresponding unwillingness to have them assimilated; and a mutual feeling of embitterment and ill will arose between the Jews and their hosts. The fact that this feeling emerged in more than one national community, goes to prove that no one particular nation is responsible for it, but rather that the Jews themselves bear the first responsibility.

The Jewish Problem, thus arose before the advent of the Jews into Palestine, was maintained during their temporary sojourn in Palestine, and grew more intense after their dispersion; and it is evident that the Jews themselves, to say the least, are not entirely innocent of the charge of having contributed to the rise of such a situation of ill will between them and the world.

The Jews, however, did not abandon their golden dream of returning to Palestine, where at last they would resuscitate the brief period of their political dominance. And, whenever circumstances proved promising, they made use of the opportunity to transform their age-long aspirations into a very pressing demand and necessity of the moment! Hence the rise of Zionism in the last century.

The history of Zionism coincides partly with the history of Palestine only after the Balfour Declaration - whereby the Jews were given access to Palestine, backed by the official pledge of the British Government of "using their best endeavours to facilitate the establishment in Palestine of a 'national home for the Jewish people' ". In this Declaration, the Palestine Problem was created. By this Declaration, Palestine was laid open for the penetration of Jews for the establishment of their national home.

Against this Declaration, and all subsequent measures inspired thereby, the Palestinians rose in protests, even at the costly price of bloodshed, martyrdom, and turmoil in the Holy Land. Through this Declaration, a supreme act of injustice, unparalleled in history, was enforced, sanctioned by the approval of the League of Nations, and realized by the mobilization of World-Jewry for the purpose, and the support of the British Government... And only by the formal abandonment of this Declaration as an official line of policy of the British Government, will the Palestine grievance be redressed and the Palestine Problem solved.

B. THE BALFOUR DECLARATION

The cornerstone of the Palestine Problem, thus, is the Balfour Declaration, the invalidity and illegitimacy of which are beyond dispute. We will not dwell here, at length, upon the various features of this Declaration which make it invalid as a political and legal document, but will content ourselves with the citation of such features:

1. The Balfour Declaration goes counter to the pledge which the British Government had previously given, through Sir Henry MacMahon, to King Hussein, in 1915.

2. The Balfour Declaration contains an inner inconsistency: for it is clear that "the establishment in Palestine of a national home for the Jewish people" is inconsistent with the condition, which the Declaration insists upon in the same breath that "nothing shall be done which may prejudice the civil and religious rights of existing non-Jewish communities in Palestine".

3. The Balfour Declaration was given at a time when the British Government was not empowered by the League of Nations to have any domination over Palestine.

4. The Declaration, when incorporated in the Preamble and the 2nd, 9th, 6th and 7th Articles of the Mandate, was in violation of the 2nd Article of the Covenant of the League

of Nations, from the provisions of which the Mandate itself emanated.

Upon these and similar legal and political shortcomings, from which the Declaration suffers, we shall not here dwell; it being considered by us that the real invalidity of the Declaration derives from the following two considerations:

1. The Balfour Declaration goes counter to the principle of nationalism and national self-determination, and to the very elemental rights of national existence and sovereignty. Our rejection of the Balfour Declaration arises from this starting-point: the trespassing against the national rights of the Palestinian people. What we reject is precisely the arbitrary treatment of Palestine, and the determination of its destiny by powers not authorized to interfere in the fate of that country. The rights of the Palestinian people in their country are natural national rights, derived from their social interaction in the land, and their occupation thereof from time immemorial - and not contingent political rights, which can be acknowledged or denied by the arbitrary declarations given by irresponsible and incompetent authorities. The destiny of Palestine is not an internal British problem, which Britain is authorized to settle arbitrarily, and concerning which the British can give promises and issue declarations; and consequently, the Balfour Declaration is an illegitimate document, which may bind the British Government, but which certainly does not bind the Palestinians at all; and the Palestinians have rejected the Declaration, and will continue to reject it, backed by the support of the whole Arab World; and if they will succumb to it at all, it is a submission to the force of might, rather than to the authority of justice and right!

The Balfour Declaration is, thus, invalid, by virtue of the incompetence of its issuing authorities; it is consequently an unjust document, an eternal symbol of injustice and transgression, an eternal sin against humanitarian conscience, as well as against the principles of national existence and international behaviour and cooperation. The unanimous and persistent rejection of the Declaration by the Palestinians demonstrates its illegitimacy and invalidity.

Any attempts to justify the Declaration retrospectively, by emphasizing the alleged progress and economic prosperity in Palestine brought about by the advent of the Jews, are beside the point entirely: for, in the first place, it is highly debatable whether economic prosperity is preferable to national existence, and whether a prosperity necessarily attended by such far-reaching national dangers as the 'Jewish nationalization of Palestine threatens the country with, is worthwhile at all; and, in the second place, it is an inalienable right of the people concerned to determine freely whether it would accept economic prosperity as a by-product of the ambitious scheme of the nationalization of the country by an alien people, seeking to establish in that country a national home of its own. The Palestine people has decided the last question, by giving its emphatic refusal to be made economically prosperous at the expense of being reduced to the status of a ruled minority in its own homeland!

2. The Balfour Declaration has facilitated the rise of a system of life in Palestine, which contradicts essentially the principles upon which true democracy and genuine international brotherhood rest – those principles for the safeguarding of which the last war has been fought and millions of lives have been sacrificed.

For, in the Holy Land, and under the auspices of the British Government, a community has developed and organized itself upon the principles of racialism - racial segregation and exclusiveness, racial superiority and domination. A regime of extreme racialism has been established, in this corner of the globe, under the auspices of that same British Government which led, only a short time ago, the most heroic war against racialism - and, so the paradox of history would have it, this regime has been established by the very first victims of Nazi racialism, those victims whose help, and the alleviation of whose sufferings, have been sought by all humanitarian peoples; those victims, in the name of whose rescue many a moving appeal to the conscience of the world is made! And, in this same Holy Land, and under the same Zionist regime, a ruthless terrorist movement has been organized, which declared war on the British forces and institutions and civilian citizens for the reluctance of the British to sustain the Jewish racial cause to the extreme ends that these terrorists want.

History will record this embarrassing paradox with reproach pointing out emphatically to the unreasonableness of that policy of encouragement and support which has been adopted towards the Jewish cause: a cause which builds itself upon the viscous principles of racialism, and threatens, in a spirit of arrogant and pugnacious racialism, the very existence of a people into whose land the Jews have been allowed to come as refugees from a ruthless campaign of racial persecution.

For these two reasons, it would clearly appear to any impartial observer that the Balfour Declaration, the cornerstone of the Palestine Problem, - apart from being void of any legal validity - is a violation of the sacred rights of national existence, and the equally sacred principles of international cooperation and brotherhood.

Proposals For The Solution Of The Palestine Problem

The above analysis of the Palestine Problem, we believe, is a guide to its just solution.

The Palestine Problem is not intrinsically insoluble: its true understanding is the guarantee of the understanding of its just settlement. Its settlement requires courage to face facts, a sense of justice, and a sincere determination to enforce it - even though the enforcement of justice may involve difficulties, entail sacrifices, and lead to a period of insecurity and turmoil.

The Palestine Problem, we have shown, is a serious grievance; and only a sincere resolve to redress this grievance will restore justice; and, in the long run, peace and good will, to the Holy Land.

We are fully confident that your honourable Committee will not fail to recommend the measures imposed by the sense of justice.

With this confidence, we offer, in conclusion, our proposals for the just settlement of the Palestine Problem:

1. The abandonment of the Balfour Declaration and all the obligations it involves. Such an abandonment will necessarily involve:

    (a) - the cessation of Jewish immigration into Palestine, and the combating of illegal immigration relentlessly;

    (b) - the facilitation, for all Jews desirous of leaving the country, to depart without any governmental difficulties or any impediments by Zionist organizations;

    (c) - the prevention of all transfers or sales of land or property, directly or indirectly, to the Jews, all over Palestine.

2. The recognition of the independence of Palestine, and the facilitation of the establishment of a democratic system of self-rule.

Conclusion

Gentlemen

You are entrusted with an extremely serious and historic responsibility, which is nothing less than the restoration of justice to a country that has been unjustly treated.

Appendix

It is the sincere hope of the National Party that the aspirations of all peace-loving people in the Arab World will not be frustrated by your honourable Committee.

And nothing short of a radical solution (which will courageously restore justice and redress the grievances of the Palestinians) will bring back security and peace and prosperity to the Holy Land, and good will towards the Western Democracies in the Arab World.

9

OUR NATIONAL REVIVAL
'TO BE OR NOT TO BE'

Today, at the heart of every human society, two major tendencies are locked in a struggle for dominance. These two tendencies compete in the depths of each human civilization and imprint each civilization and cultural trend with the stamp of the dominating and vanquishing current. The character of each civilization and the orientation of each society are determined by the degree of dominance achieved by each of these two currents. Ultimately, the abode of this decisive conflict is humans, for the currents are active in human societies and civilizations only because they are active in the human soul.

The two tendencies are not mere philosophical notions or purely artistic or scientific outlooks. Rather, they are ontological attitudes that man holds up toward himself. Thus, he sees himself, appreciates his values and activity, and interprets society and civilization. Accordingly, he determines the type of society to live in, the form of its institutions, and its principle orientation. Hence, the two tendencies represent man's attitude towards his entity as a human being. In light of them, he decides all the efforts and deeds that emanate from his human entity. The soul of each person is, thus, the place where these two tendencies contend and compete, and the identity of man is their subject matter.

*****

The conflict between these two tendencies has accompanied humankind from primordial times. It is concomitant with the existence of man, his societies, and his civilizations. The modern era is characterized by the crystallization of these two tendencies in a most aggressive and comprehensive manner, which renders their conflict fundamental and prominent. Our age arrived in the aftermath of a major historical shift where one current was instigated into revolt against the dominance of tendencies in the other in a preceding epoch. Just as the other current had reflected itself, this instigation was reflected in all human activities: religion, philosophy, science, arts, and social, political, and economic systems. With the end of this period of uprising, a period of chaos prevailed in which each of the two tendencies lost its dominance and withdrew to regain momentum.

Our age, then, is a historical one and perhaps unique among the different historical epochs. Our age came in the aftermath of an era when each of the two tendencies materialized in a full, prominent, and conspicuous manner and engaged in a basic clear conflict. In other words, our age arrived after humankind had experienced both tendencies at their height. Hence, their conflict is not an invisible one shrouded with reservations and ambiguity, but rather, a conflict of two tendencies that have expressed themselves fully unmasked in all manifestations of life. This scenario is similar to a judge deciding a case in which the two litigants have completed their pleading and defense. The judge has all the evidence before him and is able to justify his judgment clearly to the court. Our age, then, is witnessing not an elusive and invisible conflict, but a conflict that is both clear and obvious.

Moreover, given this situation, our age is laboring to give a final conclusive decision. The destiny of man is now at stake. All preparations for this decision have been made. All tests have been conducted. Nothing remains but for man to decide.

This is the situation of man in this stage, after the conflict of the two tendencies that will determine his fate has emerged from silent obscurity into clear visibility and has abated. Man is now set to give his final word about himself.

It is a formidable historical period. Truly, the destiny of man hinges on his impending decision. Today and only today, man faces this problem: "To be or not to be". It is a labor of life for the destiny of man, as a man will be determined by his decision: either to allow himself to be himself, to be human, or to eliminate the possibility of being himself to enslave his humanity to non-human elements.

*****

In this crucial stage of human history, our nation awoke and realized the huge distance that separates it from the current level of humanity. It surged forward, scrambling and trying to catch up with the rest of the world. Naturally, this same conflict developed in it in a forceful way, perhaps more fundamentally than in other societies, because whatever way our nation tries to catch up with the modern world embodies its response to this problem. In other words, the manner by which our nation revives represents our nation's attitude toward the problem, and it will determine which of the two tendencies will dominate our life. We cannot first revive and then later face this problem. Rather, in our striving for revival, we are bound in advance to confront this problem and take a certain attitude toward it.

Our national revival, represented in our institution, has indeed taken an active position towards the problem. In its basic philosophy, our revival has unconditionally embraced one current and categorically rejected the other. It is an embracing affirmed and clearly articulated in both its struggle and self-expression through the tendencies it has instigated. Finally, by instituting a Department for Culture and Fine Arts, at this point in its history, our revival has taken a decisive step toward acknowledging its unequivocal embracing of this current.

As the first dean of the newly created department, I will now analyze each of these two tendencies as they manifest themselves in all aspects of human activity.

APPENDIX

II

In each of us, two dynamic human beings are challenging and buoyant, each trying to control us and leave its imprint! I have previously called these two human beings "two tendencies" and "two attitudes" that man takes toward himself and through which he interprets all his human activities. Now I will analyze these tendencies or attitudes in abstraction and highlight their implications and affirmations.

*****

The first attitude sees man as a comprehensive totality. It sees man's diverse activities - religion, philosophy, art, science, volition, social work, politics, economics, professions, and all other conditions of his existence - as expressions of his entity. In other words, different manifestations or aspects of human effort, categorized as "man's self declaration" or "self expression" or "being oneself". Also, this attitude sees man as an entity in a comprehensive world or cosmos that he communicates with in each moment of his existence. He expresses his communication in the manifestations of the activities mentioned above. Man, thus, is a comprehensive entity in a comprehensive world with which he communicates, interacts, and adapts.

The other attitude sees man as consisting of abstract and disjointed parts, tossed in a strange and complex world, like a partner one neither is related to nor is in harmony with. In this case, man entertains an abstract and independent perspective of himself: a perspective that is not consistent with itself or with the cosmos. From this viewpoint develops a theoretical independent man who is concerned only with abstract thinking. For example, a philosopher engrossed in reflection, a logician devoted to analyzing his logical constructions, a scholar absorbed in explaining natural phenomena, an artist associated with an independent world of abstract beauty, a social being unappreciative of personal manifestations of art in society who confines himself to social behavior that is independent from such manifestations, or an economic being solely concerned with investing his efforts for lucrative ends. The cosmos (rich in space) and the human nature (rich in values) are thus dwarfed into independent abstractions, which confines human activities to their scope.

*****

The first attitude regards the process of refining or upbringing as a process of building a human being completely developed in talents, fully open to and connected with values, and fully expressive in his different activities of all human aspects. It seeks this perfection (fulfillment) as a human objective and produces a person who sees a painful manifestation of his deficient humanity and limited nature in the urgency to focus on various aspects of his entity. This attitude aspires to build individuals who appreciate all these aspects in their human entity and yearn to express them fully in their life. It regards the building of people of this kind, who appreciate values and attune their lives to them, as the aim of refinement. It aims to develop their sense of responsibility and enable them to accommodate values and make crucial decisions inspired by their human dignity.

The other attitude aims to build beings disconnected from the totality of the human personality. It aims to develop an abstract thinker, artist, or politician consumed by political considerations or specialized in an occupation that secures him a living in his political life. It is an attitude where one element of human character inflates and dominates the human entity independently of other elements.

*****

The first attitude looks at society as a comprehensive human totality, whose life is composed of human interactions forged from various aspects of humanity. It secures the society's interests and facilitates all manifestations of its activities. From within the life of this society, and as manifestations of it, specific efforts, interests, and institutions (the state and economic, cultural, religious, and social systems) emerge to secure these political, economic, and cultural interests and other interests of the society. These manifestations and institutions are not separate from each other, nor are their interests final or their standards independent. Rather, they are all manifestations that develop from within the comprehensive life of society. The interests are ultimately the comprehensive interest of society: the interest of the comprehensive entity of man.

In relation to this human entity, the value of these social manifestations is measured. This attitude sees human entity as the avenue that is available for man to redress his personal deficiencies and individual limits and to cooperate with other humans to express his own entity. This avenue is available for one to return from within this rich human life to himself at moments of seclusion and to attain within his innermost being a connection with the spiritual entity existing in the depth of the universe (i.e. the ultimate reality connected to the depths of human character).

The other attitude does not see this basic unity in society that encompasses all aspects of its life. It sees these manifestations and the institutions that ensure them as independent systems that are neither connected nor coherent. It sees a state that works and dominates by and for its own interests, enslaving people and institutions to its will and laws. Alternatively, it sees an economic system that espouses a certain ideology, functions, and exploits social classes while denying their rights to life and freedom, acknowledging only the interests of the institutions or individuals who run it. Otherwise, it sees practical science and its by-products of mechanical civilization as the ultimate objective and idol of man rather than a means to make human life easy. It sees these idols (state, economics, and applied science) taking over and enslaving the entity of the person and acquiring the status of a self-existing entity.

III

These two tendencies contend in the human soul. They emanate from two different perspectives of human nature, take shape in two different types of upbringing and social structure, and form two different civilizations.

As we gaze from our country at the Western world, we do so from a level of preparedness to take an attitude toward its conflict. In recent years, at the height of its turmoil, our nation reverted and adopted the second attitude. The dangers surrounding our nation have pushed it into choosing this easy way, deluding it into believing that the only weapon we can face impending dangers with is through political alliance, the application of mechanical civilization, or economic prosperity. Our nation has clearly forgotten that these are the paths to its doom, not its salvation. It has forgotten that its living message to attain sublimity is not in its contributions to these domains; but rather, in its rush to build humans with full human potential and in its consideration of them as its real wealth, real source of pride, and real weapon in combating corruption. The path that our nation has opted for is the easy way. It is the external, superficial, and misguided path. In reality, the correct path is the practical, internal, and spiritually challenging human way.

Our national revival, centered on our institution, has endorsed this other path as our nation's duty and course to its salvation. It has proceeded to build the sound person and thrust him into daily life as a messenger of the nation's new life in the midst of the prevailing corruption. Our institution, in its members, agencies, the currents it has set off, and the illuminating lights it has emitted, is the nucleus of the new nation. This new nation has taken a stand on the conflict of the two basic human tendencies, knows how to demonstrate its humanity, and has rejected the disfigured form of humanity that turns society into an inhuman apparatus that eliminates man and enslaves him to idols that he created for his own enslavement.

Appendix

Our national revival is established on the principle of respect for man as he is. It develops man in a way that coheres with his real nature. It thus declares that man in this country will 'be'!

In doing so, our national revival has realized that our nation's recent descent into the easy way is a peculiar descent from its eternal spiritual heritage.

*****

Our nation, standing as it is at a crossroad today, finds in our national revival a decisive decision that we will be a human society, that we will have human spiritual courage, and that from the heart of this nation, real humans will emerge instead of deformed creatures who have decided to eliminate their own humanity.

In this lies the merit of our national revival.

Bibliography

Special Resources

Abo, Fouad. "Desertification and Water Management: The Challenge in the Middle East," Paper presented at the AMESA 12th Annual Conference, Deakin University (Melbourne 1993).

Abu Fakhr, Sakr. "The triumph of Freedom over Ideology (Arabic). *Al-Safir* 'Palestine', 2012.

Andrew Killgore, " 25 Years After His Death, Dr. Fayez Sayegh's Towering Legacy Lives On." (*Washington Report on Middle East Affairs*, Dec 2005, Vol. 24, Issue 9).

An-Nahar, 1947.

As'ad Abu Khalil, "Before Edward Said: a Tribute to Fayez Sayegh." (*Al-Akhbar*, Tuesday, December 9, 2014).

Bhandari, D. R. "Existentialist Perception of the Human Condition: With Special Reference to Sartre" (unpublished lecture at Proceedings of the 20th World Congress of Philosophy, Boston, 1998).

Brown, L. Walter, (Ed.), *Lebanon's Struggle for Independence*, Part II, 1944-1947 (Documentary Publications, North Carolina, 1980).

Leroi-Gourhan, A. "Vegetational history in SW Syria and Lebanon during the upper Quaternary." (*Sahi Institute of Paleobotany*, special publication No. 5, 1974).

Lewis, Paul. "U.N. Repeals Its '75 Resolution Equating Zionism With Racism." (*The New York Times*, December 17, 1991).

LIFE, Jan 28, 1957.

Nolte, H. Richard. review of *Arab Unity: Hope and Fulfillment* by Fayez A. Sayegh. In *Middle East Journal*, Vol. 14, No. 1 (Winter, 1960), pp. 100-101.

Purdue, A. W. The Transformative Impact of World War II, in: *European History Online* (EGO), published by the Leibniz Institute of European History (IEG), Mainz 2016-04-18. URL: http://www.ieg-ego.eu/purduea-2016-enURN: urn:nbn:de:0159-2016041204

Sa'adeh, Antun. *Complete Works*, vols.1-16.

Sada an-Nahda. (Beirut: 1946-1947).

Sayegh, A. Fayez. "For the Record." (*The Caravan*, Brooklyn, N. Y., Thursday, January 15, 1959).

The Greater Syria Scheme, The Syrian Social Nationalist Party (Information Bureau), Beirut, 6 December, 1946.

Zionism: "A Form of Racism and Racial Discrimination" Four Statements Made at the U.N. General Assembly." (Office of the Permanent Observer of the Palestine Liberation Organization to the United Nations, 1976).

SSNP *Information Bulletin*, No. 4, 15 August, 1947.

SSNP, *Al-Nashrah al-Rasmiyah lil Harakat al-Qawmiyyah al-Ijtimae'yah*. (Beirut: Vol. 1, No. 2, December 1947).

SSNP, *Nashrat Imdat al-Iza'a*. (Beirut: 1947).

The Link, Published by Americans for Middle East Understanding, Inc. (Volume 36, Issue 2, April-May, 2003).

Dissertations

Makdisi, Nadim. *The Syrian National Party: A Case Study of the First Inroads of National Socialism in the Arab World.* (Ph.D., American University of Beirut, 1960).

Sayegh, A. Fayez. "Existential Philosophy: A Formal Examination." (Georgetown University, 1949).

Sayegh, A. Fayez. "Personal existence: An Essay." (unpublished M.A. Thesis: American University of Beirut, 1945).

Internet

http://www.al-akhbar.com/node/7770.

http://www.berdyaev.com/berdiaev/berd_lib/1936_408.html

http://www.ieg-ego.eu/purduea-2016-en

http://www.jewishpress.com/indepth/media-monitor/media-monitor-51/2002/08/07/0/?print

Articles and Book Chapters

Ansari, Zafar Ishaq. "The Movement For Arab Unity: A Review Article." (*Pakistan Horizon*, Vol. 13, No. 3 (Third Quarter, 1960).

Berger, Elmer."Memoirs of an Anti-Zionist Jew." (*Journal of Palestine Studies*, Vol. 5, No. ½, Autumn, 1975 - Winter, 1976).

Beshara, Adel. "A Great Man Has Died: Fakhri Maluf (Brother Francis Maluf) 1913-2009." (*Al-Mashriq: A Quarterly Journal of Middle East Studies*, Vol. 9, No. 34, September 2010).

Cooper, Barry."Ideology and Technology, Truth and Power." In Frederick Copleston and Anthony Parel, *Ideology, Philosophy and Politics* (Waterloo: Wilfrid Laurier University Press for the Calgary Institute for the Humanities, 2008).

Di-Capua, Yoav."Arab Existentialism: An Invisible Chapter in the Intellectual History of Decolonization." (*American Historical Review* 117(4), 2012).

Grimes, Alistair."Ideological Disputes." (*New Blackfriars*, vol. 63, no. 740, February 1982).

Hamid, Jafarian Yasar, Faghihi Alireza, Seifi Mohammad, "Prediction Of The Organizational Effectiveness Of The Primary Level Schools By The Factor Of Philosophical Mindedness Of The Educational Directors." (*IJBPAS*, December, 2015, 4(12), Special Issue): 888-912.

Hughes, A. Richard. "Nikolai Berdyaev's Personalism." (*International Journal of Orthodox Theology* 6:3, 2015).

Macaulay, Stewart."Non-Contractual Relations in Business: A Preliminary Study." (*American Sociological Review*, vol. 55, 1963).

Malik, C. Habib. "The Reception of Kierkegaard in the Arab World." In Jon Stewart (ed.), *Kierkegaard's International Reception: The Near East, Asia, Australia, and the Americas.* (London: Ashgate Publishing Limited, 1989).

Mitoma, Glenn. "Charles H. Malik And Human Rights: Notes On A Biography." (Biography, Vol. 33, No. 1, winter 2010): 222-241.

Morgenthau, J. Hans. "The Paradoxes of Nationalism". (*The Yale Review*, XLVI, 1957).

Plamenatz, John."The Philosophical Element in Social Theory and Practice." In Frederick Copleston and Anthony Parel, *Ideology,*

Philosophy and Politics. (Waterloo: Wilfrid Laurier University Press for the Calgary Institute for the Humanities, 2008).

Sartre, Jean-Paul. "Existentialism is a Humanism" (lecture given in 1946). In *Existentialism from Dostoyevsky to Sartre*, ed. Walter Kaufman. (Meridian Publishing Company, 1989).

Weiss, Max. "The Historiography of Sectarianism in Lebanon." (*History Compass* 7/1, 2009).

Wilkinson-Ryan, Tess."Legal Promise And Psychological Contract." (*Wake Forest Law Review,* vol. 47, 2012).

Books

Anderson, S. Betty. *The American University of Beirut.* (University of Texas Press, 2011).

Berdyaev, Nicolas. *Essai de Métaphysique eschatologique.* (Aubier, Paris, 1941).

Slavery and Freedom. (Semantron Press; 2nd edition, 2009).

Bounni, A. & K. Al-As'ad K, *Palmyra: History, Monuments and Museum*, 2nd ed. (Damascus; n.p., 1988).

Casson, Stanley. *Ancient Cyprus: Its Art and Archaeology.* (London: Methuen & Co. Ltd, 1937).

Copleston, Frederick and Anthony Parel, *Ideology, Philosophy and Politics.* (Waterloo: Wilfrid Laurier University Press for the Calgary Institute for the Humanities, 2008).

Dayeh, John. Sa'adeh wa mafakiru an-nahda: Tajribat Fakhri Maluf. (Beirut: Dar Nelson, 2008).

El-Khazen, Farid. *The Communal Pact of National Identities: The Making and Politics of the 1943 National Pact.* (Oxford: Centre for Lebanese Studies, 1991).

Eyre, S. R. (1986), *Vegetation and Soils: A World Picture* (London: Edward Arnold, 1975).

Godolphin, Francis. *The Greek Historians: The Complete and Unabridged Historical Works of Herodotus.* (New York: Random House 1942).

Golomb, Jacob and Robert S. Wistrich, (Ed.) *Nietzsche, Godfather of Fascism?: On the Uses and Abuses of a Philosophy.* (Princeton: Princeton University Press, 2002).

Grant, P. Christina. P. *The Syrian Desert: Caravans, Travel and Exploration.* (London: A & C Black Ltd, 1937).

Green, G. Samuel. *Bible Lands* (London: The Religious Tract Society, 1879).

Gyekye, Kwame. *Tradition and Modernity: Philosophical Reflections on the African Experience.* (New York: Oxford University Press, 1997).

Jreige, Gibran. *Haqa'iq Ain al-Istiqlal: Ayyam Rashayya*, 4th edition. (Beirut: Dar Amwaj, 2000).

Kassim, F. Anis. (Ed.), *The Palestine Yearbook of International Law, 1998-1999.* (Brill: Martinus Nijhoff 1984).

Khairallah, Shawki. *Memoirs.* (Beirut: Dar al-Jadid, 1990).

Khallaf, Samir. *Lebanon's Predicament.* (Columbia University Press, 1987).

Maritain, Jacques. *Existence and the Existent: An Essay on Christian Existentialism* (*Court traité de l'existence et de l'existent*), translated by Lewis Galantiere and Gerald B. Phelan. (New York: Pantheon Books, 1948).

Marshall, Peter. *Demanding the Impossible: A History of Anarchism* (London: Harper Collins, 1992).

Marten, Michael. *Attempting to Bring the Gospel Home: Scottish Missions to Palestine, 1839-1917.* (London: I. B. Tauris, 2005).

Panteli, Stavros. *A New History of Cyprus: From the Earliest Times to the Present Day.* (London: East-West Publications, 1984).

Paris, Bernard. *Dostoevsky's Greatest Characters: A New Approach to Notes from Underground, Crime and Punishment, and the Brothers Karamazov.*(New York: Palgrave Macmillan, 2008).

Penrose, Edith & E. F. *Iraq: International Relations and National Development.* (London: Ernest Benn, 1978).

Qaddura, Adib. *Haqa'iq wa Mawaqif.* (Beirut: Dar Fikr, 1989).

Qubersi, Abdullah. *Memoirs*, Vol. 2. (Beirut: Dar Fikr, 1982).

Rittenhouse, P. Bruce. *Shopping for Meaningful Lives: The Religious*

Motive of Consumerism. (Eugene: Wipf & Stock Publishers, 2013).

Rustom, Suheil. *al-Nidham al-Markazi wa Wihdat al-Amal* (Beirut: Dar Fikr, 2014).

Sayegh, A. Fayez. *al-Baath al-Qawmi.* Second Edition. (Beirut: Dar Fikr, n.d.).

Al-ta'ifiyya: Bath fi asbabiha wa-akhṭariha wa-'ilajiha (*Sectarianism: A Study into its Causes, Dangers, and Treatment*) (Beirut: Manshurat Maktabat al-Wajib, 1947).

Ila Ayn? (Whither to?). (Beirut, Dar al-Kitab, 1947).

Zionist Propaganda in the United States. (Pleasantville, NY: The Fayez A. Sayegh Foundation, 1983).

Nida' al-Aamak: Nadharat fi al-Insan wa al-Wujud. (Beirut: Dar al-Fikr, 1947).

Zionist Colonization of Palestine. (Beirut: Research Center, Palestine Liberation Organization, 1965).

al-Baath al-Qawmi. (Beirut: Dar Fikr, 2nd ed. n.d.).

Sayigh, Rosemary. (ed.), *Yusif Sayigh: Arab Economist Palestinian Patriot, A Fractured Life Story.* (Cairo: The American University in Cairo Press, 2015).

Sunayama, Sonoko. *Syria And Saudi Arabia: Collaboration and Conflicts in the Oil Era.* (London: Tauris Academic Studies, 2007).

Wallace. Mike, and Gary Paul Gates, *Close Encounters: Mike Wallace's Own Story.* (William Morrow & Co, 1987).

Yammut, Ibrahim. *Ḥasad al-Murr: Qssat tafattut qiyadat ḥizb wa-tamasuk 'aqidah.* (Beirut: Dar al-Rukn, 1993).

Zuwiyya. Yamak, Labib. *The Syrian Social Nationalist Party: An Ideological Analysis.* (Harvard University Press, 1966).

Index

A
Abdel Nasser, Gamal 5
Abdul Satir, Mustapha 42
Abu Jawdeh, Khalil 57
Abu Khalil, As'ad 21
Al-Ashqar, Asaad 42
al-Khal, Yusif 82-83
al-madrahiyyah 100
Al-Said, Nuri 121
American University of Beirut 3, 11, 17, 33, 39, 57, 69, 146, 153, 173
Anglo-American Committee of Inquiry 43, 48, 59, 228
Arab Committee Against Zionism and Racism 27
Arab Group 187
Arab nationalism 6, 33-35, 187-189
Arabian Desert 116
Azkoul, Karim 147

B
Badawi, Abd al-Rahman 159
Balfour Declaration 60, 235-240
Beethoven 125
Bilad as-Sham 112-113, 117, 119
Boghaz Keui 119
Buddhism 131

C
Camus, Albert 138
Casson, Stanley 119, 254
Christian-Islamic Conference (1946) 60
Christianity 19
Communism 2, 6, 8, 27, 42-47, 52, 55-57, 124, 173-174, 188

Communist Manifesto 122
Conservatism 124, 226
Cooper, Barry 132, 253
Cragg, A. Kenneth 12
Cultural Forum (al-nadwa al-thakafiyya) 68
Cyprus 78, 110, 114, 118-119, 254-255

D
De Beauvoir, Simone 138
Dostoyevsky, Fyodor 138-139, 157, 254

E
Edde, Emile 68
Existentialism 1, 7-8, 29-31, 75, 78, 86, 124, 137-174, 177, 179-181, 185-186

F
Fertile Crescent 113-121
Fertile Crescent Plan 121

G
Gates, Gary Paul 20-21
Georgetown University 12, 31, 161
Gold Coast (Ghana) 78, 81, 101
Greater Syria Scheme 48-49, 70-71, 121

H
Heidegger, Martin 138, 153

I
Islam 19, 131, 233
Issawi, Charles 142

J
Jaspers, Karl 138
Judaism 19, 60, 131

K

Khairallah, Shawki 76, 87
Kharaba 11
Khoury, Beshara 68-71
Kierkegaard, Søren 1, 30-31, 81, 128, 138-139, 142, 149, 153
Killgore, Andrew 5, 21
King Abdullah 48, 70, 121
Kuhn, Thomas 111

L

Larry King Live 20
League of Arab States 6, 33, 48, 189, 194, 212
Lucian of Samosata 7, 112

M

Macalester College 5, 12
Malik, Charles 7, 12, 18, 29-32, 82, 142, 146, 153
Malik, Habib 30-32, 149, 153
Maluf, Fakhri 96, 147, 253-254
Maluf, Fawzi 126
Maluf, Hilmi 86
Marx, Karl 46, 55-56, 100, 122
Morgenthau, Hans 151
Mubarak, Farid 42

N

Nahda Club 54
National Socialism 100, 124
Nazism 26, 153
Near East 30, 48, 115, 149, 153, 228
Nietzsche, Friedrich 138, 155
Nikolai, Berdyaev 138, 157-158
North Africa 116

O

Organization of Arab Students (US) 14
Orthodox Club 49

Oslo Accords 28

P
Palestine Liberation Organization (PLO) 16, 26, 28, 36, 187
Palestine Research Center 16-18
Panteli, Stavros 119
Phelps, Christina 116-117
Protestantism 131

Q
Qubersi, Abdullah 42, 76, 82-83, 86

R
Raad, Inaam 27
Reform Club 53

S
Safad 11
Sartre, Jean-Paul 138-141, 156, 157, 162
Sayegh, Anis 41
Sayegh, Fuad 39
Sayegh, Yusif 39, 41
Scots College 11
Sea of Galilee 11
Second World War (WWII) 176
Social Nationalism 101, 105, 108, 122-123, 138, 158, 161-162
Sufism 159
Suleiman, Fuad 82-83
Susskind, David 21
Sykes-Picot Agreement 11
Syrian Desert 112-118
Syrian nationalism 6, 8, 25, 33, 35, 39, 187, 189

T
Taiwan 119
Thabet, Naimet 73
Tiberias 11

INDEX

Totalitarianism 8, 94, 123, 153, 156
Tueini, Ghassan 82, 86, 98, 146, 169

U
UN Resolution 3379 25, 27
United Arab Republic (UAR) 34
United Nations 6, 12, 22,-23, 26, 36, 187, 189
United Press 49
University of Utah 2, 19, 146

V
Von Braun, Werner 5

W
Wallace, Mike 20-21
Weiss, Max 51

Y
Yale University 12

Z
Zionism 1-2, 6, 8, 25-28, 36, 39, 42-43, 47, 52, 58-60, 174, 211, 235
Zuwiyya, Labib Yamak 85, 133

www.ingramcontent.com/pod-product-compliance
Lightning Source LLC
Chambersburg PA
CBHW050135170426
43197CB00011B/1845